Teaching Character and Virtue in Schools

Teaching Character and Virtue in Schools addresses the contemporary issues of quantification and measurement in educational settings. The authors draw on the research of the Jubilee Centre for Character and Virtues at the University of Birmingham in order to investigate the concern that the conventional wisdom, sound judgement and professional discretion of teachers is being diminished and control mistakenly given over to administrators, policymakers and inspectors, which in turn is negatively affecting pupils' character development.

The book calls for subject competence to be complemented by practical wisdom and good character in teaching staff. It posits that the constituent virtues of good character can be learned and taught, that education is an intrinsically moral enterprise and that character education should be intentional, organised and reflective. The book draws on the Jubilee Centre's expertise in support of its claims and successfully integrates the fields of educational studies, psychology, sociology, philosophy and theology in its examination of contemporary educational practices and their wider effect on society as a whole. It offers sample lessons as well as a framework for character education in schools.

The book encourages the view that character education is about helping students grasp what is ethically important and how to act for the right reasons so that they can become more autonomous and reflective individuals within the framework of a democratic society. Particularly interested readers will be educational leaders, teachers, those undertaking research in the field of education as well as policy analysts with a keen interest in developing the character and good sense of learners today.

James Arthur is Professor of Education, Deputy Pro Vice Chancellor (staffing) and Director of the Jubilee Centre for Character and Virtues at the University of Birmingham, UK.

Kristján Kristjánsson is Deputy Director at the Jubilee Centre for Character and Virtues and Professor of Character Education and Virtue Ethics at the University of Birmingham, UK.

Tom Harrison is Director of Education at the Jubilee Centre for Character and Virtues at the University of Birmingham, UK.

Wouter Sanderse is Associate Professor of Teachers' Professional Ethics at Fontys University of Applied Sciences, Tilburg, the Netherlands and a former Research Fellow at the Jubilee Centre for Character and Virtues at the University of Birmingham, UK.

Daniel Wright is Deputy Head (Staff), St George's College, Weybridge and formally a Research Associate at the Jubilee Centre for Character and Virtues at the University of Birmingham, UK.

Citizenship, Character and Values Education
Edited by James Arthur and Wing On Lee

This series provides a platform for discussion and debate on the latest issues, challenges and developments in Citizenship, Character and Values Education across the globe. The series facilitates continued conversation on policy and politics, curriculum and pedagogy, review and reform, and provides a comparative overview of the different conceptions and approaches to Citizenship, Character and Values Education around the world. The volumes in this series will appeal to teacher educators, researchers, teachers, school leaders and policymakers. They will also facilitate decision-making in the practical steps necessary to develop Citizenship, Character and Values Education curricula in different national contexts.

1 The State of Global Education
Edited by Brad Maguth and Jeremy Hillburn

2 Teaching Character and Virtue in School
James Arthur, Kristján Kristjánsson, Tom Harrison,
Wouter Sanderse and Daniel Wright

Teaching Character and Virtue in Schools

James Arthur, Kristján Kristjánsson,
Tom Harrison, Wouter Sanderse and
Daniel Wright

LONDON AND NEW YORK

First published 2017 by Routledge

2 Park Square, Milton Park, Abingdon, Oxfordshire OX14 4RN
711 Third Avenue, New York, NY 10017

Routledge is an imprint of the Taylor & Francis Group, an informa business

First issued in paperback 2017

British Library Cataloguing in Publication Data
A catalogue record for this book is available from the British Library

Library of Congress Cataloging in Publication Data
A catalog record has been requested

ISBN: 978-1-138-90761-4 (hbk)
ISBN: 978-0-8153-6091-9 (pbk)

Typeset in Galliard
by Deanta Global Publishing Services, Chennai, India

Contents

Acknowledgements

We would like to thank David Lorimer for assisting us with the final editing of the text. David reviewed all the chapters and helped with the coherence in style as well as offering suggestions on the content at various points. We are most grateful for his advice and guidance.

Introduction

Most people say that it is the intellect that makes a great scientist. They are wrong: it is character.

Albert Einstein

Teaching Character and Virtues has emerged from the work of the Jubilee Centre for Character and Virtues, founded in 2012 by Professor James Arthur, with a multi-million-pound grant from the John Templeton Foundation. The Centre is a unique institution which is leading the world in examining how character and virtues impact individuals and society. The authors in this volume are all present or past colleagues at the Centre, which has a dedicated team of 30 academics from a range of disciplines, including philosophy, psychology, education, theology and sociology. The Centre takes a robust and rigorous research-and evidence-based approach that is both objective and non-political.

In this book, we argue that the virtues that make up a good character can be learned and taught, that education is an intrinsically moral enterprise and that character education should be intentional, organised and reflective. We believe that character virtues are the basis of individual and societal flourishing and that schools and teachers can and should play a fundamental role in developing these in their students. This reflects the widely held view that character can be taught and caught in schools. We take the view that schools and teachers should see character cultivation as a core part of their role and that teachers themselves should be trained to serve as role models and moral exemplars. In this way, the cultivation of good character can come to permeate all subject teaching and learning.

This book unpacks both caught and taught aspects of character education, showing the importance of school values, ethos and culture, which inform how teachers and students relate to each other. We give examples of whole school approaches involving community learning, service and volunteering, as well as how character can be taught effectively through curriculum subjects. We clarify our view on character education based on the Aristotelian concept of 'good sense' or 'practical wisdom' (*phronesis*), which incorporates the capacity to choose intelligently between alternatives when the demands of two or more virtues collide. Hence, character education is about helping students grasp what is ethically important in situations and how to act for the right reasons, with the help of *phronesis*, so that they can become more autonomous and reflective individuals.

We emphasise our view that character education is *not* about moral indoctrination or mindless conditioning, but rather the development of critical, reflective and applied thinking that makes for better persons and creates the social conditions where all human beings can flourish within the framework of a democratic society. The more people exhibit good character and virtues, the healthier our society is. As we explain in this book, we categorise the character virtues into the four areas of moral virtues, performance virtues, intellectual virtues and civic virtues. Although performance virtues such as grit and resilience are important, we believe that they must be underpinned by the primacy of moral virtues and good character.

For this reason, we regard the exclusive instrumentalist emphasis on attainment, measurement and outcomes as inadequate. Although research indicates that character education also has a positive impact in this respect, we insist on its intrinsic value independent of any connection with attainment. We are concerned that quantification and measurement have replaced wisdom in teaching and that the discretion and wise judgement of teachers has been replaced by the judgement of administrators, policymakers and inspectors. Subject competence needs to be supplemented by practical wisdom and good character. Recent developments in the UK do indicate a renewed interest in moral education in general, and character education in particular, on the part of all main political parties – and a recognition that the true purpose of education means preparing young people for the tests of life, not simply for a life of tests. A recent Populus poll (Jubilee Centre, 2013a) showed overwhelming support on the part of parents for schools to be involved with character education and the moral development of their children, and we give examples of the benefits of schools partnering with parents on character education.

Character education forms a broad church and incorporates various approaches that nevertheless have some common elements. We explain the relationship between values, moral and character education, defining character education as a subset of moral education concerned with the cultivation of positive traits of good character called 'virtues'. We argue that character traits are *developmentally*, *logically* and *motivationally* prior to more general moral concerns. We provide a historical background of character education and policy in the UK and explain the distinctiveness of an Aristotelian virtue ethics approach based on human flourishing. As we have already indicated, this approach goes beyond the instrumentalism of much recent educational policy.

We propose a list of prototypical moral virtues as a sound basis for character education, underpinning other forms of virtue. We argue that the terms 'character' and 'virtue' are by no means old-fashioned and that they should be retrieved as part of the development of 'virtue literacy' in terms of moral sensitivity, moral judgement, moral motivation and moral character. We explain the Aristotelian background of virtue ethics and human flourishing as a form of moral naturalism and its advantages as secular rather than overtly religious in the present social context.

We outline the achievements and limitations of Lawrence Kohlberg's work on moral development and describe our own virtue-based model of moral development that is firmly grounded in Aristotelian ethics and based on the Character Development Ladder with its four levels: moral indifference, emerging self-control, self-control and virtue. Our own programme uses a spiral curriculum model enabling students to look at previous learning and experience in a new light, and at new learning from the perspective of previous experience. This entails a spiral of engagement, action, ideas, reflection and refinement by means of which these practices become internalised and habituated. We introduce the conceptual tools of growth in virtue in terms of virtue knowledge, virtue reasoning and virtue practice. This provides a solid basis for creating a curriculum around the cultivation of virtue and the building of character, rather than simply the acquisition of subject-based knowledge and skills.

Later in the book, we address the challenge of measuring and evaluating the effects of character education programmes, with special reference to an Aristotelian approach and to young moral learners. We highlight the shortcomings of self-reports and propose a triangulated approach including these but adding peer reports and more objective measures. Towards the end of the book, we give a comprehensive guide to resources in the field and provide sample lesson plans for primary and secondary teachers. We also reproduce the Centre's 2013 *A Framework for Character Education in Schools* and the more recent *Statement on Teacher Education and Character Education* (Jubilee Centre, 2015b).

We hope that readers – and especially teachers – will be inspired by our reflections and find a renewed sense of personal and professional purpose.

1 Wisdom in the craft of teaching

For do teachers profess that it is their thoughts which are perceived and grasped by the students, and not the sciences themselves which they convey through thinking? For who is so stupidly curious as to send his son to school that he may learn what the teacher thinks? ... Those who are pupils consider within themselves whether what has been explained has been said truly; looking of course to that interior truth, according to the measure of which each of us is able. Thus they learn, and when the interior truth makes known to them that true things have been said, they applaud.

St. Augustine, *De Magistro*, 389AD

Now this is what some great men are very slow to allow; they insist that Education should be confined to some particular and narrow end, and should issue in some definite work, which can be weighed and measured. They argue as if everything, as well as every person, had its price; and that where there has been great outlay, they have a right to expect a return in kind.

John Henry Newman, *The Idea of a University*

Summary

This chapter argues that education and teaching are intrinsically moral enterprises. The moral dimensions of teaching are often hidden or ignored, but they can never be avoided and must be made more transparent. Society takes an interest in the character of people who become teachers. Teachers are expected to exhibit a high level of moral responsibility and are held to a high standard of conduct. We are concerned that quantification and measurement have replaced wisdom in teaching and that the discretion and wise judgement of teachers have been replaced by the judgement of administrators, policymakers and inspectors. Subject competence should be supplemented by practical wisdom and good character. Professionally, teachers need relational as well as contractual incentives. We explain the four types of virtues – moral, intellectual, civic and performative – and the ways in which teachers can convey these by example. Accepting that teaching has a moral purpose therefore highlights a need to include character education as an integral part of teacher education. Teachers provide support for classroom learning that goes beyond the mere mechanics of teaching. They must have a moral commitment to serve the interests of their pupils, as they contribute to their moral development.

The nature of teaching and learning

The basic premise of this chapter, and indeed of the book as whole, is that all teaching is a moral enterprise, as is education itself. Parents entrust their children to the care of teachers for the purposes of education, so it is not surprising that they are concerned about the kinds of people who are employed to teach. Schools are therefore sites of moral interaction, and teachers are moral agents. The teacher–student relationship is an inherently moral one and the teacher, like the parent, assumes a moral responsibility for pupils. Teachers also seek to influence pupils, and this influence is woven into the personal development of their pupils. Consequently, society and schools are also naturally concerned about the kinds of people who should teach. In addition, because schooling is compulsory and pupils are susceptible to influence, the qualities of the would-be teacher are worthy of careful consideration. What kind of person must he or she be? What is required of the teacher?

We are also concerned about the conduct of teachers, because such conduct carries moral significance in the classroom. The importance of a teacher's role lies not only in what they teach directly, but also in what they model in practice as ethical exemplars. This is why many national governments retain the power to deny or withdraw teacher certification from those they consider not to be of good character. In addition, since all teachers engage in some tacit form of moral education, even when there is no discrete class in moral education on the curriculum, we are clearly interested in the character of the teacher. This chapter attempts to conceptualise teaching as a moral activity: it argues that criteria beyond efficiency and competence are needed to understand the real nature of teaching.

Good teaching should challenge our minds and shape our characters, but it is sometimes argued that there are no teachers as such, only different degrees of learners; that children ought not to be passive in learning and that learning is not always the result of teaching, since learning involves thinking and understanding on the part of pupils. So a good teacher is someone who supports their students' learning. For learning can happen without teaching, but teaching cannot happen without learning. Teachers are of course learners too, and their students will eventually become independent of teachers, even to the point of forgetting their names. After all, schooling does not complete the education of a person, but is a preparatory stage in a life-long process.

A wise teacher knows that teaching is not confined to educational institutions such as schools. As Mark Twain famously quipped: 'I have never let my schooling interfere with my education.' Some of the most important teaching in life happens outside schools. As we move through life, we are all by turns both teachers and learners – in the many different roles we assume –, whether as parents or teachers, doctors or bricklayers. Nevertheless, while teaching is not confined to the professional teacher, the trained teacher does have enormous responsibilities since it is a serious moral matter to intervene professionally in a child's upbringing. Teachers are therefore naturally and rightly held accountable for their actions and decisions.

The teacher's conduct in the classroom is always a moral matter. As Halstead and Taylor (2000: 178) conclude:

> It is through relationships that children learn the importance of qualities such as honesty, respect and sensitivity to others. Children are most likely to be influenced by teachers whose qualities they admire. Such qualities include tolerance, firmness and fairness, acting in a reasonable manner and a willingness to explain things and, for older pupils, respect, and freedom from prejudice, gentleness and courtesy, and sensitivity and responsiveness to the needs of pupils.

The act of teaching therefore reveals the centrality of a teacher's moral and intellectual character. Since the teaching role implies a high degree of public trust, the general expectations of society are greater than for many other professions. The teacher is expected to exhibit a higher level of moral responsibility and is held to a higher standard of conduct. The greater the degree of public trust, the higher the corresponding level of teachers' moral responsibility.

Who the teacher is matters

When we presume to teach others about complex things in life, there is a great danger of getting it wrong, so teaching is not something to be entered into lightly. Subject area expertise, knowledge and concern for children and their needs, combined with practical wisdom are essential. The attempt to improve the quality of teaching through standards, inspections, incentives, performance management, competency criteria and tests – in fact, anything that is quantifiable and easily measurable – has resulted in quantification replacing wisdom in teaching. The value of teaching is nowadays largely seen in terms of the economic value of qualifications. Little attention is paid officially to purpose, to questions of meaning, and to the ends to which pupils can put their acquired knowledge, skills and understanding. The teacher is portrayed as a technician, charged with specific tasks leading to measurable outcomes rather than emphasising the teacher's personal qualities and potential. It is simply not possible to encapsulate the full range of human abilities and qualities of a good teacher within the concept of competence. Teaching is above all else a self-giving vocation that is concerned with the welfare and development of pupils. It is fundamentally a moral enterprise and cannot be entirely neutral: pupils need the example of those who care for them. However, we cannot simply assume that all new teachers will have the requisite qualities.

At this point it is worth saying that many societal expectations of schools and teachers are clearly unreasonable. Teachers are expected to help eradicate crime among the young through teaching good behaviour, to contribute to the elimination of the gap between rich and poor through equal opportunity policies and to produce citizens who participate in elections through citizenship lessons. Policymakers often see schools as a cure-all but schools are not equipped to cure society's woes. At the same time, teachers are often held responsible for these woes. More recently, teachers are even being asked to eradicate 'extremism' and 'radicalisation' in students. It is true that many schools include the promotion of social justice and human rights among their stated aims, but in reality they are forced to deliver a curriculum that is largely test-driven and imposed by central government.

The discretion and wise judgement of teachers is no longer trusted by politicians and has been replaced with the judgement of administrators, policymakers and inspectors. Ironically, the more professionalised teaching has become, the less attractive it is as a vocation. As Barry Schwartz (2010: 176) notes:

> the de-skilling of teachers produces a kind of 'de-willing' – it risks taking the fight out of some good teachers and takes other good teachers out of the fight. The danger here is a downward spiral. Good, experienced teachers leave, and idealistic and talented prospective teachers are discouraged from entering the classroom. Administrators interpret the lack of experience as evidence that more stringent procedures and rules are needed and they ratchet up the standardisation, demoralising and turning away more promising teachers. Forcing teachers to *do right by rote* risks driving the wisdom out of the practice and driving out the wise practitioners.

Schwartz is right to maintain that these kinds of policies are counterproductive for both teaching and teachers. They reduce teaching to skill, efficiency and instrumental purposes, in which *explicit* values disappear. Such developments have limited the scope of the debate about the nature of teaching by an overemphasis on the behavioural aspects of teacher competency. Wisdom is subverted by bureaucratic measures that focus on compliance with instrumental ends. Unfortunately, teacher training has suffered also and is increasingly lacking any clear moral compass.

The competency agenda

Teaching is embedded within a set of beliefs, values, habits, traditions and ways of thinking that are shared and understood by teachers already in the profession, but which are seldom articulated. Pring (1992: 17) commenting on the competence agenda for teaching says:

> These conditions make little mention of theory. They require no philosophical insights. They demand no understanding of how children are motivated; they attach little importance to the social context in which the school functions – unless it be that of the local business and the world of work; they attach no significance to historical insight into the present; they have no

place for the ethical formulation of those who are to embark on this, the most important of all moral undertakings.

Pring is making the point that the ethical intuition of good teachers is just as important as their subject knowledge and teaching skill. Reducing teaching to a set of discrete competencies fails to capture its richness.

Wilson (1993: 113) believes that teaching is in a sense the formation of 'moral dispositions':

> Moral qualities are directly relevant to any kind of classroom practice: care for the pupil, enthusiasm for the subject, conscientiousness, determination, willingness to co-operate with colleagues and a host of others. Nobody, at least on reflection, really believes that effective teaching – let alone effective education – can be reduced to a set of skills; it requires certain dispositions of character.

Teachers are major influences on pupils since they clearly require pupils to change in directions they specify in the classroom – this is reflected in what they choose to permit or encourage. Indeed, it goes deeper, since all the while teachers are engaged in teaching, they are under the close examination of pupils, who see and hear in teachers' eyes, voice and body language what they are really saying.

Moreover, a view of teaching grounded primarily in a subject knowledge base – in terms of expertise, skill and competence – does not capture the essential meaning of the occupation. Good teaching will enrich and expand the minds of pupils by encouraging reflection, self-evaluation and the practice of virtues. Schools intentionally build and promote positive moral atmospheres and encourage their teachers to exemplify the virtues that constitute their ethos. The challenge facing teachers and teacher educators in this regard is whether to allow this moral formation to occur opportunistically, letting students learn what they will, for good or bad, come what may; or whether to foster intentional, transparent and deliberative approaches that take the moral dimensions of teaching and schooling seriously. In addition to setting behavioural examples to their pupils and peers – which is critically important from a moral perspective – there are additional *independent* reasons why any good teacher would want these interactions to satisfy moral requirements: reasons concerning general moral aspirations towards others, professional aspirations and aspirations *vis-à-vis* themselves, in striving to flourish as a good human being.

Despite the contemporary technocratic policies for education, many still come forward freely to make teaching their life. They dedicate themselves with serious intent while knowing that their pay and conditions are by no means the best and that they may be punished for their students' performance. These strongly motivated teachers believe that all children are educable and that it is appropriate to cultivate virtues in them that will enable them to flourish. As Sockett (1993: 14) observes, 'many teachers have a moral vision, a moral sense, and a moral motive however mixed up they may be in any individual.' This does not imply that the teacher is morally perfect, as Guitton (1964: 1) rightly said: 'A teacher instructs you by what he gives you, yes, but he also stimulates you by his very deficiencies; he pushes you to becoming your own inner teacher.'

This echoes the quotation from Augustine at the beginning of this chapter when he said that you do not bring your child to school to learn what the teacher thinks. Essentially, good teachers must have the following qualities: they must know and like their subject and continue to learn it; they must like their pupils, know their faces and names and treat them as individuals; they must have good characters, and be kind, caring and patient so that their pupils will pick this up in their teaching. Teachers should also be determined, have a sense of humour and speak with authority – including moral authority. This moral authority must be exercised wisely and Kevin Ryan (1993: 17) sums it up when he says that 'to engage students in the lessons in human character and ethics without resorting to preaching and didacticism is the great skill of teaching.' Students will respect and trust such teachers, but will easily detect the teacher who does not display these qualities and virtues.

Contractual versus relational incentives

Teachers are increasingly given rules and standards to follow by those who are not teachers; and incentives, such as performance pay, are used to encourage them to help students perform better in exams. Many schools have become completely compliant to these external standards, and in the process have become rigid and narrow in their expectations for teachers and pupils. With too many exams, targets and assessments, teaching has become more like a business and in the process the power of education as transformation, rather than mere transmission of information, has been lost. The focus on league tables and exams has changed the way students learn and are taught.

Teaching and learning becomes superficial when the student is prepared to simply pass an exam and then forgets what has been learnt after they have passed the test. The teacher–pupil relationship has become increasingly contractual and legal, further eviscerating the noble purpose of education. The traditional idea of the teacher being in *loco-parentis* has vanished, and with it much respect from parents. The so-called cognitive domain of education is emphasised and the moral dimension increasingly ignored. Good teachers are deterred from pursuing teaching because the focus is more on the contractual than the relational dimensions of teaching and learning. We need to look again at what is missing in our teaching since it is vital that teaching supports the ethical development of our pupils.

Ethical and character formation does not happen by chance. It cannot be fostered by indifference to ethical questions in the classroom. It must embrace a deliberate and planned-for pedagogy. In 1995, the Universities Committee for the Education of Teachers (UCET) set up a working party to formulate some ethical principles for teaching. The working party outlined eleven principles that were claimed to be fundamental to teaching, which are worth summarising here (Tomlinson and Little, 2000: 152–154):

Teachers must:

1   have intellectual integrity;
2   have vocational integrity;
3   show moral courage;
4   exercise altruism;
5   exercise impartiality;
6   exercise human insight;
7   assume the responsibility of influence;
8   exercise humility;
9   exercise collegiality;
10 exercise partnership; and
11 exercise vigilance with regard to professional responsibilities and aspirations.

This list demonstrates the obligations of teachers, particularly their moral obligations, with a clear emphasis on courage, altruism, humility and integrity. However, no definitive list of relevant virtues can be given, but a list of prototypical virtues can be articulated and used for teacher education. Consider, for example, the three-year-old child in the nursery playing with a toy and refusing to share it with others. The children with whom the child refuses to share the toy feel excluded and aggrieved, and these feelings of rejection result in tears. The nursery teacher instinctively intervenes, encouraging and persuading the child to share the toy. In so doing, the child begins to learn how to socialise in a fair way – in fact, he begins to learn what justice is. Virtue and character are being taught directly to the child. In this example, building character is about developing virtues that lead pupils to good habits and to flourish as responsible citizens.

The virtues and practical wisdom

The virtues can be categorised into four types: *moral, civic, performance* and *intellectual*.[1] It is important for all four to work in collaboration for positive human flourishing and it can be argued that the fundamental purpose of education is to help students cultivate those character traits – the human excellences or virtues – that promote human flourishing. Particular schools may choose to prioritise certain virtues over others in light of the school's history, ethos, location or specific student population. Teacher education, though, should seek to prioritise the development of all four of the types of virtues.

These are:

Moral Virtues: Those virtues that enable us to respond in ethically sound ways to situations in any area of experience. These are the virtues of courage, self-discipline, compassion, gratitude, justice, humility and honesty, which every child should learn.

Performance Virtues: Those virtues that can be used for both good and bad ends – the qualities that enable us to manage our lives effectively. The virtue most commonly mentioned in this category is resilience – the ability to bounce back from negative experiences. Others include determination, confidence and teamwork. These virtues should derive their ultimate value in being enablers and vehicles for the moral virtues.

Civic Virtues: Those virtues necessary for engaged and responsible citizenship. They include service, citizenship and volunteering. These civic virtues assist the flourishing of each person and promote the common good of society. Sometimes civic virtues are seen as a specific subset of the moral ones (see Chapter 3).

Intellectual Virtues: Those virtues that are rational prerequisites for right action and correct thinking, for example, autonomy, reasoning and perseverance. We want students to think and react in the right way so that they do the right thing, and in so doing promote human flourishing for all. These intellectual virtues are required for the pursuit of knowledge, truth and understanding and include how to interpret, analyse, evaluate, compare and judge – all essential to a well-formed mind that can reason well.

It is important to single out what the Greeks called *phronesis*, but we can call 'good sense,' or practical wisdom. This is an overall quality of judgement – knowing how best to handle a situation. For example, choosing the best course of action when the demands of two or more virtues compete with one another, and to integrate such demands into an acceptable course of action (see Cooke and Carr, 2014). Living with good sense entails considered deliberation, well-founded judgement and the vigorous enactment of decisions. It reveals itself in foresight, and in being clear-sighted and far-sighted about the ways in which actions will lead to desired goals. The ability to learn from experience and mistakes is at the heart of 'good sense.' It is, therefore, an essential virtue for the education of teachers. We explain *phronesis* in moral detail in Chapter 2.

At the start of their careers, many teachers are motivated to choose the profession for its moral content (Sanger & Osguthorpe, 2011); moreover, research demonstrates that people enter the teaching profession motivated by the desire to make a difference to children's lives and to help mould them into good people (Arthur *et al.*, 2015a). Sadly, however, this early moral aspiration is not being adequately developed in teacher training and beyond. There is also a reported lack of moral *self-knowledge* among teachers. Indeed, Sockett and LePage (2002) found that a number of teachers, at the beginning of a non-traditional graduate programme, were unable to reflect on themselves critically as moral agents. The ideal good teacher is a certain sort of person, a person who exhibits pedagogical *phronesis* in their dealings with students. Such a view of teaching as a moral profession clearly calls for a richer account of the nature and requirements of teacher training, and even for the revival of the time-honoured idea of teaching as a moral vocation. Research by Revell and Arthur (2007: 85) found that while student teachers thought that teaching was a moral endeavour, their training courses did not cover this area.

Accepting that teaching has a moral purpose highlights a need to include character education as an integral part of teacher education. Recent research by the Jubilee Centre (see Arthur *et al.*, 2015a) highlights the guiding principles by which teacher education ought to address the moral complexities of the teacher's role through:

- providing a focus on the development of the moral agency of teachers;
- including academic input concerning the integral role of moral virtues in teaching;
- providing space for critical, moral reflection on practice;
- greater recognition of the moral importance of mentoring in the education of teachers;
- offering continued professional development that retains a moral focus throughout the teaching career.

However, philosophers continue to debate whether virtues can be taught in schools. The debate hearkens back to Socrates and Plato. Both question whether virtue, moral excellence, can be taught. Plato's Socrates raises this doubt in the *Meno* – that virtue cannot be knowledge and therefore it is not teachable. If there is no knowledge then there can be no teachers of virtue, but Socrates changes his mind by the end of the *Protagoras*. He starts with the idea that virtue is not knowledge and concludes by believing that virtue is in fact knowledge and must therefore be teachable. We need to recognise, though, that both Socrates and Plato are talking about the acquisition of virtue by young men – they are not concerned here with children aged between three and sixteen years. They are dealing with students who have already experienced schooling and have already been partially formed by parents and teachers. What they experience from Socrates and Plato is dialogue, a rigorous and shared inquiry into the nature of virtue and its acquisition as part of the final stages of their moral education.

For Aristotle, virtues are developed by an individual over time and the process requires direction as well as knowledge from the teacher. In modern discussions about character, since the time of the influential moral psychologist Lawrence Kohlberg, who was a sceptic about character and virtues, most writers tend to polarise this ancient debate between Plato and Aristotle. Plato's focus is then seen to be on the teacher helping to improve the pupils' thinking skills, while Aristotle's central idea is the teacher helping the pupil practise good actions. The implication is that one emphasises moral reasoning without moral action, and the other conformity without inner conviction. This misconstrues and overstates their differences, as they both agreed that character could and must be cultivated in the young.

The moral dimension of teaching

Today there are widespread assumptions among many teachers that moral points of view are neither true nor false – only chosen positions on an issue. Nevertheless, as we observed above, teachers intervene instinctively to encourage and persuade (teach) the three year old that sharing is the best option. So there are clearly some situations where it is not obviously a matter of opinion or viewpoint, but about the transmission of practical knowledge from one generation to the next. We cannot accept a view of teaching based on the kind of extreme relativism that undermines our confidence in universal ethical principles, such as kindness, respect and justice. It is also difficult to separate the moral integrity of the teacher from the effectiveness of his or her teaching, as teachers will always express moral virtues in their interactions and relationships with pupils. Indeed, it is in these interactions that moral qualities are shaped. Fallona (2000: 684) believes that a teacher is a moral exemplar and that we ought to develop and nurture the following virtues in them: 'bravery, friendliness, wit, mildness, magnificence, honour, generosity, temperance, truthfulness, and justice.'

Halstead and Taylor (2000: 29), in reviewing the evidence for teacher interactions with pupils affecting their moral development, conclude:

> It is through relationships that children learn the importance of qualities such as honesty, respect and sensitivity to others. ... Children are most likely to be influenced by teachers whose qualities they admire. Such qualities include tolerance, firmness and fairness, acting in a reasonable manner and a willingness to explain things.

We could add here other desirable teacher qualities, such as patience, being a good listener, being likeable, showing compassion, caring – the list is almost endless. It would be inappropriate to produce a definitive checklist of these and other associated virtues by way of a blueprint for all schools. Nevertheless, what teacher would not strive for these admired virtues in teaching? As they develop one of these virtues, other complementary virtues are developed alongside. The danger is that when the State prescribes the list of virtues to be taught, they will inevitably be taught in a '*techne*' fashion, focusing on skills and mechanics, with little emphasis on the development of '*phronesis*', good sense and judgement in all spheres of life.

We appear to recognise that the child often fails to share because of some moral weakness and that we need to teach them to share. The child may be ignorant of the good thing to do in the situation, or alternatively the child may know what is good in the situation, but sets out to do the opposite. In both cases teaching is necessary and teachers generally do not hesitate to teach virtue in these circumstances. Some will claim that they simply present children with various moral problems and then allow them to decide what their own value preferences are – but in practice, this method of teaching the virtues is problematic and not as common as is purported. Schools are communities of teachers and learners that cultivate virtues together. They generally do not present a thousand moral choices to explore, but possess rather a fairly settled vision of the good.

Carr (1993) argues that since values are inherent in teaching, it is unlikely that pupils will be able to avoid the moral influence of teachers completely, even if teachers do not see themselves as moral exemplars. All teachers are involved inevitably in moral education and all teacher actions have moral import. Good teachers exhibit settled dispositions that shape their interactions with pupils – the way teachers establish classroom routines, and how they form groups, enforce discipline and encourage excellence. This is done instinctively and spontaneously in teaching, as teachers have a deeply embedded commitment to caring about children as individuals and a desire to help them become their best possible selves as students and as persons. As Campbell (2003: 138) concludes:

> Moral agency... concerns the dual, but interrelated, commitment of the teacher to be both a moral person and a moral educator and, by means of combining the two, an inevitable exemplar and a model of virtuous conduct and attitude.

The overall argument we are advancing is that the teacher provides support for classroom learning that goes beyond the mere mechanics of teaching. Teachers must have a moral commitment to serve the interests of their pupils and they contribute to their moral development. Indeed, teaching can only be counted as a profession insofar as it is committed to promoting an important human good – education. As Sockett (1993: 14) observes: 'Many teachers have a moral vision, a moral sense, and a moral motive however mixed up they may be in any individual.' Good teachers sense the importance of acquiring a wider perspective on human values and know that values are unavoidable in teaching. That is why it is crucial that the values and virtues in the act of teaching are clearly described and understood. Coby and Damon (1992: 300) also identified five criteria that characterise persons who could be seen as moral exemplars, which could be applied to teachers. They are:

1 a sustained commitment to moral ideals or principles that include a general respect for humanity, or a sustained evidence of moral virtue;
2 a disposition to act in accordance with one's moral ideals or principles;
3 a willingness to risk one's self-interest for the sake of one's moral values;
4 a tendency to be inspiring to others and thereby to move them to moral action;
5 a sense of realistic humility about one's own importance relative to the world at large, implying a relative lack of concern for one's own ego.

Teaching as virtue in action

Good teaching will enrich and expand the minds of pupils, encouraging reflection, self-evaluation and the practice of virtues. Schools intentionally build and promote positive moral atmospheres and encourage their teachers to exemplify the virtues that constitute their ethos (we elaborate on this in Chapter 5). This school ethos can only be constructed through the pervasive moral attitudes of teachers, which in turn profoundly influence pupils. School ethos and teachers are recognised by almost all character educators to be a vital dimension of character education. As Wynne (1991) pointed out, there is no such thing as a value-free school. The non-academic aspects of schooling are just as important for the development of students. The influence of school on character formation is based on the belief that adults have a duty to teach virtue and help children develop good habits (Wynne, 1991). Role modelling of values by teachers through setting examples – further discussed in Chapter 3 – are known to be key instruments in values development (Lickona, 1991; Rose, 2004; Arweck *et al.*, 2005; Kristjánsson, 2006a). According to Huitt (2004) and Campbell and Bond (1982), the most tractable sources of influence in a young person's life are schools and teachers. The influence of family (for example, important adults and older siblings) is least tractable, and hence most difficult to alter.

The Jubilee Centre (2013; Framework for Character Education) argue that character is more caught than taught. A number of them underlined the importance of being a good role model for pupils by exemplifying the behaviours they wished to see in their pupils or in society at large. A primary teacher commented:

> [...] if we can set a good example to the children by being the kind of person that we would want them to be, by showing them the kind of qualities they need to have in life, then it gives them a role model, something to aspire to. I do know in my role that children do copy adult behaviour. So the more we can produce as a role model for them the better the world is going to be in the future.

While primary and secondary teachers share common views regarding their role in pupils' character development, there are clear differences too. Primary teachers tended to focus on their moral agency as a person in helping pupils to develop values. The majority of secondary teachers, on the other hand, viewed their role in pupils' value development within the context of the curriculum: this means the extent to which they provided appropriate and challenging work, the way they taught the lesson or the ways in which they addressed team work or sharing where pupils worked together. In secondary schools there was a stronger awareness of helping pupils to make good choices, and taking responsibility for projects and their personal decisions. Teachers recognise that resolving dilemmas in the classroom forces them to prioritise between the conflicting wants, needs and interests, not only of their students, but between parents and fellow teachers. Helping students to reason morally through all curriculum subjects is essential and Stoll and Beller (1998: 24) recognise that:

> moral reasoning does not promise behavioural change, but it does promise individual soul-searching and reflection on personal beliefs, values, and principles. Without this process, cognitive moral growth will not increase, behaviour change will never occur, and the potential for consistent moral action becomes little more than a hit and miss proposition.

We discuss character education across the curriculum in Chapter 4.

Conclusions

Teaching is inherently moral and ethical in nature because it implicitly imparts values when the teacher selects or excludes topics, when they insist on answers being accepted as correct and when they encourage students to seek the truth. The moral dimensions of teaching are often hidden or ignored, but they can never be avoided and must be made more transparent. Virtues – understood as an acquired disposition to do what is good – are really taught by example. In this sense, the good is not just something to reflect on, but something to be put into practice. The virtues are therefore values that we embody, live and enact. As the Jubilee Centre (2015; Statement on Teacher Education) notes: 'The single most powerful tool you have to impact a student's character is your own character.' Since teachers intervene in the lives of pupils and may require them to change direction, they need to reflect on and be conscious of the moral purposes of education. Pupils are observing and listening to teachers, which means that teachers ought to be morally disciplined since morality is not a private practice in schools. Clearly, any view of ethics for teaching should have broad public and professional support. There is much more to teaching than subject knowledge and technical skills, so there is a strong case for a virtue-based rather than simply a competence-based conception of teaching.

Objectives reached

By the end of this chapter you should have clear ideas about:

- how all teaching is a moral enterprise and teachers have moral responsibilities as exemplars;
- why the character of teachers matters and why character education should feature on teacher education courses;
- the danger of current instrumentalist policies driving dedicated teachers out of the profession;
- why the competency agenda needs contextualising within a wider vision of the purpose of education – not just competence-based but also virtue-based;
- why teachers are more motivated by relational than contractual incentives;
- the four types of virtue – moral, intellectual, civic and performative – and the importance of *phronesis* as practical wisdom or good sense.

Questions for reflection

- To what extent do you agree that teaching is a moral enterprise and that teachers should be moral exemplars?
- Do you agree that character education should form part of teacher education courses?
- How would you situate the competency and moral agendas in policy terms?
- How do you see the relative importance of the four types of virtue?

- Do you agree with the 1995 UCET list of teacher qualities? Which in your view are the most important? Would you add any?
- Do you agree with Thomas Lickona's remark that 'The single most powerful tool you have to impact a student's character is your own character'?

Note

1   As defined in *A Framework for Character Education in Schools* (2013b) available via: http://jubileecentre.ac.uk/userfiles/jubileecentre/pdf/character-education/Frame work%20for%20Character%20Education.pdf (accessed 20th July 2015).

2 What is 'character education'?

Summary

Character education forms a broad church and incorporates various approaches that nevertheless have some common elements. We explain the relationship between values, morals and character education, defining this as a subset of moral education concerned with the cultivation of positive traits of good character called 'virtues'. We argue that character traits are *developmentally, logically,* and *motivationally* prior to more general moral concerns. We are now seeing renewed interest in moral education in general, and character education in particular, although recent programmes are rooted in different disciplines. We provide a historical background of character education and policy in the UK and explain the distinctiveness of an Aristotelian approach to virtue ethics based on human flourishing. This approach also goes beyond the instrumentalism of much recent educational policy. We define virtues as stable *dispositional clusters*, concerned with praiseworthy functioning in a number of significant and distinguishable spheres of human life and with a special emphasis on emotions and achieving a golden mean between extremes and the development of *phronesis* – practical wisdom or good sense. We compare Aristotelian character education with other variants and respond to some common criticisms of the field.

Introduction

The present chapter and Chapter 3 present an overview of the theoretical and conceptual foundations of character education, as well as a brief account of its history. We start in this chapter by offering a specification of 'character education' and some of its variants. We explain why we favour an Aristotelian approach to character education. Chapter 3 then digs deeper into the nuances of some of its underlying concepts, such as 'character' and 'virtue'. After reading these two chapters, readers should have got to grips with the philosophy and psychology underpinning character education, and appreciate some remaining controversies that divide character educationists among themselves as well as from character-education sceptics.

Definition of character education and its relationship to values education

Character educationists form a broad church and do not see eye-to-eye on everything. Nonetheless, they will tend to agree on a number of significant points (see further in Jubilee Centre, 2013b), such as that:

- Character is educable and its progress can, in principle, be measured holistically.
- Character is important in contributing to individual and societal flourishing.
- Character is largely caught through role-modelling and emotional contagion; school culture and ethos are therefore essential, although character can also be taught.
- Character lays the foundation for better behaviour and increased employability.
- Character results in academic gains, such as higher grades, as a happy by-product.
- Character empowers students, is liberating and promotes democratic citizenship.

Unless you subscribe to these basic tenets, you should probably not consider yourself an actual or potential character educator. However, this list simply articulates a faith in an educational ideal, and does not argue for its legitimacy. Such arguments will be added at various junctures in the present chapter and in Chapter 3. Moreover, this list may create the false impression that character educationists form a discrete cult with a fixed credo. Nothing is further from the truth: character education is, as already noted, a broad church and incorporates various approaches and variants. Indeed, in the present book, 'character education' is used as an umbrella term for any approach to moral education that highlights the cultivation of good character in a broad sense. Notably, we avoid applying the term in the narrow sense in which it is often used in educational discourse to designate a certain US-based approach to moral education, which became popular in the 1980s and that some commentators have written off as overly nostalgic and conservative.

We will say more about the different variants of character education and the approach that the present authors favour in later sections of this chapter. Let us continue first to spell out the general contours of the concept, by way of Figure 2.1.

According to this specification, *values education* is the broadest term relevant to the purposes of the present book. It designates any education 'in' or 'about' values. Those values may be aesthetic, religious, political, environmental, etc. Most national curricula for compulsory education across the world include references to a number of such values that students are expected to learn about – and in some cases ideally adopt – at school.

Moral education designates education focusing on a subset of values specifically relevant to the moral sphere. Although it is difficult to define the word 'moral' definitively, most people will have an intuitive grasp of what distinguishes moral values from non-moral ones. Under the general rubric of moral education,

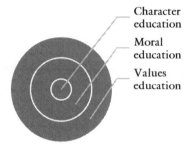

Figure 2.1 The relationship between general approaches to values education.

a range of courses are taught in schools in the world, variously designated as 'moral education', 'human rights education', 'peace education', 'citizenship education', 'life-skills education' and so forth.

Character education is best understood as a subset of moral education, concerned with the cultivation of positive character traits called 'virtues'. Both of the key terms here, 'character' and 'virtue', contain complexities that we will explore in due course, but we can rely for the moment on an everyday understanding. Discerning readers may question, however, whether character education is best defined as a subset of moral education, since character education typically aims to cultivate a number of personal qualities that are not necessarily considered moral: intellectual qualities or virtues such as curiosity, and performance-related qualities such as resilience. We maintain, however, that because character education is not about the cultivation of any particular character type, but of a generally *good* character, any traits addressed in proper character education need to be informed by moral constraints. So, we do not consider building the resilience of repeat offenders to be true character education. Therefore, we consider it helpful, for classificatory purposes, to consider character education as a specific form of moral education, or – more precisely – moral education with a special target and focus.

Why prioritise character education?

If there are so many types of moral education, why should we prioritise the cultivation of moral *character*? Why not start with citizenship education or human-rights education, for example? We, the authors, want to make it clear that we consider all those variants important. However, we suggest three reasons below why character education may be the best starting point in moral education, based on the assumption that character traits are *developmentally, logically* and *motivationally* prior to more general moral concerns:

- *Development.* Children learn to apply a moral vocabulary – and gradually internalise its content as part of their character – in small-scale situations such as the home and the classroom before they learn to apply it to society at large. For instance, three-year-old Jack may complain that it is 'unfair' that his sister Beth got a bigger slice of cake than he did long before Jack starts to think about issues of unfairness in society.

- *Logic.* Character concepts are what philosophers call 'thicker' than other moral concepts and serve as logical grounders for them, rather than vice versa. For example, a complex moral/political theory about fairness can be logically critiqued for not corresponding to everyday ideas by laypeople about what fairness is. It would be odd to critique Jack's conception of fairness from the standpoint of a complex moral theory, however. This is why some theorists have argued that teaching children citizenship education before they are taught character education is putting the cart before the horse.
- *Motivation.* From a psychological point of view, we have reasons to believe that people will not be reliably motivated to feel or do the right things unless it is deeply ingrained in their character, or forms part of their 'moral identity'. A merely intellectual commitment to abstract ideals is motivationally fragile.

To reinforce the point above, however, these reasons should *not* be taken to mean that character education is ultimately more morally/socially 'important' than, say, citizenship education. Human beings are social animals, not Robinson Crusoes; nor is adult moral association limited to small-scale interactions around the kitchen table or in the classroom. Yet everything has its time and place, and the younger the student the better the reason to prioritise the cultivation of good character over other facets of moral education.

The problem of a conceptual labyrinth and the need for a GPS

If we examine education systems around the world, we see renewed interest in moral education in general, and character education in particular. The exclusive focus on exam results is often considered very much a twentieth century obsession and other, character-related, factors are seen to hold the key to twenty-first century employability. For example, in the U.K., all the major political parties now say they support character education in schools.

However, if we look at the actual programmes and interventions on offer, a more complex picture appears. For example:

- Some of the programmes are geared towards preschool and/or primary education while others are exclusively aimed at students in secondary education.
- Some have been dressed up as new, discrete school subjects, while others function as add-ons to those already in existence.
- Some are part of the compulsory curriculum, while others are optional elements.

These *formal* differences are compounded by apparent *substantive* differences between recent programmes, based on the fact that they are rooted in different *disciplinary paradigms* and are frequently engaged, internally, in turbulent factional strife:

- Some are explicitly *moral*, giving rise to programmes such as character education.
- Some are rooted in *psychological* theories, giving rise to programmes such as social and emotional learning (SEL) and positive education.
- Some are *political*, giving rise to programmes such as civic or citizenship education.
- Some are *health*-related, giving rise to programmes such as physical, social and health education (PSHE).
- Some are *religious*, giving rise to programmes of religion-based moral education.
- Some are of an *eclectic* disciplinary provenance, such as well-being education and life-skills/life-competence education.

An obvious question to ask, then, is whether moral education is swimming in a sea of hopeless heterogeneity. Is there anything distinctive to be found in this prodigious plurality of approaches – any putative common point of departure? The eminent American character educationist Marvin Berkowitz (2012) has stated this problem in stark terms: 'I have found the language of moral education to be a semantic minefield', he says. 'There is no moral GPS to help with such semantic navigation. I have lectured, written, etc. under quite a set of terms. The terminology varies geographically and historically. And there are many overlapping terms used.'

This semantic minefield no doubt confuses many teachers. They do not know where to start and some of them suffer from initiative fatigue. With each new minister come new approaches that are supposed to develop 'the whole child', but after a few years they fall out of fashion and are replaced with something else. While we are well aware of this 'problem of heterogeneity' and cannot simply wish it away, we propose to offer readers a possible GPS to extricate them from the conceptual labyrinth. Our GPS is based on time-honoured Aristotelian conceptions about the cultivation of moral character in young people. Before we explain this approach in more detail, it will be instructive to recap some facts about the history of character education in the UK.

Historical background and policy developments

The formation of character could be regarded as the goal that all general education has historically set out to achieve. While the Scottish Enlightenment focused on the study of character in human beings, it remained the case that one of the principal goals of nineteenth century elementary schools for the poor was the production of characters suited to the needs of work. Attempts at this kind of character education showed up in schools through strict discipline, punishments and rote learning and were misapplied, particularly to the poor, as a form of social control rather than character building. The Victorian period was certainly a high point in character education, or perhaps more accurately in the use of the language of character. The Victorians meant many things by 'character' and many of these meanings did not apply to schooling. They were principally concerned with the idea of the will and its power over good conduct. It was generally assumed that people knew the difference between right and wrong and that it was only weakness of will that caused them to do wrong.

The Victorian theory of character formation led to much ambiguity and contradiction in behaviour. Robert Owen's (1824) experiment in the social reconstruction of character through integrating character with society was an example of a utopian theory of character formation. Beside his factory in New Lanark, Scotland, he built a 'school', which opened on 1st January 1816, with the title 'Institute for the Formation of Character'. This was the first explicit attempt to transform the characters of the poor, but it did not last long. Much more widespread was the view that character equalled a socialisation in good manners and, in a particular, a form of social conduct. Whilst there was a recognition that human nature could be directly shaped by education, the notion of character was largely embodied in laws, institutions and social expectations.

The concept of schools as a place to train character was totally new, but it eventually came to distinguish the English private school. The growing middle classes realised that money alone would not secure them the coveted status of the 'character of a gentleman'. Increasingly, they sent their sons to the rapidly expanding number of independent schools. There was a marked revival of interest in character formation for middle class children in the 1820s, which first began in some reformed public schools (Rothblatt, 1976: 133–134). Thomas Arnold, the Headmaster of Rugby, gave voice to middle class aspirations by emphasising that the educational ideal should be the production of the 'noble character', the 'man of character' or more precisely the Christian manly spirit, better known as 'muscular Christianity'.

His aim was no less than the formation of the Christian character in the young through 'godliness and good learning'. As David Newsome (1961) notes, it was a movement to re-unite religion and morality. The school as a place for the explicit training of character came to distinguish the English public school from all other Western school systems. Supporters of Arnold were strong adherents of character formation. As well as instituting stern disciplinary regimes in their schools, they encouraged the reading of selected great authors to discern the essential core of 'common' values. The Clarendon Commission (1864: 56ff), which reported on the nine principal public schools, found that among other virtues it was partially 'their love of healthy sport and exercise' that helped 'in moulding the character of the "English gentleman".' There was a strong belief that games developed manliness and inspired, *inter alia*, the virtues of fairness, loyalty, moral and physical courage and co-operation. Games in the private schools were thus constituted as a course in practical ethics.

The public schools also socialised young men into the habit of good manners. In this view, character was a form of social and moral capital, and the function of the school was to provide the right environment in which the 'right' people could, at an early stage, get to know one another. The upright stance of the Victorian gentleman seemed to provide the external confirmation of an acquired well-formed character. It often amounted to little more than the visible sign of conformity to a set of public virtues, revealing nothing of any inner moral qualities. For many, character was not an ideal, but a display of the required manners solely to those they considered their elders and betters. This was an education designed for the social elite and generally for men. Rothblatt (1976: 135 and 102) reminds us that it was in the 1860s that character formation made a forceful appearance in Oxford and Cambridge Universities, but it often resulted in conduct by undergraduates and dons alike that was 'self-consciously painful'. This class-bound society was changing rapidly and it remained impossible to develop workable notions of character for all. There is a long history of ill-conceived, ineffective and failed efforts at character education in Britain. The kinds of character that teachers and educational thinkers espoused and the training methods they used also varied enormously.

The government's provision for elementary schools from 1870 onwards was directly concerned with outlining the goals of this kind of public education. The Board of Education's Handbook from 1906 onwards continued to make explicit that: 'The purpose of the Public Elementary School is to form and strengthen character.' The handbook emphasised that the corporate life of the school should avoid anything that undermines character formation, and listed the habits of industry, self-control, duty, respect for others, good manners, fair play and loyalty as the kinds of virtues that should be cultivated.

In 1949 the Ministry of Education published a paper entitled 'Citizens Growing Up: At Home, At School and After', in which it is stated that 'good citizens must first be good men.' The document has a section on character that briefly details why and how it must be improved and there is an appeal to 'public virtues' and an exhortation to develop an improved moral tone in schools. The Ministry's (1949: 11) yearbook also advocated the introduction of 'social activities' in schools in order to develop character. After 1950 it is difficult to find any references to character in government education publications, until 2001. Nevertheless, interest in character education continued outside government circles and in 1951 the editors of *The Yearbook of Education* at the Institute of Education in London produced a *Yearbook* that sought to examine 'the ways in which…the school contributes to the formation of moral character, sentiments, attitudes, ideals and ethical standards' (see Lauwerys and Hans, 1951). In one of the edited papers, T. H. Pear (1951: 313) claimed that it was still generally assumed by most English teachers that they were involved in the training of their pupils' characters.

The reasons for the subsequent omission of 'character education or building' from government policy documents in education are complex. By the 1950s and 1960s cognitive psychology became a discipline and gave great emphasis to Lawrence Kolhberg's theories, helping to make them popular in education. The success of Jean Piaget, Lawrence Kohlberg and Eric Erickson was due to their themes of development, indicating progress. These themes satisfied the cultural demands of the time and influenced government policy on education. British culture and society had become more pluralistic and therefore schooling became more sensitive to the growing diversity of children in many schools. Many involved in education believed that the lack of substantive content for character education made it less susceptible to criticism from ethnic and religious groups in society. The 1960s and 1970s were concerned with values clarification and procedural neutrality in the classroom, and there was a widespread presumption in favour of moral relativism.

In 1996 the Conservative government encouraged the Schools Curriculum and Assessment Authority to enter the public debate about morality by establishing the National Forum. This was not intended to increase children's knowledge of morality, but to improve their behaviour (Marenbon, 1996). Whilst this endeavour began under a Conservative government, it was continued under New Labour, with Tony Blair suggesting that a fourth R should be added to education – the teaching of Responsibility (see Arthur, 2001). In describing the core values that it believed society would agree upon, The National Forum for Values in Education and the Community sought a consensus on the principles for developing virtuous conduct. The Forum produced a set of core values, which, it claimed, were applicable to all, irrespective of class, sex, gender, race or religion. The values included: friendship, justice, truth, self-respect, freedom, and respect for the environment, but as William Glasser (1969) said 'certain moral values can be taught in school if the teaching is restricted to principles about which there is essentially no disagreement in our society.'

New Labour also sought to implement a policy of 'education with character', which it claimed lay at the heart of its policies on education. In the White Paper (Department for Education and Skills, 2001), the government recognised that schools may not be the ideal learning environments for building character and it advocated experiential learning about informed participation in communal affairs. All of this aims to build character by developing 'rounded individuals'. In summary, the New Labour government was not neutral about its view on the good life: it desired citizens of a particular type with certain capacities, habits and virtues that allow them to contribute to communal, economic and institutional life in society. It identified the school as the main institution in society responsible for fostering these virtues. In the previous chapter we mentioned how this can overreach the role of the school as a panacea for social ills.

Both Labour and Conservative political parties in the UK have, to varying degrees, begun to employ character and virtue terms in statements and speeches about education policy. The Coalition and current Conservative government have spoken of the need for character development to form part of the school day. Nicky Morgan, the Secretary of State for Education, has established a character unit in the Department of Education and has made character education a fifth aim of the whole department.

It is not therefore surprising that some discussions of moral or character education have been somewhat controversial, with disputes about definitions and methods. Nevertheless, it is recognised in modern British liberal society that the development of a person's character is not entirely a private matter for individuals or their families. It is accepted that character is intimately linked to the ethos of society itself and shaped by public forces. Public values have an influence on private life, albeit indirectly, because everything a government does is founded on the notion of it being of some benefit to the people it represents. Character is connected to the political system through the medium of schooling, which modern government oversees. It is also a major component in the making of a citizen. The decisions made by a government have a significant impact on the whole community and on individual citizens, including children. The attractiveness of character education rhetoric for politicians is also evident. Moreover, the quality of political life in a democracy is largely determined by the quality and character of its people. Governments are therefore concerned with citizens and whether the quality of their citizens' characters is improving or deteriorating. As we observed in Chapter 1, the quality of teachers' characters is of special concern in this respect.

What is distinctive about an Aristotelian approach to character education?

It may at first seem odd to seek inspiration for character education today in the ideas of the great philosopher Aristotle who lived more than 2,300 years ago. However, a closer look reveals some striking analogies between aspects of Greek society in Aristotle's time and our own. After all, the Athenians had experimented with democracy and were faced with many of the same challenges that we encounter in modern Western democracies, including demagoguery and public disaffection or apathy. In addition, Aristotle was a great believer in supporting philosophical and educational approaches with empirical evidence rather than constructing them within academic ivory towers. His ideas therefore have a strong resonance with twenty-first century sensibilities and lend themselves well to scientific updates in the light of new social scientific evidence. It is precisely such a renewed and reconstructed form of Aristotelian character education that we present in this book.

Below, we give *five reasons* why we consider an Aristotelian approach to character education to be well grounded, practical and plausible. In Chapter 3, we then explore some of its key concepts in more detail.

First, Aristotelian character education is rooted in a clear conception of human flourishing (or what the ancient Greeks called *eudaimonia*) as the ultimate good and unconditional end of human beings, for the sake of which they do all instrumentally desirable things. An action or a reaction is morally right if and only if it enables human flourishing. According to Aristotle, by analysing empirically the proper 'function' of human beings (just as we analyse the proper function of a good knife or a good field of wheat), we can ascertain that human flourishing consists of the realisation of virtues of thought and character and the fulfilment of other specifically human physical and mental potentialities over the whole course of life. In a nutshell, *eudaimonia* is 'a certain sort of activity of the soul expressing virtue' (Aristotle, 1985: 23). Moreover, as the virtues are both conducive to and constitutive of *eudaimonia*, it is an explicitly moral notion. It is impossible to achieve *eudaimonia* without being morally good – that is, without actualising the moral virtues. However, while necessary for flourishing, moral virtues are not sufficient; we also need good friends, family, health, basic material provisions, satisfactory education, a decent political society and sufficient supplies of 'luck in life' to thrive.

Alternative accounts of character education often highlight the extrinsic benefits of virtuous living or, at best, make fleeting and cryptic references to the final end or purpose of the good life. Aristotelian character education does not underestimate the complementary instrumentalist benefits of character education in terms of higher grades and increased employability. However, it has the distinct advantage of upholding a clear view of the intrinsic value of virtuous character traits: that virtue is, so to speak, its own reward. This assumption neatly and flatly contradicts the currently dominant technicism and instrumentalism in education, which we described in detail in Chapter 1. That is perhaps the reason why we sometimes find it difficult to convey the idea of intrinsic value to policy-makers and politicians. Teachers, however, generally understand that there is more to education than exams, exams and more exams. They realise that schooling should prepare students for the tests of life rather than just a life of tests, as we have already argued.

To convince the 'instrumentalists', however, there is considerable empirical evidence, which suggests a link between (morally informed) character education and traditional academic achievement (e.g. grade attainment). A study of 681 elementary schools in California showed that schools with higher total character-education implementation tend to have higher academic scores by a small, but nonetheless discernible margin (Benninga *et al.*, 2003). According to Park and Peterson's research (2006), lessons in character education can apparently result in a 16 percent improvement in academic achievement. Snyder and colleagues (2012) present findings highlighting how character-development programmes improve academic achievement, as well as an array of other, positive behaviours. Findings from a meta-analysis of 213 USA school-based social and emotional learning (SEL) programmes (most of which include, at least, *some* moral-character relevant ingredients) showed that compared to controls, SEL participants demonstrate significantly improved social and emotional skills, attitudes, as well as behaviour *and* academic performance that reflects an 11-percentile-point gain in achievement (Durlak *et al.*, 2011). Put simply, promoting the development of morally good character traits in schools seems to lead to higher attainment – as a happy side-effect.

Second, Aristotelian character education makes it clear that character education is about the cultivation of *virtues* as specifically human excellences. What sort of capacities are virtues? Unfortunately, most of the general terms that have been used to describe them carry unfortunate connotations. The closest answer is perhaps 'traits', but in psychology the term 'trait' typically refers to attributes that are (at least partly) inherited. The virtues, however – or so the Aristotelian story goes – are *acquired*, first through upbringing, and later through one's own repeated choices, coalescing into stable patterns (Aristotle stated that we are what we habitually do). 'Habits' is another possible answer, but 'habit' carries the connotation of a mere behavioural trait, which virtues are not. 'Dispositions' is a more neutral term and perhaps apt here, although the idea of self-cultivated dispositions is not common in educational psychology. The virtues, however, form complex dispositional clusters. It is no wonder that many theorists have given up on technical psychological language and simply refer to them by the Greek term '*hexis*', namely 'states of character', which may sound pretty bland but can at least be fortified with meaning.

Let us say, then, that the virtues constitute stable *dispositional clusters* concerned with praiseworthy functioning in a number of significant and distinctive spheres of human life. Each virtue is typically seen to comprise a unique set consisting of perception/recognition, emotion, desire, motivation, behaviour and comportment – or style, applicable in the relevant sphere – where none of these elements (not even 'correct' behaviour) can be evaluated in isolation from the others. The person possessing the virtue of compassion, for example, *notices* easily and *attends to* situations in which the fortunes of others have been undeservedly compromised, *feels* for the needs of those who have suffered this misfortune, *desires* that their misfortune be reversed, *acts* (if humanly possible) for the relevant (ethical) reasons in ways conducive to that goal and *exudes* an outward aura of empathy and care.

It is difficult to say which of those 'spheres' or 'components' of virtue is most important as, ideally, they form a coherent whole. However, if pressed, the Aristotelian answer will be that *emotion* is the component which really sets virtue apart: a compassionate person would still count as one even if she became paralysed and could not engage in any compassionate behaviour. Conversely, a person could display compassionate-seeming behaviour without the relevant emotional engagement – simply for the sake of getting praise from others, for example – in which case she would not be exhibiting the virtue of compassion.

Aristotelian character education offers the additional benefit of an attractive account of virtue architectonics: the *golden-mean* structure. Each moral virtue thus constitutes, in Aristotle's schema, a specific medial character state (e.g. courage), flanked by the extremes of deficiency (e.g. cowardice) and excess (e.g. foolhardiness). There is only one way – the medial way – to be 'correct': to be inclined to act in the right way, towards the right people, at the right time. But there is a plethora of ways in which to be 'bad' (Aristotle, 1985: 44). From our experience, the aspect of Aristotelian virtue theory that teachers find most appealing is precisely this golden-mean structure. As a very similar architectonic can also be found in Confucian virtue ethics (Yu, 2007), one may wonder whether this aspect taps into deeply entrenched public conceptions.

Diametrically opposed to the virtues are the *vices*: habitual desires for and practices of evil, albeit typically under some euphemistic description like 'taking care of one's own interests'. Vice can be characterised as deep alienation from virtue (Annas 2011, Chapter 7), rather than simply the absence of virtue. It is, therefore, misleading to talk about young moral learners as possessing 'vice'; nor can one attribute 'full virtue' to them. Young people are *developing towards* virtue or vice. We have already described the different *types* of virtues in Chapter 1 and we say more about common stages in the development of character in Chapter 4.

The *third* proposed advantage of Aristotelian character education, as already suggested, is how it attributes a unique role to *emotions* in moral development, in contrast to many other forms of character education that concentrate on mere behavioural modification. Although Aristotle nowhere produces a definitive list of all the character states that can pass as moral virtues, it is crucial that not only proper actions but also proper reactions are conducive to and constitutive of *eudaimonia*. Emotions are central to who we are, and they can, no less than actions, have an 'intermediate and best condition' when they are felt 'at the right times, about the right things, towards the right people, for the right end and in the right way' (Aristotle, 1985: 44). If the relevant emotion is 'too intense or slack', we are badly off in relation to it, but if it is intermediate, we are 'well off' (1985: 41); and persons can be fully virtuous only if they are disposed to experience emotions in this medial way on a regular basis. Some virtues, such as compassion (pain at another's undeserved plight) are simply a cluster of emotions, and they can constitute a full-blown virtue, as already noted, even if one may not have the ability to do anything about the plight in question.

Emotional traits are seen as reason-responsive and educable; the individual (even the young child) is not simply prey to ungovernable passions. Accordingly, character education – in its early stages at least – will above all involve sensitisation to appropriate emotions which, in turn, start to function as moral barometers and motivators by developing into automatic response routines. For example, the child who develops an understanding of and sensitivity to gratitude automatically perceives – as the response routine is triggered – relevant events in grateful ways. This focus on the emotional nature of moral motivation and general moral functioning is very much in line with current state-of-the art research in moral psychology that has demonstrated how moral emotions function like an autopilot mechanism, typically steering moral reactions in a particular direction before moral reasoning has had time to kick in.

Fourth, Aristotelian character education pays more attention to the adjudication of virtue conflicts than most other approaches. Some less sophisticated forms of character education depict young people as consistently being faced with choices between virtue and vice. We believe, however, that the typical dilemmas young people face are between conflicting virtues, which cannot easily be juggled. For instance, teenagers often experience conflicts between *loyalty* to friends – which surely is a virtue in its golden-mean form – and *honesty* to authority, for example at school. In Aristotelian character education, the demand for reflective holism is stringent and clear. In the case of fully developed adults, their conduct does not count as virtuous unless it is chosen for the right reasons from 'a firm and unchanging state' of character, is motivated by the right emotions and has been overseen and adjudicated by the intellectual meta-virtue of *phronesis* (good sense or practical wisdom as already explained in Chapter 1) which acts as a moral integrator when two virtues, such as loyalty and honesty, clash (Aristotle, 1985: 40).

Aristotle is actually quite unwavering on this point. We cannot be 'fully good' without *phronesis*, nor can we possess *phronesis* without virtue of character (1985: 171). In order to take the step from merely externally taught ('habituated') virtue to full virtue, we must learn to choose the right actions and emotions from a *phronesis*-guided reflection – which eventually becomes an internalised routine. This process takes time, as those who have learnt a virtue through habituation 'do not yet know it, though they string the [correct] words together; for it must grow into them' (1985: 180). Stripped of its link to the moral virtues, *phronesis* degenerates into a cunning capacity – a mere performance virtue – that Aristotle calls 'cleverness'. Cleverness involves the capacity to act or react in such a way as to 'promote whatever goal is assumed and to achieve it'; hence, both the *phronimoi* (persons exhibiting *phronesis*) and the unscrupulous can be called clever (1985: 154, 168–169).

To live with the good sense of *phronesis* is to be open-minded and to recognise the true variety of things and situations to be experienced (Schwartz & Sharpe, 2010). To live without 'good sense' is to live thoughtlessly and indecisively. 'Bad sense' shows itself in irresoluteness, failure to carry out decisions and/or in negligence and blindness to our circumstances. To live without 'good sense' is thus to be close-minded; it can reveal itself in a 'cock-sure', 'know-it-all' attitude (see Jubilee Centre, 2013b). Good sense gradually matures, if all is well, and explaining how it develops in the individual psyche provides Aristotelian character education with the beginnings of a theory of developmental levels of moral functioning, to which we return in Chapter 4.

This theory may explain not only the difference between habituated and *phronetic* virtue, but also how young people can be reasonably developed morally, at least for their age, without having reached the highest level. Being *self-controlled*, for example, involves making the right moral decisions, albeit reluctantly and with effort, even possibly with resentment or boredom. While not the ultimate moral ideal to aim at, we can perhaps consider a rebellious teenager well on the way to moral virtue if she succeeds in keeping reasonable tabs on her rebelliousness. Thus, just as temperance in diet is not the same for the Olympic athlete and the sedentary office worker, so 'optimal' moral functioning in a teenager may differ considerably from what would count as its optimal expression in a fully mature person.

The *fifth* advantage is the essential educational emphasis of the moral theory underlying Aristotelian character education. Obviously, all forms of character education are, by definition, about *education*. In Aristotelianism, however, character education is not an extraneous addition to an understanding of morality or the study of moral philosophy; it is, rather, what such understanding and study are all about. We progress towards moral excellence only if we are educated from an early age – indeed from birth – to do so. A study of morality would, by Aristotle's light, be an entirely fruitless enterprise if it did not gauge the educational implications of its findings. Contemporary moral philosophy is commonly criticised – by moral psychologists for example – for its lack of attention to developmental issues and its almost complete neglect of childhood. Aristotle's stance is so radically different here that he could almost be accused of the opposite error: of reducing moral philosophy to character education. For him, it is more precious to know how virtue arises than to know what it is. More specifically, with respect to moral inquiry as such, its purpose 'is not to know what virtue is, but to become good, since otherwise the inquiry would be of no benefit to us' (1985: 35). We cannot think of a more suitable platform from which to launch an approach to character education.

Aristotelian character education compared with other variants

Some introductory texts about moral education take a fairly dim view of 'character education', equating it with a variant that became popular in the USA in the 1980s, already mentioned at the beginning of this chapter. According to this textbook description, character education is a) backward looking (nostalgic), b) grounded in conservative politics, c) only ever concerned with fixing individual shortcomings, d) aims at behaviour modification, e) uses habituation/conditioning as the method of instruction and f) flags patriotism as the main moral value.

Although we have yet to find a theorist who subscribes to all those tenets, it is worth distancing Aristotelian character education from them. On the view espoused in the present book, developed in the UK at the Jubilee Centre for Character and Virtues, character education is first and foremost a) forward-looking, b) grounded in progressive politics, c) concerned with both individual and societal change, d) aims at a change of emotional make-up, e) uses a variety of methods geared towards the development of *phronesis* and f) promotes specific universal moral values and virtues.

In the corridors of Whitehall and in some political circles in the U.K., an alternative view of character education has been forming in the last few years, according to which 'character' is referred to by the labels of 'soft skills' or 'non-cognitive competencies'. Unfortunately, neither label is particularly well suited. The so-called 'soft skills' do not seem 'softer' in terms of being easier to administer or learn than their allegedly 'harder' counterparts. As someone once quipped, after the skull, character seems to be the hardest part of the human body. Moreover, so-called 'non-cognitive competencies' are not raw feelings and desires, but rather certain attitudes, such as self-confidence and resilience, based on complex self-beliefs and beliefs about the world. These are anything but non-cognitive, because 'non-cognitive' means 'not based on cognitions (beliefs, judgements)'. For example, self-confidence is not just a non-cognitive feeling, like a toothache, but involves 'cognitions' about what future tasks people think they can master. Perhaps, then, 'non-cognitive' is simply meant to denote 'non-academic' – but this is a different notion altogether.

If we dig deeper, this 'Whitehall' view of character seems to seek academic justification in a much-cited book by Paul Tough (2013). Tough's book describes the successful focus on a particular subset of character skills in the so-called KIPP ('Knowledge-Is-Power-Program') charter schools in the US and how this focus has transformed the lives of disadvantaged kids in terms of their future study and career prospects by enabling them to 'climb the mountain to college' (2013: 50). The main skills in question are grit/resilience and self-confidence. Tough is impressed by the way in which character has here been severed from 'finger-wagging morality' and how the new approach is 'fundamentally devoid of value judgment' (2013: 60).

From an Aristotelian perspective there is a deeper issue here, however, than how useful a certain programme of character education is in getting kids into college. To be sure, resilience helps young people to bounce back from negative experiences, and self-confidence makes them more efficacious in achieving their ends. The deeper Aristotelian worry is that such 'performance virtues' (as we defined them in Chapter 1) can be positively dangerous if they are freed from moral constraints. The missing element in the character make-up of the 'banksters' in the run-up to the financial crisis, or even the average dictator, is clearly not a higher level of resilience and self-confidence. What we want to instil in young people is hardly the grit of the repeat offender. The truth is, as the proverb has it, that the higher the ape climbs, the more he shows his tail. If the choice is between an immoral high climber and a moral low climber, Aristotelian character educationists will opt for the latter.

Although we have been concerned in this chapter with fleshing out the conceptual and substantive repertoire of Aristotelian character education – distinguishing it from other variants of character education and other, more distant, approaches to moral education – we do not want to leave readers with the impression that there are as many irreconcilable types of character education as there are character educationists. Most, if not all, forms of character education refer back in some way to Aristotle, and in the end, there are typically more areas of convergence than divergence between those views. However, they do *prioritise* differently the character virtues to be promoted.

Objectives reached

At the end of this chapter, you should have clear ideas about:

- the difference between values education, moral education and character education;
- some reasons for prioritising character education;
- the history of character education in the UK;
- five distinct advantages of Aristotelian character education; and
- how Aristotelian character education distinguishes itself from some other variants.

Questions for reflection

- Do you believe in the claims about character and character education, expressed in the bulleted list at the beginning of this chapter? If yes, why? If no, why not?
- Should character education really come before citizenship education, or is this just a chicken-and-egg question?
- What does it really mean to say that something is intrinsically valuable, in addition to its instrumentalist benefits?
- What could be the link between character and employability?
- Is *phronesis* something that you can teach, or can it only be picked up gradually from experience?

3 Digging deeper into the purpose and meaning of character and character education

Summary

In this chapter we review the history of character within psychology and distinguish it from self and personality, stressing that character traits are moral and educable and that moral character can continue to grow and develop. We propose a list of prototypical moral virtues as a sound basis for character education underpinning other forms of virtue. We argue that the terms 'character' and 'virtue' are not old-fashioned and that they should be retrieved as part of the development of virtue literacy. We explain the Aristotelian background of virtue ethics and human flourishing as a form of moral naturalism and its advantages as secular rather than religious in the present social context. We refute the charges of conservatism, individualism and paternalism levelled at character education, and respond to critiques from the stances of cultural relativism and situationism. We set out four criteria for successful character education, commenting that further work needs to be done to integrate the concept within moral psychology and educational practice.

Introduction

As the title suggests, this chapter digs deeper into some of the core concepts of character education. The practically minded reader might be tempted to skip this chapter and jump straight to the more 'applied' chapters to follow. That could be unwise, however, as all practitioners of character education will, from time to time, meet with sceptical colleagues, parents or students who call into question the very endeavour in which they are engaged. This chapter provides grist to the mill for responding to such scepticism.

More specifically, the chapter provides further psychological and philosophical backbone to the application of the core concepts of character education; it offers a more nuanced taxonomy of the virtues relevant to character education; and it defends the very idea of the cultivation of moral character at school against some common objections, often based on misunderstandings or 'myths'. The most obvious question to start with is the meaning of 'character' and its role in human psychology.

Character and human psychology

In Chapter 2, we explored the challenges associated with the notion of 'character education', but we spoke as if it was pretty clear what character education is meant to be education *of*. That may have been a bit hasty – and it is time to provide further justification.

'Character' is not a commonly explored subject in contemporary psychology. To explain why, we need to go back to the 1930s when personality psychologist Gordon Allport provided *character* with a concise specification as 'personality evaluated' – and *personality*, in turn, as 'character devaluated' (Allport, 1937: 52). Since then, in social science, 'character' has been used to refer to a certain subset of personality that is morally evaluable and supposed to provide persons with moral worth. Most philosophers and educationists will take that to mean that those traits are reason-responsive and educable. So, to give an example, *conscientiousness* as a personality trait (one of the famous Big-Five traits in personality psychology) refers to the state of being generally disciplined, reliable and predictable. None of these descriptions is meant to carry moral connotations. A crook can be conscientious as such, and reliable in dealings with fellow crooks. Moreover, conscientiousness as a personality trait is partly inherited and may be hard to educate into or out of people. In contrast, conscientiousness as a character trait (or moral conscientiousness) is a learned quality, a *virtue*, that of channelling the general conscientiousness into practical, moral contexts of daily life. So even if it turned out that 50 percent of the personality trait of conscientiousness could be explained genetically, this would not mean that the same applied to the virtuous subset.

In the early part of the twentieth century, psychologists were highly interested not only in general personality, but also in the subset of (moral) character, but then character fell into disrepute because psychologists – entering the heyday of so-called 'value-free' social science – became concerned that by studying and promoting character, they would stop being scientists and turn into moralists. This trend may now be changing again, especially within so-called positive psychology, which argues for the resuscitation of character constructs (Peterson & Seligman, 2004). Yet, it would be premature to celebrate the reintroduction of character into mainstream social scientific discourse; for instance, until recently, character education only evoked interest among a small number of mainstream educational psychologists.

That said, quite a few psychologists harbour concerns about the practical arbitrariness of standard personality constructs for making sense of individual difference – at least the sort of difference that interests ordinary people. For example, research shows that people regard moral virtues, such as honesty, higher than the Big-Five traits when looking for a potential spouse on dating sites (Baumeister & Exline, 1999). As Hofstee (1990: 82) observed a long time ago, 'the science of individual differences is deeply rooted in morality' (for recent empirical evidence on this, see De Raad & Van Oudenhoven, 2011; Goodwin, Piazza & Rozin, 2014). Our own research in the Jubilee Centre indicates that primary-school children in the UK even choose their friends partly on the basis of moral character virtues.

The basic problem is that by excluding moral properties from their potential list of traits that comprise our everyday personhood, personality psychologists risk obscuring and diluting what is central to us. To take a parallel example from the field of education, considerable emphasis used to be placed on the difference between a teacher's classroom *style* (that was supposed to reflect non-moral personality traits) and a teacher's *manner* (meant to capture what was moral in relation to the teacher's conduct). A closer look revealed, however, that the two could not be separated for any relevant purposes. In so far as a teacher's 'style' matters in the classroom, it is because of its moral implications: namely, its impact on student well-being (Kristjánsson, 2007: 152–155).

Figure 3.1 aims to capture the constructs that explain psycho-moral individual difference via different levels of personhood (see Kristjánsson, 2010). First of all, each of us possesses a unique profile of personality traits, some of which are inborn. Conscientiousness is one of those, as explained above. Others include extraversion, openness, agreeableness and neuroticism. Character traits form a subset of the general personality traits, and the most highly developed of those are the so-called virtues. As character traits are morally evaluable and educable, they are the subset on which most of character education focuses. The deepest level of personhood is sometimes referred to as 'self' or 'selfhood'. The 'self' comprises the emotional and moral traits that most characteristically set us apart as individuals, many of which remain beneath the threshold of consciousness (although our closest friends and family are often more aware of these than we are). A change of selfhood does occur occasionally in the moral development of individuals; this is referred to as a 'Damascus experience' or 'moral epiphany', and is sometimes inspired by a charismatic teacher, like John Keating in the film *Dead Poets Society*. However, such radical changes are rare as there are various psychological mechanisms that protect the self, for instance through our strong preference for self-verifications. More specifically, individuals typically seek out people who confirm rather than challenge their own conceptions of selfhood (Swann, 1996), guarding them like birds guard their nests. This explains, for example, why bullied children sometimes seem to seek out the company of bullies – those who confirm the low opinions they have of themselves.

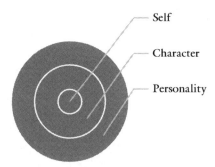

Figure 3.1 Three levels of personhood.

Although character education only rarely penetrates to the deepest level of personhood, this should not make us pessimistic about its efficacy. The younger the child is the more likely character education will influence all the levels of personhood. With older students, character education is more focused – as, indeed, its name suggests – at the level of character traits, helping students to re-evaluate, polish, and further develop these traits through the critical thinking of *phronesis*. Even at the secondary and tertiary levels of education, considerable scope remains for manoeuvre: although we are all born with the makings of a distinct personality, and our deepest selfhood often remains intact after early childhood, moral character continues to develop gradually through moral upbringing, education and experience. In this field, even old dogs can be taught new tricks.

Different types of virtue

In a well-formed character, the most prominent features are the virtues. In Chapter 2, we provided a specification of virtue as a dispositional cluster combining a number of elements. Not only does each virtue contain multiple features, there are also a great number of different virtues, each concerned with potential spheres of significant human experience. As those spheres may change over time – for instance, in recent years, with the looming threat of environmental degradation calling for new 'environmental virtues' – Aristotelian character education suggests a flexible and open-ended list of virtues, which may also vary according to context. For instance, particular schools may decide to prioritise certain virtues over others in light of the school's history, ethos or specific student population. Nevertheless, a list of *prototypical* virtues – that will be recognised and embraced by representatives of most cultures and religions – can be suggested and drawn upon in character education. The list below (derived from the Jubilee Centre's *A Framework for Character Education in Schools*, 2013b – see Appendix A) contains examples of such virtues that have been highlighted in some of the most influential philosophical and religious systems of morality – and that also resonate well with current efforts at school-based character education:

Virtue	Definition
Courage	Acting with bravery in fearful situations
Justice	Acting with fairness towards others by honouring rights and responsibilities
Honesty	Being truthful and sincere
Compassion	Exhibiting care and concern for others
Gratitude	Feeling and expressing thanks for benefits received
Humility/modesty	Estimating oneself within reasonable limits

Those above are all examples of *moral* virtues. This is suitable for the present purposes as we are exploring the virtues in the context of an education aimed at promoting *good character*. A subset of the moral virtues is formed by the so-called *civic* virtues, such as citizenship and volunteering, which focus on the moral effects on society at large. However, other virtues are also necessary to achieve the highest potential in life. For example, all developing human beings will need to possess a host of *intellectual* virtues, such as curiosity and critical thinking, which guide their quest for knowledge and information. We explained in Chapter 2 how one of those intellectual virtues, namely *phronesis* or good sense, occupies a special position in Aristotelian character education and builds a bridge between the moral and the intellectual. Finally, there are the *performance* virtues, such as co-operative skills and resilience, which enable us to manage our lives effectively and achieve our goals, whatever they are. Recall also the specification of those four virtue categories in Chapter 1.

As stressed in Chapter 2, good programmes of character education will *include* the cultivation of performance virtues, but it also needs to be explained to students that those virtues derive their ultimate value from serving morally acceptable ends, in particular from being enablers and vehicles of the moral virtues. Generally speaking, the internal cohesion of one's virtue system is of crucial importance – more so than the exclusive nourishing of individual virtues. This is why we are sceptical of character-education programmes that empha- sise the further strengthening of the virtues that one already possesses – so- called 'signature strengths' – rather than the overall strengthening of the whole system or the meta-virtue of good sense. A chain is never stronger than its weakest links.

Why 'character' and 'virtue' are not redundant or old-fashioned

Some theorists find the language of 'character' and 'virtue' old-fashioned or even redundant. In our work with policymakers, practitioners, parents and students, we have not encountered much resistance to the language of character; some do initially find the language of virtue however, rather quaint and Jane Austenesque. As the same does not apply to the names of individual virtues, such as 'honesty' and 'compassion', we have tried to explain to sceptics that since a general term for such traits is badly needed, 'virtue' seems to be the obvious contender, so that, even if it has fallen out of use, it may be worth retrieving.

Sometimes, retrieval of old language can have significant benefits. For example, our own successful programme of character education in the UK, the *Knightly Virtues*, gained plaudits from parents for its brushing up of the nuances of moral language. In interviews, parents explained that while the 'thin' concepts of 'the good' and 'the bad' were often 'covered' or 'done' at home, the introduction of more complex ('thicker') vocabulary helped their children verbalise their ideas in more robust terms (Arthur *et al.*, 2014; cf. Carr & Harrison, 2015). Children themselves also seem aware of their lack of vocabulary to talk meaningfully about psycho-moral issues. What is more, when provided with such a vocabulary, they cherish it and enjoy the opportunity of using it, rather than finding it archaic, dull or bookish (Arthur, 2010a: 79–84). This is not surprising; many of us will have experienced the eureka-feeling of coming across phrases, previously unfamiliar to us, that enable us to say exactly what we mean. Sophia Vasalou (2012) has recently argued persuasively that *learning* or, if necessary, *recovering* an apt moral terminology is a task that each of us needs to pursue in our efforts at character self-education – and the education of others – and in that endeavour traditional 'thick' virtue terms may turn out to carry the greatest moral force. Thus, it is a myth that aspirations to breathe new life into concepts that have been forgotten by an individual or a culture necessarily count as old-fashioned.

A recent study of the use of general and specific virtue words in 5.2 million books published between 1901 and 2000 seems to show a steady decline in the use of traditional virtue terms (Kesebir & Kesebir, 2012). A closer look at the findings shows, however, that while it is true that many specific virtue terms – in addition to the generic terms 'character' and 'virtue' – have declined in use, a few have had a significant positive correlation with time ('compassion', 'integrity', 'fairness', 'tolerance', 'selflessness', 'discipline', 'dependability', 'reliability') and others have remained stable over time ('loyalty', 'trustworthiness', 'forgiveness', 'respect', 'determination'). There is, therefore, no compelling evidence for the redundancy of the virtue-vocabulary *as such*. What seems to have happened, rather, is that its focus has shifted to fewer and more general virtue terms, while at the same time, the overall rationale provided by the genus-terms '(good) character' and 'virtue' seems to have gone astray. We have good reasons for trying to reverse that trend if we think that using terms such as 'character' and 'virtue' really help us make sense of, and navigate our way through, our everyday moral landscape.

A brief detour into moral philosophy: virtue ethics and moral naturalism

Although the term 'virtue' seems to have lost some of its mooring in everyday language and may stand in need of retrieval, it has been making a spectacular comeback on philosophical agendas. This is not the right place to delve very deeply into moral philosophical theory. However, as the version of character education promoted in this book is explicitly grounded in a particular moral theory, *virtue ethics*, some observations about that theory are in order. At the end of this section, we also make some observations about the differences and similarities between grounding character education in a secular virtue ethical theory and in religious forms of virtue ethics.

Virtue ethics, harking back to Aristotle's *Nicomachean Ethics*, started to re-emerge as a serious contender to the dominant paradigms of Kantianism and utilitarianism in moral theory after the middle of the twentieth century. According to virtue ethics, an action is right not because it can be universalised in light of a rational principle (Kantianism), or because it makes the greatest number of people happy (utilitarianism), but because it enhances virtue and contributes to a flourishing life – as opposed to a languishing or floundering one. Indeed, the focus is no longer on the correctness of individual actions, but rather on their role in a well-rounded life and on their roots in the 'inner world' of the agent – in stable states of character that incorporate motivational and emotional elements (as explained in Chapter 2). In terms of moral evaluation, the crucial factor is not merely observable behaviour, but the emotions with which an action is performed, the motivation behind it and the manner in which it is performed. Moreover, the virtues are not understood primarily as complexes of duties, but rather as goals of personal/moral aspiration that yield themselves to cultivation and coaching. This assumption carries significant implications for how virtues and/or programmes of character education can be evaluated, as we discuss further in Chapter 7.

It is difficult to be more precise about the contours of virtue ethics without becoming too technical and philosophical. We want to flag here, however, the fact that subscribing to (Aristotle-inspired) virtue ethics involves a number of distinct assumptions, such as:

- An objective view of human flourishing – rather than just subjective well-being – as the final end of education and worldly life in general.
- Moral realism, more specifically moral naturalism, according to which moral 'facts' exist outside of the human mind and are grounded in our nature and the environment in which we live. Morality is not just 'a matter of taste', or a mere set of subjective preferences.
- Self/character realism, according to which who we are deep down is not the same as the set of beliefs we may hold about who we are deep down (that is, 'self' is not the same as 'self-concept') – although those beliefs also form a *part* of who we are. For example, simply boosting self-esteem does not necessarily make our underlying 'self' stronger.
- Evidential naturalism, according to which all moral theorising needs to take account of evidence from social scientific research. Virtue ethics and character education cannot just be argued for and designed from the convenience of the philosophical armchair. For example, character education cannot be studied and argued for without drawing on a lot of empirical evidence about actual classroom practice.
- Irreducibility of the moral to the expedient, and the idea of the intrinsic (i.e. non-instrumentalist) value of certain states of character (the moral virtues), as already explained in Chapter 2. In other words, being moral is not just a means to other ends.

According to this virtue ethical approach, moral notions cannot be comprehended in abstraction from human ethology and the natural environment in which we live, and we need considerable fence-crossing between philosophy and social and biological science to understand what really makes people flourish. The same applies, obviously, to the content of character education aimed at engendering a flourishing life. Although vexing questions remain about the exact division of labour between philosophy and social science at the borderline in question, the general naturalistic assumptions of Aristotelian virtue ethics – its distinctive worldliness – will be music to the ears of most social scientists and education-ists, not to mention philosophers who subscribe to recent forms of virtue ethics. Representatives from all these camps can then, ideally, gather around a variant of character education which is forthrightly *interdisciplinary:* integrating insights from philosophy, psychology, sociology and education. It is important also to mention the role of practitioners – in this case, especially teachers – in the inter-disciplinary endeavour. Only *teachers* can bring to the table the required experi-ence and expertise to turn character education from an academic mind-game to a lived reality for young people.

In short, Aristotelian character education assumes that there cannot be a ser-viceable social scientific theory of virtue, or of its constitutive elements without significant input from philosophical virtue ethics, any more than there can be a reasonably developed philosophical theory of virtue without grounding in the empirical knowledge of how people actually think about virtues and the way they inform their character. The downside to this assumption, however, is that char-acter education cannot be seen to reside conveniently in a cloistered realm of its own, and its success will be dependent upon *both* academics and practitioners delivering the goods.

So where are we at the present point in time? We think it fair to say, in order to catch the spirit of what is now afoot in the academic fashion industry, that we are entering the era of the *flourishing child* (Walker, Roberts and Kristjánsson, 2015). This ideal has many historical and intellectual roots apart from the recent upsurge of virtue ethics in moral theory, such as the new positive psychology/ education movement and disillusionment with mere subjective criteria of well-being in economics and public policy. Yet the influence of recent developments in academia towards an ethics of virtue – and its educational incarnation as character education – should not be underestimated.

For some people, the term 'an ethics of virtue' may carry religious connotations. We have deliberately chosen to give character education a secular grounding by rooting it in Aristotle's non-religious theory of human flourishing. In today's mul-ticultural climate, that seems to be a reasonable option. There is no reason to shy away from the fact, however, that notions of moral character and virtue are a main-stay of all the world's great religions, and that many people gravitate towards con-siderations of good moral character through religious motivations and inspirations. Generally, that should be seen as an advantage rather than a disadvantage. For one thing, religious aspirations to virtues are often more ambitious and demanding than secular ones; witness the relatively higher contributions of religious people to charitable giving. For another thing, religious schools and individuals typically score higher on measures of moral development and virtue than non-religious ones (Arthur *et al.*, 2015b). Our own research indicates, however, that this may have more to do with higher levels of virtue literacy (linguistic familiarity with virtue talk) than with an all-round mastery of virtue. In any case, the difference between religious and non-religious participants seemed to lessen considerably after a fairly short intervention to boost virtue literacy (Arthur *et al.*, 2014).

It would be churlish to complain if individuals prefer to ground their conception of the flourishing life in a religious framework than in Aristotle's secular one. All the widespread religious systems of the world profess doctrines that are conducive to virtue; only non-mainstream radicalised interpretations provide exceptions to that rule. Nevertheless, the idea that 'character' and 'virtue' do not make sense or cannot be justified outside a religious context does not bear historical scrutiny.

From a practical perspective, we should be less concerned with the designation of a school as religious or non-religious than with what actually takes place in the name of character education within the school gates. Our extensive research into the moral development of secondary school students in the UK shows, for example, that just as in the case of binaries such as state–independent, city–rural and large–small, schools that characterise themselves as either religious or non-religious find themselves in the list of the top- and bottom-performing schools on moral development. A stronger indicator of success in this area than any of the binaries in question is the presence of a leading person in the school, ideally the head teacher, making character education a school priority (Arthur *et al.*, 2015b). In brief, some religious schools do character education well, some badly. Each school needs to be judged on its own actual merits rather on how it labels itself.

Conservatism, individualism and broader social concerns

In Chapter 2, we explained what we consider to be the difference between character education and other forms of moral education (for example citizenship education). We also provided reasons (motivational, developmental and logical) why we believe character education should be prioritised over the other forms, especially at the early stages of schooling. Some critics are sceptical of considerations of this kind and think they betray a *conservative* and/or overly *individualist* stance. Is character education then all about 'fixing individual kids' and forgetting broader social concerns – which would mean that it constitutes a *reactionary* approach to schooling? Although we take the view that these concerns are based on myths about character education, they are worthy of a serious response.

To begin with the charge of conservatism: the first and most obvious meaning of 'conservative' is 'supportive of the status quo'. Is the emphasis on character, virtue and character education conservative in that sense? From a *political* perspective, that seems not to be the case at all. The philosopher Martha Nussbaum (1990) has, for instance, argued convincingly that Aristotle's own virtue-and-well-being theory, if transposed to the modern world, would have radically reformative and progressive implications, and that its practical policies would most likely resemble those of Scandinavian social democracies. From an *educational* perspective, it seems equally far-fetched to saddle character-education theories of an Aristotelian bent with service to the status quo. There is little doubt that the status quo in today's education is technicist and instrumentalist in approach (critiqued by Oancea & Pring, 2008; Arthur, 2003; and in Chapter One above). An Aristotelian character-based approach would, in contrast, highlight the role of normativity and values – not only within character education, but in all educational efforts – and prompt us to understand education itself non-instrumentally as having intrinsic value. It would also call for a radical overhaul of the training of prospective teachers towards more explicit immersion in moral and cultural values: philosophy, art and literature (Carr, 2012). An approach can hardly be more anti-status-quo than that.

Another meaning of 'conservative' is simply 'inspired by, or in line with, the agenda of conservative political parties'. To be sure, when US-style character education was first introduced in the late 1980s, one of its torchbearers was William Bennett, Education Secretary in the Reagan government; it cannot be denied that he and many of his colleagues put their own ideological spin on the movement's agenda. However, such connection to the political right seems to have been entirely contingent. The history of character education initiatives in the UK, for instance, shows that liberals and progressives have been the primary advocates – as we reviewed briefly in Chapter 2. In any event, in current UK political circles, the order of the day seems to be that we are 'all Aristotelians now' (Arthur 2003, chap. 11; Evans, 2011). In other words, all the main political parties support character education (although they may not all understand it exactly in the same way), as witnessed in the 2015 UK general elections.

Regarding the related worry about an *individualist bias* in character education, it may seem odd to fault an Aristotle-based paradigm for individualism. Aristotle himself was anything but an individualist, claiming instead that the good life could only be realised in a certain kind of society with a certain kind of moral upbringing, public education and political arrangement. Moreover, the ideal breeding ground for character is a community in which a vision of the good life is at least broadly shared. Aristotle would have liked the African proverb that it takes a village to bring up a child.

Neither is Aristotelian character education individualistic *vis-à-vis* an excessive focus on how to make oneself a better person. For Aristotle, there is simply no way that one can exercise one's personal virtues without benefiting others at the same time; in the case of friends, even the distinction between one's 'self' and the 'selves' of significant others becomes blurred, as a true friend acts as one's 'second self'. Nevertheless, contemporary efforts at character education commonly find themselves under attack for their inherent individualism. The idea of virtue is seen as focusing excessively or exclusively on the capacities of individual students in isolation from their socio-cultural contexts or *habitus*, thus neglecting issues of gender, class, ethnicity and power relations. Conversely, vice is allegedly located in individual failings rather than in social, economic and political structures, and improvement is sought through personal change (or 'kid-fixing') rather than political reform.

Notably, those objections are rarely aimed directly at the sort Aristotelian character education espoused in this book but rather at the (perhaps) more vulnerable targets of, first, US-style character education of the late twentieth century kind and, second, current positive psychological virtue theory. Yet, even in the case of those 'softer' targets, the objections are largely misplaced. The reason for the apparent foregrounding of an inward gaze and individual development in both movements seems to be the same, at least if its advocates are to be taken at their word. They all insist that the question of individual versus societal reform is a chicken-and-egg one. We need to start somewhere, and for pragmatic reasons, it is more feasible to start with the individual child, student or classroom than the whole school system or society at large. Both in US-style character education and positive psychology, the eventual goal is, however, said to be 'social change' or the 'creation of positive institutions' (see citations and discussions in Kristjánsson, 2013, chap. 2.5). We made similar points in Chapter 2, where we emphasised that we did not see character education as 'more important' than citizenship education, although we considered it the ideal starting point of all moral education. Once again, the charge in question turns out to be a myth.

Having said all that, we do need to be more forthright about the effects of *social background* and *gender roles* on moral development. Most empirical research into moral development or pro-social attitudes – including our own – reveals a link to a socio-economic-cum-social-capital background. Children with educated and relatively well-off parents score better than poor kids; so do girls compared to boys (Arthur *et al.*, 2015b). Perhaps this is not surprising; some of this is perhaps due to a 'social desirability bias', with girls and middle-class children being more concerned about 'pleasing' researchers. It is surprising, however – and here we agree with the critics – how few programmes of character education attack this cultural issue head-on. Why is more attention not paid, in moral education in general, to ways in which the varying socio-economic, ethnic and gendered self-concepts (or *habitus*) that children take with them to school can be turned into a moral resource rather than a source of disadvantage? We need to engage practitioners in a debate about those issues and help them devise means to make moral education in general – and character education in particular – more sensitive to the social and cultural features that affect character development.

Paternalistic intervention – or what children and parents want?

Yet another possible – and indeed often heard – objection to character education is that it is *paternalistic*. Now, paternalism is one of philosophy's trickiest concepts. We assume here an everyday understanding according to which an intervention is paternalistic if it involves *A*'s forcing a choice upon *B* against – or at least without regard for – *B*'s own will, under the pretext that the choice is in *B*'s best interest. Is teaching young students about good character at school paternalistic in this sense? If so, is this a task that should be left to the discretion of their parents, or left undone until they have become mature enough to decide for themselves? The first issue to be determined here is whether character education at school is against the will of parents (who typically act as proxies for younger children) *or* of the students themselves. The evidence suggests it is neither.

Parents are typically happy if character issues are addressed at school. In a recent UK poll of 1,000 parents, nearly nine-in-ten agreed that schools should develop character rather than just deliver academic results. 95 percent of parents agreed that it is possible to teach children values and shape their characters in positive ways, and 84 percent believed that it is the teacher's role to encourage good morals and values in their students. Importantly, that minority of parents who expressed doubts or disagreed did so not because they thought grades matter more than character, but because they considered themselves better equipped to instil character than teachers (Jubilee Centre, 2013a). This is by no means the first poll to show overwhelming parental support for character education. Yet, parents may be less than adept at getting their view across, as children and teachers often seem to think that, when push comes to shove, parents only care about grades.

One can only make an educated guess as to what motivated those parental views. Below is an unsystematic collection of some possible (but by no means exhaustive) explanations for which there is anecdotal evidence:

- A perceived increase in youth depression and social disaffection, culminating in events like the London 2011 riots, indicates problems that some parents may interpret as a sign of moral decline in need of rectification;
- Internationalisation and multiculturalism have created a need for universal values;
- More secularisation and individualisation (witness the so-called 'me' generation) have formed the perception of a spiritual void or a 'value gap' that needs to be filled;
- More female employment has led to increased demands on schools to help 'bring up' children;
- Finally, the 2008 financial crisis was a wake-up call for many parents, who viewed it as being caused more by general character flaws than financial bad judgement, and who want to make sure that their children do not fall prey to the same temptations.

Moreover, students themselves, in our extensive *Learning for Life* and *Knightly Virtues* studies, have shown great eagerness to learn more about the virtues at school (Arthur, 2010a; Arthur *et al.*, 2014). Perhaps none of this should surprise us, for, as Carr (2012: 262) puts it, it is in a way:

> *much* clearer why it is important to encourage children to be honest, tolerant and fair than why they should be taught mathematics or science, for although not all children will develop an interest in or a need for science, *all* human beings require an interest in honesty or fairness.

Let us suppose, however, for the sake of argument, that evidence showed the opposite; namely, that parents and students would prefer schools not to address issues of good character at all. The idea that the school could then inconsequentially leave such issues aside betrays a peculiar conceptual and psychological misconception: namely, that the character of children can simply be held in abeyance at school until they reach the age where they have become wise or autonomous enough to decide for themselves. This is a misconception both about the meaning of the terms 'character' and 'education' and about the psychology of character development. Character is gradually formed from birth through the interactions of children with others; they become just or unjust, as Aristotle reminded us, by engaging in just or unjust acts and through the example of role models (parents, siblings, peers, teachers). When character is not formally *taught*, virtues and vices will still be *caught*. There is no alternative type of education that children can be exposed to at school than character education (although deep questions obviously remain about the right form of character education). Character education will always take place, and although it can obviously be done either well or badly, concerns about all character education being paternalistic are simply red herrings.

To sum up, no teachers can either logically or psychologically dissociate themselves from the practice of character education (cf. Carr, 2012: 243–258). The sensible question that we can ask about a school's, or an individual teacher's character education strategy is not whether such education does occur, but whether it is 'intentional, conscious, planned, pro-active, organized and reflective' or 'assumed, unconscious, reactive, subliminal or random' (Wiley, 1998: 18). It does not require deep knowledge of curriculum theory to know which of those two strategies is more propitious for learning.

But is good character not culturally relative?

Cultural relativism has been the proverbial spectre haunting all moral theorising since the time of the Greek sophists. Is talk of good character and virtues not relative to time and place? Is the basic question to ask, then, not always this: *whose virtues, which character?* Apart from academic scepticism about the universality of moral virtues, it is often said that most teenagers go through a 'relativist' period – questioning all received values – causing a temporary dip in their moral development (Arthur *et al.*, 2015b).

Some virtue ethicists have not so much tried to lay cultural relativism to rest as to take it on board, most notably Alasdair MacIntyre (1981). According to his social constructivist interpretation, virtues (and vices) differ over times and societies or, more specifically, among the prevailing social practices of different cultures. Nevertheless, a more common tack taken in contemporary virtue ethics is to follow Aristotle's (1985: 208) empirical universalism about human nature, captured in his much-quoted observation that 'in our travels we can see how every human being is akin … to a human being'. The case for such anti-relativism has recently been bolstered considerably by extensive empirical work in positive psychology on the conceptions of virtues in different societies, religions and moral systems. In light of this work, positive psychologists claim that people are more or less the same wherever they go, and that the spheres of human life where our virtues and vices play out have remained essentially constant throughout history (Peterson and Seligman, 2004; McGrath, 2015).

Perhaps little more than a thought-experiment would have sufficed to elicit that same conclusion, for it is surely impossible to envisage human societies where character strengths, such as conscientiousness or courage are not needed, recognised, or held in esteem. This does not mean that there cannot be varying interpretations or instantiations of a virtue, given different circumstances in different societies. To take a specific example, in some societies, people drive on the right side of the road, others on the left; yet it would clearly be a myth to claim that there is no such thing as a good driver (cf. Carr, 1996: 359). This observation can easily be transferred to the educational arena. Nobel Peace Prize winner Malala Yousafzai has, for instance, done much lately to highlight the danger of seeing educational opportunities as a good that is somehow relative to cultures, religions or genders.

Aristotelian character education is particularly well suited to meet the relativist challenge. It couches its account of flourishing, character and virtue in terms that are both non-religious and essentially universal. 'Essentially' is a crucial modifier here, because Aristotle's 'thick but vague' theory of the human good (Nussbaum, 1990) leaves sufficient space for cultural and individual variance to satisfy all but the most radical relativists. In Carr's (2012) well-chosen words, in the Aristotelian model of moral virtue we do not actually have to know what another person (whether Muslim, communist or atheist) actually values or believes across the board in order to judge whether she is honest, just, courageous, temperate or compassionate; we only need to know that she is inclined to tell the truth, deal with others fairly, stand up for her principles under threat, control her appetites or care for others. The Aristotelian language of virtue thus provides an effective cross-cultural currency of moral evaluation. This is an important advantage for contemporary multicultural societies like the UK, which function badly without some common core of generally accepted values.

But is there such a thing as character? The situationist challenge

So-called *situationism* is often considered to pose a more immediate threat to character education than cultural relativism. Situationists say there is no such thing as stable and consistent states of virtues and vices making up character; rather, all human behaviour ('moral' or otherwise) has now been shown in psychological experiments, such as the famous Milgram-experiments, to be completely situation-dependent (Doris, 2002).

In the Milgram-experiments, participants were encouraged to administer what they knew were life-threatening electric shocks to stimulate the learning of persons who were supposed to be studying in another room. All that was needed for most of the participants to comply was the firm voice of an authority figure in a white gown. This experiment was meant to show what actually happened when the majority of apparently good-natured people in Nazi Germany decided to follow a charismatic but immoral leader. Much older experiments, dating back to the early part of the twentieth century, had shown a similar effect for young students; namely, that their presumed honesty was situation dependent; they would turn out to be honest in one context but not another. Is moral character then essentially chameleon-like and malleable? Is there any use in trying to cultivate cross-situational character traits?

Let us first give situationism the credit that it deserves. First, all personality psychologists seem to agree nowadays that behaviour is a function both of *character* and *situation*. Since situations are the arena where character plays out, it would be a conceptual as well as an empirical error to maintain that character is completely situation-independent. Second, it seems undeniable that the point of good character education is not only to help students develop virtuous traits, but it also teaches them to learn to steer clear of perilous situations with which they have no previous familiarity and which might land them in trouble, given the common-sense insight that the more extraordinary features a situation presents, the more extraordinary and 'out of character' our reactions are likely to be. There may be some truth to the old excuse that a teenager begins to behave badly after 'falling in with the wrong crowd'. However, the lesson from that is not the fatalistic one of simply waiting and hoping for the best, but rather of helping young people stay away from situations that may corrupt them.

Recent empirical research seems to be turning the tide away from radical situationism. It indicates that most people do, in fact, possess stable dispositional clusters of the sort under present discussion (Jayawickreme *et al.*, 2014) but that, with the exception of the most and the least perfect amongst us, those clusters rarely coincide completely with standard designations of, say, honesty or dishonesty *as such*. Rather, most people possess what Miller (2014) helpfully calls 'mixed traits': clusters that, to a smaller or larger degree, resemble the idealised form but incorporate various person-specific and interrelated mental-state dispositions pertaining to the relevant domains (say, the domain of honesty). Most importantly, each mixed trait embodies certain 'enhancers and inhibitors' (Miller, 2014: 52), which influence motivation in trait-relevant ways. Each person thus possesses, so to speak, a different cluster of dispositions, relevant to a moral domain (such as truth-telling), and presents herself to the outside world with a unique individual character profile of psycho-moral preferences and saliences, under whose sway her behaviour oscillates.

Take the honest 14-year-old Jack, for example, who can be consistently relied upon to tell the truth, except when the interests of his best friend Ali are at stake. Jack would be strongly inclined to lie, if needed, to get Ali out of trouble. This theory of mixed traits explains both the apparent unpredictability of behaviour with respect to standard virtues, such as honesty – often found in psychological experiments – and the common-sense intuition that our reactions are almost tediously predictable for those who know us well. Jack's apparently aberrant reaction in cases affecting Ali is thus not so much an indication of the *lack* of a character trait as of the *strength* of one (see Murphy, 2015). Understood in this way, becoming more virtuous in a given sphere does not mean taking on a virtue wholesale but, rather, gradually moving closer to an *ideal*. Conversely, becoming less virtuous does not mean dropping virtue like a mantle but rather growing baser by degrees.

It so happens that Aristotelian character education is better equipped than other theories undergirding character education to counter situationism. First, Aristotelianism assumes that robust global character traits only appear at the highest level of moral development (that of 'full virtue'), to which most people can only aspire, but that various lower levels (to be explored in Chapter 4) still have considerable moral worth compared to the baseline of the morally undeveloped. Second, Aristotelians will want to measure the exercise of character traits, not just through behaviour (as typically done in situationist experiments), but rather through the combination of reason, emotion and action (see Chapter 7). A person who seems to act well may not do so for the right reason, and hence may not possess the respective virtue. Conversely, a person who seems to act badly in a psychological experiment may have been temporarily misled by panic or unfamiliarity. If she feels strong remorse afterwards, she may still possess the character virtue that she failed to exhibit in the experiment.

There is an even more fundamental problem of which the situationist challenge falls foul, which is to do with the very concept of a 'situation'. Situations can range from the narrowest ('picking up papers that someone else has dropped in front of a phone booth after you have found a coin in the booth') to the broadest ('being a citizen in Nazi Germany'). Typically, situationists deliberately choose to focus on situations that are not only *broad* but also *passive* (the agent is a victim rather than a creator of the situation), *extraordinary* (the situations presents features that the agent has never experienced before and is never even likely to experience in real life) and/or involve *strong* social expectations of compliance (for instance, being subjected to orders from an acknowledged authority-figure). After tilting the evidence in their favour in this way, it is no surprise that the situationist experiments yield the findings that they do. This is scarcely even a matter that requires empirical corroboration; rather, it is what the very terms 'broad', 'passive', 'extraordinary' and 'strong' seem to *mean* when applied to situations. They are used in our language precisely to denote classes of situations where people's reactions are less easily predictable than they normally are. We should not labour under the illusion that evidence gathered in this way poses a serious threat to the ideas of character, virtue and character education. Indeed, we agree with Russell (2014b) that, as far as Aristotelian character education is concerned, the so-called situationist challenge has generated considerably more heat than light.

Virtue attuned to individual dispositions – and a reminder of the invaluable role of *phronesis*

Although relativism and situationism – in their radical forms at least – seem to constitute mere myths, different types of individual and cultural variance need to be built into any viable form of character education. Thus, if we understand the virtues of character as (ideal) excellences that people need in order to live well – individually *and* together in ways that are peaceful, neighbourly and morally justifiable – then what counts as a proper display of virtues will to a certain extent be different depending on individuals, developmental stages and social circumstances. For example, temperance in eating will be different for an Olympic athlete and an office worker; what counts as virtuous behaviour for a teenager may not be so for a mature adult; and the virtues needed to survive in a war zone may not be the same as those in a peaceful rural community.

We also need to be aware of *genetic variance*. Psychologists sometimes accuse character educationists of not taking sufficient account of genetic factors. We pointed out earlier that even if the basis of our broad personality trait of conscientiousness is genetic, there is considerable scope left for character education to channel this general trait into specific moral outlets – namely, *what*, precisely, the student is conscientious *about*. We did not mention there, however, the other side of the coin: what about students who are not hardwired with a strong disposition to general agreeableness or conscientiousness? Character educationists often rely on the mantra that 'virtue must be within the reach of anyone who really wants it' (cited and critiqued in Adams, 2006: 163). This mantra harks back to Comenius's (1907: 90) rose-tinted observation that 'the gardener can unfailingly train a struggling shoot into a tree, by using his skill in transplanting'.

It may be reasonable to doubt, however, whether a person very low in innate agreeableness (*as a* Big-Five personality trait) can ever acquire the full Aristotelian moral virtue of agreeableness (as explained in Kristjánsson 2007, chap. 10). She may force herself successfully to act in agreeable ways, but having to force oneself to do *x* is not to do *x* virtuously. Conversely, a person high in congenital agreeableness – while privileged with regard to moral agreeableness – may find herself at a disadvantage with regard to some other moral virtues, such as honesty, as she will find it extremely difficult to call a spade a spade, when needed, in front of a person who will take offence. To give another example, a person high on neuroticism, prone to see her glass half-empty, will most likely never turn into a half-full-glass sort of a person, however hard we (as educators) and the person herself try or how many character-education exercises she labours through. Given these considerations, there may be *some* individual virtues which – for *some* people – it is extremely hard to develop (see Adams 2006, chap. 9). One takeaway lesson for Aristotelian character educators is that virtue must be seen as relative to individual dispositions (see Chen, 2013) – as Aristotle did indeed himself acknowledge.

Another takeaway lesson is that the development of individual virtues may in the end be less salient than the development of the intellectual meta-virtue of good sense or *phronesis*. For most reasonably developed young people, for example, the hard everyday choice is not between virtue and vice but between different virtues when these collide. The standard historical image of moral conflict is of the Manichaean conflict between full-blown virtue and vice. The mixed-trait view, suggested in the preceding section, and recent empirical research suggest a more mundane and complex picture. Internal moral struggles are thus more commonly between, say:

- An overall virtuous cluster and a certain inhibitor or blind spot within it. For example, although I consider myself generally temperate, I know I am terribly weak-willed when it comes to ice cream.
- Two generally virtuous clusters. For example, shall I display the virtue of honesty or the virtue of considerateness when my friend asks my opinion about the ugly dress she has just bought for the ball?
- A virtuous cluster applied to a new, out-of-the-ordinary situation. For example, knowing nothing about hospital procedures, I am suddenly asked by a doctor for my opinion about end-of-life decisions relating to a dying parent.
- A virtuous cluster tested in a situation involving strong social norms of compliance. For example, as a callow army recruit I am ordered by an army sergeant to do something that I consider immoral.

The above examples have been chosen from the lives of adult persons who have considerable life experiences to draw upon. One can only begin to imagine how much more difficult such struggles are for young moral learners: namely, the people who are normally targeted in the discourse on character education (although such education should ideally be seen as a life-long process).

We do concede that orthodox Aristotelianism (based only on actual textual evidence) does not have a very strong developmental story to tell about the gradual cultivation of critical, intellectual faculties in the student. However, we wish to emphasise that the Aristotelian character education espoused in this book is beholden to a powerful and uncompromising idea: that without the eventual development of the integrative and adjudicative faculty of *phronesis* – good critical sense of autonomous decision-making – virtue remains but a charade. More specifically, the cultivation of moral virtues without the cultivation of the intellectual virtues of *phronesis* is not really character *education* on our understanding, but rather an inferior form of character *conditioning*. We will say more about this issue when we turn to practical methods of teaching character in later chapters of this book.

The need for further integrative work

We hope that the observations and arguments presented in this chapter have given the reader sufficient ammunition to counter most of the common 'myths' about character education. Fortunately, in recent years, suspicions that character education constitutes either a conspiracy from the *right* (of blaming individual kids rather than social structures for moral ills) or the *left* (of inserting a Trojan horse of touchy-feeliness into educational discourse to undermine traditional standards) have been fading away, at least in the UK. Yet various negative conceptions about the notions of character, virtue and character education do remain in *some* academic circles, especially outside the specific fields of moral education and moral psychology, and even more so among the 'chattering classes' of bloggers, media pundits and politicians, who still cling fiercely to some of the old myths.

Despite rising interest in academic and political circles – not to mention among practitioners – the paradigm of the flourishing child, which undergirds the writing of the present book, has so far failed to make a significant dent in educational *policy making* and *teacher training* in the UK. Indeed, contemporary policy discourse, with its amorally instrumentalist, competence-driven bent, seems to shy away from any perspective that embraces normative visions of persons in the context of their whole lives. The lack of teacher-training establishments with a coherent approach to any character education – let alone of the Aristotelian kind – is most likely the result of more dominant legitimating principles of grade attainment and classroom management. This seems a lost opportunity, however, given the hunger among trainee teachers to make a moral difference (Sanger & Osguthorpe, 2011).

That said, politicians are notoriously sensitive to subtle changes of opinion among the electorate. If polls such as the one commissioned by the Jubilee Centre for Character and Virtues (2013a) continue to show strong parental support for school activities aimed at character education, and politicians interpret those findings as evidence of true opinions rather than simply lip service paid by parents to ideals that they do not really support in practice, one can expect more and more politicians to adopt the principles of the flourishing child paradigm and to filter them into educational policy (although they might meet with some *Yes-Minister*-style resistance there from the mandarins). Schools tend to be conservative institutions, however, and are as difficult to move quickly as large aircraft carriers. That is generally a good thing. We do not want educational institutions to jump on just any approaching bandwagon and to adjust themselves slavishly to the flavour of each new month. Yet this conservatism can easily degenerate into an indiscriminate resistance to any new ideas, especially radical and controversial ones. While we would hesitate to categorise the call for Aristotelian character education as 'radical', since it is built on the accumulated experience of generations of educators about what makes children flourish and does not require the whole fabric of schooling to be torn up, it does necessitate a turn away from high-stakes testing as the ultimate measure of school success. For some people – including some politicians – this may be a bridge too far. Hence, their tendency, noted in Chapter 2, to favour forms of character coaching that make good character instrumentally subservient to grade attainment. However, as we have argued consistently throughout this book, character without non-instrumental moral features is like Hamlet without the prince.

We hypothesise that in order to be truly successful, any paradigm of moral education needs to satisfy four main criteria. It must:

1   Align with public perceptions and speak to the dominant anxieties and vulnerabilities of the given era. In most cases, connecting to the spirit of the times involves tapping into prevalent concerns about perceived moral decline and how it can be reversed.

2   Meet with a relatively broad political consensus and attract political interest, ideally both on the political 'left' and 'right'.
3   Be underpinned by a respectable philosophical theory, providing it with a stable methodological, epistemological and moral basis.
4   Be supported by a dominant psychological theory, explaining how the ideals of the educational theory fit into actual human psychology and are, as such, attainable.

In our view, Aristotelian character education satisfies criteria (1)–(3) quite well, but (4) much less so. Aristotelian character education (1) aligns with public perceptions about a moral 'value gap' in the wake of the financial crisis and, more generally, with concerns about the current state of the social-media savvy but social and morally deprived 'me' generation. (2) meets, in the UK at least, with an increased political consensus where 'character' is becoming a buzzword across party lines. It is (3) underpinned by a distinct philosophical theory that is – as has been shown in this chapter and Chapter 2 – particularly resourceful in providing foundations for educational efforts. Moreover, the contribution of recent virtue ethics has further revitalised the field of character education and renewed its confidence. We consider (4), however, to be the elephant in the room. Contemporary psychological theory is, as yet, not distinctively virtue-friendly. More generally and crucially, perhaps, serious doubts tend to be entertained in psychological circles about the very idea of moral education and how efforts at such education are typically designed in isolation from the best available psychological evidence.

There is rising interest in character and virtue in some psychological circles, as we have already noted (Peterson & Seligman, 2004; Fowers, 2005). There is a long jump, however, from pointing out – correctly – that *some* psychologists are now finally showing *some* interest in the re-accommodation of virtue, to claiming that we have already reached that stage in the development of Aristotelian character education where all the four criteria listed above have been met. It is probable that psychologists will heed a call from practitioners more so than a call from fellow academics. Much of the future of character education thus lies in the hands of the teachers who are reading this book, rather than in the hands of the academics writing it.

Objectives reached

At the end of this chapter, you should have clear ideas about:

• the difference between personality, character and self;
• the difference between various types of virtue;
• the debate on whether or not the terms 'character' and 'virtue' are old-fashioned;
• how to respond to the objection that character is radically subject to cultural and situational variance;
• how good sense or *phronesis* may be more important than the existence of individual virtues.

Questions for reflection

- Do you know examples of individuals who have undergone a radical moral self-change due to the influence of a charismatic teacher?
- Can an immoral person be a good teacher – as long as she knows her subject well?
- Do you think secondary-school students will understand the meaning of most common virtue words? If not, what should we do about it?
- Can character education be paternalistic? If so, what sort of character education would fall under that description?
- Why do so many people believe that there are no universal moral virtues?
- What might motivate such a view and how can we argue against it?

4   How does children's moral character develop?

Summary

Engaging in character education shapes children's moral development. We explain the achievements and limitations of Lawrence Kohlberg's essentially reason-and-duty-based work on moral development and describe in more detail another virtue-based model of moral development that is firmly grounded in Aristotelian ethics. The model, which is called the 'Character Development Ladder' has four stages of virtue development: moral indifference, emerging self-control, self-control and virtue. Kohlberg characterised children's responses to moral dilemmas in terms of levels of moral reasoning about what the just thing to do is. Carol Gilligan criticised this approach as ignoring the emotional and caring dimension, while David Carr pointed out that Kohlberg had ignored *self*-regarding concerns such as moderation and courage. We elaborate on the Character Development Ladder and show how it can be applied to the kind of situations that might arise in a school. The chapter will help teachers understand what it means for children to develop morally, making it easier to recognise the various developmental stages of their students. This in turn will enable teachers to adjust their teaching methods, so as to stimulate all students in ways that will help them progress.

Introduction

To engage in character education means to shape and even to interfere with students' moral development. What does this actually mean in practice? What is the normal course of children's moral development? What can be done to stimulate it, and what, in the end, does it mean to be 'morally developed'? In this chapter, we address these questions so as to give an insight into the outcomes in students' lives when we educate their characters in a deliberate, explicit and structured way.

'Moral development' is a complex notion, so where is the best place to start? The term calls to mind the 'cognitive development model' designed by Lawrence Kohlberg in the 1960s and which is still the reigning fashion in mainstream educational psychology books used in initial teacher training today. While we can acknowledge Kohlberg's achievement in drawing attention to the importance of children's moral development in both educational theory and practice, we think that his work has serious limitations. In this chapter, we will use Kohlberg's developmental model as a springboard to describe in more detail another virtue-based model of moral development that is firmly grounded in Aristotelian ethics. This is the so-called 'Character Development Ladder', describing four stages of moral maturity, from 'moral indifference', to 'emerging self-control', to 'self-control' and, eventually, 'virtue'.

This chapter will help readers – and especially teachers – understand what it means for children to develop morally, making it easier to recognise the various developmental stages of students. This in turn will enable teachers to adjust their teaching methods, so as to stimulate all their students in ways that will help them progress. Without sufficient knowledge of the process of moral development, educational efforts to promote character can easily misfire. Finally, in the Character Development Ladder, we describe how the interactions between the 'components' of virtue, such as sensitivity, judgment and motivation, change when a person morally matures. In this way, our account of moral development may help readers gain a deeper understanding of the concept of virtue.

Moral psychology and development

Before we look in more detail at a virtue-based model of moral development, we will review the work of the American Lawrence Kohlberg (1927–1987), the founding father of twentieth-century moral psychology. Contrasting his model with our own will help readers understand more clearly the distinctive features and merits of the Character Development Ladder elaborated below. Readers only interested in the virtue-based model may want to skip this section.

Kohlberg's model of moral development

In the late 1950s, Kohlberg formulated universal moral criteria that could be used to challenge the idea that 'good' and 'bad' are relative to subjective preferences or cultural conventions.

First, we give an example of subjective preferences. In teacher training, teacher educators have to judge whether students will make good teachers. The qualifier 'good' has a technical dimension in the sense that teachers need all kinds of professional knowledge and skills. However, the idea of a 'good' teacher also has moral overtones. In our experience, most teacher educators will characterise a morally good teacher as a person who is patient instead of impatient with students, who is reliable rather than unreliable etc. However, they are reluctant to judge students in terms of these moral character traits. Who are they, they will argue, to evaluate students' characters, and in particular their lack of virtue? Even when a teacher educator thinks that one of the students lacks a caring or friendly attitude, he will quickly conclude that 'this is just my opinion'. They feel they lack a criterion to back up their intuition that care or friendliness are objective features of any good teacher. This view is known as 'moral subjectivism'.

Next, Kohlberg was particularly concerned about another widespread idea, namely 'conventionalism' or 'moral relativism', a view to which we already implicitly referred in Chapter 1. In this case, the meaning of 'good' and 'bad' depends not so much on an individual's taste, emotion or opinion, but on the conventions of one's culture(s), such as those of a football team, a school or society at large. There is certainly something valuable in cultural conventions. Take, for example, a community of teacher educators who share a conception of what a 'good teacher' is. In this case it will be much easier for individual teacher educators to justify their professional moral judgments about student teachers. While communities can foster the development and exercise of the virtues, they can also be problematic since they are open to corruption by narrowness, complacency and prejudice against outsiders: what a community *believes* to be good *is* not necessarily good (MacIntyre, 1999: 142).

Of Jewish descent himself, Kohlberg (1981: 407) explained that his own interest in moral education arose partly in response to the Holocaust. Kohlberg believed that the Nazis could only exterminate the European Jews because many people at that time had come to believe horrible things about Jews. The educational system was partly responsible for this, he believed, since it had uncritically initiated children into the conventional morality of the 1930s. Kohlberg wanted to prevent a similar eventuality by formulating an empirically valid account of moral development in which 'conventional morality' was not the best or final stage. He saw conventional morality as an intermediate stage in a process with a 'principled' or 'post-conventional' understanding of morality as its goal.

In his view, people who have reached this highest level are intellectually and socially *autonomous*: they can justify their moral judgments from an overall just and impartial point of view by taking the perspectives of everyone affected into account. This way of thinking about morality was not new. For this central idea about what makes moral development 'moral', Kohlberg relied on philosophical ideas borrowed from scholars in the deontological tradition (*to deon* is Greek for 'duty'), dating back to the German Enlightenment thinker Immanuel Kant. Kant argued for an ethical theory that based the moral worth of an action on the adherence to rules or principles that can be universalised.

Deontological theories are commonly contrasted with teleological theories, which do not follow the logic of duty, but rather of a *telos*, which is Greek for 'goal', or 'destiny'. For Aristotelian virtue ethicists, the moral worth of an action or a virtue depends on whether they enable people to achieve their goal, i.e. a happy or flourishing human life. Tracing these philosophical roots makes it clear that Kohlberg's model has a rather different point of departure from the Aristotelian account of virtue and virtue education promoted in this book. This will become clearer in what follows.

Kohlberg's model was certainly not exclusively based on philosophical theories. As a psychologist, Kohlberg (1958) investigated the moral development of children empirically, initially in 72 boys aged 10, 13 and 16, in Chicago. He later extended the sample with younger children, delinquents and boys and girls from other American cities and other countries. His method was to interview children after they had read three hypothetical dilemmas, of which the so-called 'Heinz dilemma' has become the most famous. In Chapter 7, we explain how Kohlberg's followers developed this time-consuming oral interview into more efficient pencil-and-paper dilemma tests. In the original dilemma story, Heinz's wife is close to death from a very serious disease, but the pharmacist who has just discovered a life-saving drug is charging a lot of money for it as he wants to profit from his discovery. However, Heinz is unable to raise enough money to buy the drug. The experimenter then asks the children whether he should actually steal it in order to save his wife's life, and, if so, why.

Kohlberg discovered that children of different ages use different forms of arguments to justify their answers. He was less interested in the actual judgment than in the reasoning children used to justify these judgments. He categorised these reasons in a model, ordering them hierarchically in such a way that the answers given by people at the highest stage would be exactly those predicted by a deontological theory about the goal of moral development. Kohlberg's moral development model counts three levels, each divided into two stages: see Table 4.1.

Kohlberg believed that the stages form an invariant sequence regardless of culture or religion. Moving through these stages is not just the inexorable unfolding of a child's natural abilities. It is only through the interaction with others, and in particular through the confrontation with higher kinds of moral reasoning, that children can grow morally (Sanderse, 2012: 45).

At the first, *pre-conventional level*, children are responsive to cultural rules and labels of good and bad, and are sensitive to the possible consequences (i.e. punishment, reward) of their actions. At Stage 1, children basically want to avoid punishment, and obey authorities. Children at this stage will point out that it would be wrong for Heinz to steal the drug because 'it's against the law' or because 'it's bad to steal'. At Stage 2, children point out that what is good is relative: 'Heinz might think that it's right to take the drug, but the pharmacist would not', so they think that everyone should pursue their own needs and interests.

At the second, *conventional level*, children perceive that maintaining the expectations of their family, peer group or nation is valuable in its own right, regardless of immediate and obvious consequences. At Stage 3, children want to be good people in their own eyes and those of others. For example, they will say that Heinz was right to steal the drug because 'he was a good man for wanting to save her'. At Stage 4, children express a desire to uphold laws and keep society as a

Table 4.1 Kohlberg's model of moral development

Stage	Level	Characterised by:
1	Pre-conventional level	Avoiding punishment
2		Self-interest
3	Conventional level	Good boy attitude
4		Law and order morality
5	Post-conventional level	Social contract
6		Universal principle

whole going, which would not be the case if everyone started stealing drugs. They recognise that Heinz's motives may be good, but maintain that theft is wrong.

At the third, *post-conventional level*, people define moral values and principles independent from the authority of specific groups and their identification with these groups. At Stage 5, people will be clear that they do not generally favour breaking laws, as they are based on a social contract between citizens, but that Heinz's wife's right to live is so important that it must be upheld in any society. Finally, at Stage 6, people believe that universal moral principles apply to human beings as rational persons. Laws or social agreements are only valid when they rest on principles of justice and respect for the dignity of every human being.

Towards an alternative model of moral development

It is difficult to overestimate the influence of Kohlberg's account of moral development on the theory and practice of moral education. He filled a void during a time when there was a general moral hopelessness in the wake of World War II (Kristjánsson, 2015: 9) At the end of the 1950s, he single-handedly 'moralised' psychology, which was then considered a value-free science not dealing with normative issues (for a discussion see Kristjánsson 2010, chap. 3). During the decades that followed, his account of moral development was supplemented with an account of how students' development could be stimulated in schools, initially through the discussion of hypothetical moral dilemmas, and later also through the design of so-called 'just community schools' (Power, 1998).

Although Kohlberg died in 1987, his legacy lives on in the works of many present-day 'neo-Kohlbergian' psychologists and educationalists (see Chapter 7). Despite the value of his ground breaking work, there are many reasons to be critical of Kohlberg's ideas about moral psychology. We will briefly examine two major arguments against his model as an overture to our alternative, virtue-based model of moral development. This critical overview explains why this virtue-based model needed to be developed in the first place.

First, Carol Gilligan, one of Kohlberg's colleagues at Harvard, argued in the early 1980s that Kohlberg's theory did not adequately describe the concerns of women, as it was initially based on empirical research using only male participants. While men are likely to be moved by abstract principles of justice, women would be more concerned with caring for particular others, such as children, family and friends, and by extension caring about strangers as well. Gilligan (1982) pointed out that the voice of care is just as important in moral concerns as justice. Whether or not there is a difference between men and women with regard to morality, she hit the nail on the head by arguing that our moral lives are much richer than concerns about the right thing to do from an impartial point of view. Kohlberg had effectively reduced the moral domain to justice, neglecting *other-regarding* concerns that are also clearly moral – though not impartial – such as love, care and friendship (see Fullinwider, 1989). In character education terminology, we could say that Kohlberg was only interested in one virtue, that of justice. Moreover, virtue ethicists such as David Carr (1991) added that Kohlberg not only restricted the domain of *other*-regarding concerns to justice, but he had also completely ignored *self*-regarding concerns such as moderation and courage. From a virtue ethical perspective, 'morality' is about more than treating *others* fairly, since it takes into account how we can enhance *our own* lives as well.

Second, Kohlberg's theory emphasised moral reasoning to such an extent that he underestimated other processes that are equally part of moral functioning. Kohlberg was only interested in the kind of *reasoning* that children used in a response to dilemmas. This meant that his research was not primarily about children's moral awareness, feelings or actions. Admittedly, 'moral functioning' is a complex notion, so from a scientific point of view, it arguably makes sense to concentrate on a single aspect. However, theoretical choices have practical implications. Someone confronted with a hypothetical moral dilemma might be able to reason on a post-conventional level, but this is no guarantee that they will actually act on this reasoning when experiencing a real moral dilemma. In an often-cited review study, Augusto Blasi (1980) pointed out that there is only a weak relationship between people's scores on Kohlberg's dilemma tests and their actual behaviour. In other words, children might be great moral reasoners, but that does not mean that they behave well in the classroom. Later, Kohlberg's followers admitted this shortcoming, and came to see moral reasoning as one of the components of a more encompassing 'Four Component Model' of moral functioning, including moral sensitivity, moral motivation and moral courage (Narvaez & Rest, 1995; Curzer, 2014). In this way, Kohlberg's heritage came closer to an Aristotelian account of moral development (Lapsley & Narvaez, 2006: 268; Thoma, 2006).

A virtue ethical account of character development

What can we learn from this overview of Kohlberg's cognitive development approach? Kohlberg's critics have already highlighted what we are looking for in an account of moral development: namely, an account that covers children's moral development in a *broad* sense, both in moral and psychological terms. In this section, we will argue that virtue ethics does indeed provide such a broad account. Consequently, this account of moral development is also more complex. This makes it difficult to measure empirically (see Chapter 7), but it gives a fuller and more adequate picture of the nature of our moral lives.

The advantage of a virtue ethical approach

In the previous chapter, we defined a virtue as a settled trait of character (*hexis* in Greek, *habitus* in Latin), concerned with morally praiseworthy functioning in a significant and distinctive sphere of human life. Allocating limited resources is, for example, one of these spheres, and 'justice' is the virtue required to achieve this optimally. An example of a limited resource can be something as ordinary as a pie, but it also applies to one's attention. Teachers' attention is limited, and they have to somehow divide it between the students in their classrooms. This prompts the question: who deserves what, and on what basis? Teachers need a sense of justice to determine this on a daily basis. Justice is traditionally one of the four 'cardinal virtues' (*cardo* is Latin for 'hinge'), but it is certainly not the only one, since there are other significant domains. For example, 'courage' is the quality that one needs to deal with one's fear of danger, 'generosity' helps to manage one's property where others are concerned, and 'mildness of temper' is the best attitude in the domain of slights, and so forth (Nussbaum, 1993).

While in real life most people will be more virtuous in one sphere than in another, the ideal virtuous person exhibits such qualities in a fully integrated fashion. This means that, in the character of a virtuous person, a moral trait such as courage will be accompanied by other moral traits, such as justice or temperance. Second, each moral virtue comprises a unique combination of awareness, emotion, reason, behaviour and manners, where none of the factors (not even moral reasoning) can be evaluated in isolation from the others. Virtue theory includes perception, emotion and action when morally evaluating people's lives – not just their moral reasoning. To *have* a virtue is to *be* a certain kind of person with a certain complex mind-set. A virtue is a character trait, a disposition which is well entrenched in a person, something that, 'goes all the way down', as Rosalind Hursthouse (2012) puts it.

We have covered most of this area in Chapter 2. The present chapter adds to our understanding of moral virtue by explaining how those originally separate elements of our moral psychology can become intertwined as our character matures. The Character Developmental Ladder, elaborated below, describes progressive stages of moral excellence corresponding to different developmental stages of a person's moral functioning (Sanderse, 2015). This is not a strict stage theory, however, in the Kohlbergian sense of everyone having to pass through the stages in the same order. Depending on a child's early upbringing, the lowest stage might never be experienced, for example. A stage denotes a particular alignment between reason, desire and action and a corresponding kind of pleasure. The configuration of these components gradually changes as a person reaches a new stage. The reference to 'pleasure' may seem odd in this context, but this does matter when we try to judge whether a student is virtuous or not. Self-controlled students, for example, often act virtuously, but they do so with a kind of reluctance that virtuous people have overcome, as they now do what is virtuous gladly and with pleasure.

Moral development can, over time, result in a complete metamorphosis: a virtuous person sees and interprets the world very differently from someone who does not care about moral considerations. For the purpose of illustration, we restrict ourselves to the virtue of temperance (or 'moderation'), the attitude of dealing optimally with bodily pleasures such as eating and drinking. An overweight person who has developed extreme eating habits over the years will probably love eating large amounts of sugary and fatty foods. A moderate person will also enjoy drinking and eating, but will have the good sense to determine what qualifies as the best food on each occasion. They may occasionally eat French fries, but they will have developed a more refined taste, generally choosing healthy options over unhealthy ones.

The Character Development Ladder

In the sections below, we describe four qualitatively different stages of a person's moral functioning. These stages are grounded in a virtue ethical understanding of human nature and development, which makes the model theoretically sound. We have not, however, empirically investigated in what way peoples' actual moral development matches these stages. This means that we cannot address empirical questions here, e.g. about who is on what stage at what age (see, however, Arthur *et al.*, 2015b). Still, we assume that the acquisition of virtue takes place 'along a single developmental path', as Howard Curzer (2012: 359) puts it, but we think that moral development takes place for different people at different rates, and with different starting points, depending on their endowment and moral education.

Before examining our model of moral development, we will refer back to the work of Aristotle, the inspiration for present-day virtue ethics and character education. In his *Nicomachean Ethics*, Aristotle mentions several categories of people who are more or less morally developed. The most significant categories here are the *hoi polloi* (the many), *akrates* (the weak-willed), *enkrates* (the self-controlled) and *phronimos* (the practically wise). However, we cannot simply adopt these categories, for two reasons: first, Aristotle seems to present the categories as different stages of moral excellence associated with different groups. In our case, however, we are looking for stages that can be attained successively in a diachronic process by the same person. Second, the public of Aristotle's lectures on ethics consisted of ambitious young Athenian citizens who wanted to pursue a career in politics (Smith, 2001). Our primary interest, however, is in children's moral development.

In this book, we are interpreting the Aristotelian categories as progressive stages of moral excellence that children as well as adults can go through. This interpretation is consistent with virtue ethical assumptions about human nature and development, as we think that every child is potentially human and acquires, through character education, the definite 'form' of humanity. In our model of moral development, we view all children as 'in progress toward full humanity', as Nancy Sherman (1989: 162) puts it. Our four stages of moral development are called 'moral indifference', 'emerging self-control', 'self-control' and 'virtue'. In the following sections we will describe these four stages in more detail, using an example that may help teachers recognise the stages of the students in their own classrooms. For each of the four stages, we will clarify (a) whether people are committed to virtue, (b) whether they act virtuously or not, (c) whether they enjoy acting virtuously or not, and (d) which desires and reasons they have for doing so. These stages can be depicted graphically in the form of a Character Development Ladder (see Figure 4.1). The four stages depicted in Figure 4.1 are explored further below in relation to different situations:

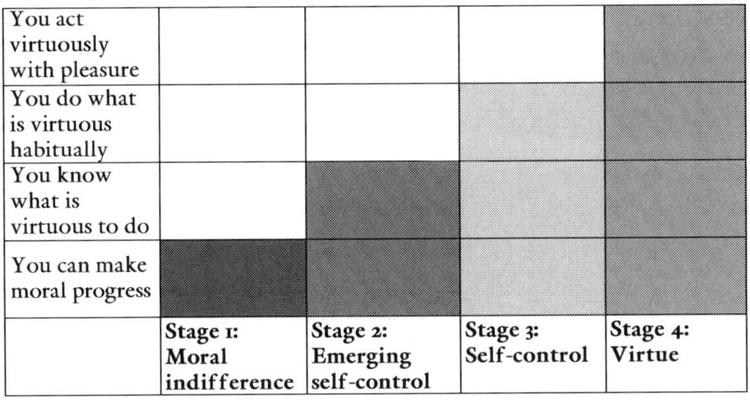

	Stage 1: Moral indifference	Stage 2: Emerging self-control	Stage 3: Self-control	Stage 4: Virtue
You act virtuously with pleasure				
You do what is virtuous habitually				
You know what is virtuous to do				
You can make moral progress				

Figure 4.1 The Character Development Ladder.

Case: gossiping about Florence

Imagine a 14-year old pupil – let's call her Amy – who wants to buy a snack in the school canteen when the end of the break is near. While she walks towards the counter, she passes a group of classmates. She can clearly hear that they are gossiping about another classmate, Florence, who has not been able to attend school for two weeks now because of a serious illness.

There are different ways for Amy to react. One option for her is to stop; another is to ignore the gossiping and walk on. If she stops, she has several new options: Will she join the group and enjoy making fun of Florence? Or will she address the group and say that their insinuations are nonsense and give Florence a bad name? In the case where Amy decides not to pay attention to the gossiping, there are again several options. Does she, for example, fail to address the classmates because she does not dare to, or does she care more about getting a snack before the break is over? Does Amy forget the incident right after it happens, or does she subsequently feel ashamed because she did not act according to her own values, one of which is to stand up for people who are in trouble? Let us take a closer look at four options.

Stage 1: moral indifference

When Amy is on the first stage of moral development, we call her 'morally indifferent'. The fate of her classmate does not affect her in any way. She hears her classmates talking about Florence, but she does not really notice that they are *gossiping*, and she walks on.

This illustrates that those who are not interested in the moral point of view are indifferent towards the good as they believe that happiness consists in something else, e.g. a life rich in pleasure, status, money or power. They are, however, not vicious, because vicious people have actually *chosen* to lead a bad life and have cultivated bad habits over the years, which makes it difficult for them to change. They have become, for example, reckless, greedy, arrogant or unreliable. The morally indifferent, however, have no evil intent. They simply do not care about virtue. They are *a*moral, not *im*moral. This means that they do not yet have stable emotional dispositions or the ability to judge what is good. Consequently, they often change their minds about the content of happiness, depending on what happens in their lives. For example, when they are ill, their health is all-important; when they lose their jobs, money is suddenly what matters most.

One way of motivating morally indifferent people to act well is to address their desire to avoid pain or punishment. Take Kevin, who is tempted to steal a sweater from a store, but notices a store clerk suspiciously looking his way. If he decides to pay, or leave the shop without the sweater, this is not because he knows it is bad to steal, but because he is afraid he could be arrested and face penalties (Garrett, 1993: 183; Damon, 1988: 18). At this stage, rules and laws can prevent people from doing bad things. Similarly, when children occasionally act well because they abide by the rules, we should keep in mind that they are not yet doing this *for the sake of* virtue. Another emotion, shame, only starts to play a role in the second stage. The morally indifferent do not experience it yet, since being ashamed presupposes that one already knows what is good whilst being unable to act on this knowledge in all circumstances.

It is clear from this description that, while we cannot exclude the possibility that some children may be on this stage, most children will already have an interest in living a good life from a very young age (Damon, 1988) and will start by at least Stage 2.

Stage 2: emerging self-control

When Amy is on the second stage of moral development, her self-control is not fully developed, but is starting to emerge. She feels for the classmate being gossiped about, but she is also hungry. She knows that the break is almost over, and in order to avoid a long confrontation with her classmates, she walks on. However, when she is back in class, she is ashamed that she did not defend Florence.

This illustrates that people who care about leading a virtuous life do not necessarily have the willpower to put that concern into action. Research has shown that most four-year-olds know that they should share some of their possessions with others, but they do not always manage to do this. For example, children may want to share food or toys, but do this only occasionally and erratically, as the needs of the self take precedence (Damon, 1988: 36). This kind of behaviour is not only typical of children; it is a condition that many grown-ups will know from experience as well. You know that smoking is bad, but you continue to smoke; you know that cheap clothes are often produced by children working under terrible circumstances, but you buy them anyway. In general, the challenge for people who are not yet self-controlled is that they know more or less what is good but are unable to act on it. We often make the wrong choices because our feelings are turned towards morally irrelevant concerns. This second stage takes seriously situations in which we 'know' in a sense what is good, but we still act differently under the influence of certain other desires.

A process of habituation is necessary – ideally under the supervision of more experienced tutors – so as to internalise moral knowledge in such a way as to act on it (Steutel & Spiecker, 2004). How does this work? Aristotle's account of shame gives us an indication. He describes shame as 'a certain fear of disrepute or discredit, that we should ideally feel when we have done things that signal vice, such as recklessness, intemperateness, vanity or boorishness' (1975 NE 1128b-11). We experience shame in particular towards those we hold in esteem such as friends, parents or teachers, and specifically towards their judgments about our worthiness. Their negative judgments about us can be a humiliating experience. Nevertheless, when these judgments are internalised in a healthy way, shame can function as a warning signal if experienced when others are not physically present. We feel it when we do not act according to what have become our *own* moral standards (Damon, 1988: 22).

Shame not only signals that a moral mistake has been made, but it can also help people to improve morally. When Amy is ashamed of herself, it can motivate her to think about how she may behave differently in the future. This function of shame contributes to the development of moral judgment and therefore towards more consistent moral action. If our thinking is future-oriented, it makes us consider what may go wrong in situations similar to the ones we previously found morally challenging. For example, imagine last week's team meeting during which you became so angry with a colleague that you were no longer in control of yourself. You lacked self-control, but right after the outburst you felt embarrassed. This may stimulate you to think about why you became excessively angry, and to prepare carefully for the next meeting. For example, after having envisaged the next meeting, you can promise yourself to do your utmost to stay calm. In this case, shame has the function of saying 'no' to an act before it is performed (Curzer, 2002: 161).

Stage 3: self-control

At the third stage, Amy is fully self-controlled. In the case of the gossiping classmates, she believes that confronting them is the virtuous (just, brave) thing to do, and she actually confronts them. Compared to the stage of emerging self-control, it is a huge achievement to have acquired this willpower. However, self-control is not the ultimate stage of moral development, as self-controlled people still need to overcome certain contrary desires. When she is self-controlled, Amy confronts her classmates reluctantly, for example because she is still afraid that they will consider her a loser who sympathises with the weak.

The capacity to control oneself is sometimes treated as a full expression of virtue (see Baumeister & Thierney, 2011), but we do not agree with this in our framework. In our view, the difference between self-control and virtue concerns the way in which reasons and feelings are connected. If your feelings reflect your sound judgments about what is valuable, then you are virtuous. If they do not, then you are merely self-controlled (Stohr, 2002: 362). We can illustrate the difference through another example. Imagine that Chris and Jane, two 16-year-olds, are engrossed in a video game at Chris' place. Ben, another friend, rings the bell because he fell off his bike, hurt himself and asks for help. Let us assume that Jane is self-controlled, while Chris is virtuous. In this case, they will both leave the video game and help Ben. For Chris, helping Ben is the only thing on his mind. Jane, however, will regret that she cannot continue playing her favourite video game, even though she knows that helping Ben is the right thing to do.

The connection between feeling and reason points towards the ideal of psychological integration and harmony. We probably make the assumption that internal conflict, stress and frustration are signs that something is wrong, and that it is better not to have these conflicts (Annas, 1993: 53). This means that for people who are self-controlled, acting virtuously is not yet completely pleasurable. We should be cautious in this respect not to think that this means that virtue is always accompanied by *sensory* pleasure. When Amy is virtuous, she experiences a kind of *attitudinal* pleasure: she finds pleasure in the belief that she did what was good, even when the consequence of her brave action may be painful for her, for example, when her classmates ignore her for a while.

Stage 4: virtue

At the fourth and ultimate stage, that of virtue, Amy sympathises with Florence, believes she should confront her classmates, confronts them, and is pleased that she has done what she knows she should do, even when her classmates make fun of her.

It is sometimes very tempting to call children 'virtuous', and Aristotle agrees that some people are endowed with moral qualities by nature. They are, for example, naturally more caring, generous or kind than others. However, he stops short of saying that children are virtuous in a *full* sense, since children lack *phronesis*, what we have explained as 'practical wisdom' or 'good sense'. Aristotle contrasts 'natural virtue' with 'proper virtue' (1975 NE 1144b3). People can only reach proper virtue when they possess good sense. Why is the possession of this capacity so important?

Good sense has two functions: one is constitutive, the other integrative (Kristjánsson, 2014a). When Amy has acquired good sense, she will deliberate about how to realise a virtue, such as justice, in practice. She considers all the details of her situation and determines what counts as justice in that case. This is the constitutive function. The integrative function of good sense helps Amy to 'act virtuously in an overall way', not only in one type of situation (Russell, 2012: 262). Without good sense, someone may be committed to virtue in one sphere, but not in another (Curzer, 2012: 359). For example, you may be a very caring husband at home, but a ruthless businessman at work; or you may treat your own two children fairly while not being able to give the students in your classroom equal treatment, because you do not know how to exhibit justice to children with learning disabilities.

These examples show that people can (and often do) function at different stages with respect to different virtues or in different situations (Miller, 2013). However, at the stage of proper virtue, good sense has forged the virtues into a complete, stable and integrated collection. So the case of Amy does not capture the idea expressed in the saying that 'one swallow doesn't make a summer', as Aristotle puts it. Acting virtuously on one occasion is not sufficient for a person to be called 'virtuous'. We can only call people virtuous who have had stable and firm commitment to the good – hitting the mean with regard to actions and emotions in all spheres – over a complete life.

There are several reasons why we should hesitate to call even people at this fourth stage 'morally developed', as if 'virtue' is a kind of finishing line that can be crossed. Virtue can better be compared to a finishing line that moves *out* of sight as soon as it comes *in* sight, spurring people on to perform even better. While we can say that the goal of moral development is a 'flourishing life', we do not know in advance what this really means, as if moral development is only about finding the means to get there. Moral development is, at this stage, also gaining a better understanding of the meaning of the goal of moral development. Alasdair MacIntyre (2007: 19) has famously phrased it in this way: '[T]he good life for man is the life spent in seeking for the good life for man'. Hence, even for the virtuous person there is room for improvement. A virtuous person's understanding of the good life can be continually refined as they acquire a more reflective understanding of the values embodied in their practical decisions. Moreover, when a virtuous person encounters new situations, there are still several ways in which they can act wrongly (Curzer, 2005). So, 'being virtuous' does not imply 'being perfect', but rather 'being good enough' (Curzer, 2012: 401). Or, as Badwar (2014: 167) puts is: virtue is 'like an A grade, which can go from A- to A+.'

Conclusion

In this chapter we have described what it means for children to develop morally, starting with Kohlberg's cognitive development model and moving on to a new developmental model: the Character Development Ladder.

While our model is not based on extensive empirical research in the same way as Kohlberg's, it has another strength: it is grounded in the long tradition of Aristotelian virtue ethics. This contributes to what is known as its 'construct validity': we articulated a set of components for virtues and told a story about the way these components *are* in fact interrelated in the virtuous person, or are *becoming* interrelated when one is not virtuous yet. Obviously, this model could be developed further. Potential next steps would be to design ways to measure the stages of virtue development proposed by our model, and to test the relations we postulated between them empirically. As this kind of empirical research into virtue development is still in its infancy (Arthur *et al.*, 2015b), we will only claim to be reasonably optimistic that our model offers the best available picture of character development to date. We discuss this further in Chapter 7.

The core message of this chapter is that developing morally is not only about becoming a more competent judge, and also not only about taking the most just course of action. It is about discovering how one can lead a good and meaningful life. Besides justice, this involves virtues such as friendship, patience, gratitude, moderation and compassion. The new account of moral development makes it clear that virtue is not synonymous with moral reasoning, nor can it be equated with moral action. Rather, it involves both, and more. To be more precise, a life well lived entails having an integrated set of virtues, called 'character', which involves not only moral thinking, but also the way we perceive, feel and act, our manner and our relationships. In this chapter, we have seen how these components of our moral psychology change as one morally matures.

How can the information contained in this chapter help teachers to teach character in schools? First, we showed that the model can help teachers recognise the developmental stages of their own students. We have seen, for example, that certain emotions can give an indication of the stages of moral development. The morally indifferent can be persuaded to act well through *fear* of consequences that may follow; those whose self-control is emerging will be *ashamed* when they don't act on their knowledge of virtue; self-controlled pupils will often act with *reluctance*, while virtuous people will find doing what is good to be self-evident, and they do it gladly. Keep in mind, though, that most students will think, act and feel in ways that do not easily fit into a single category. They might be relatively kind, generous and respectful, but lack self-knowledge, courage and temperance. This shows that they are not virtuous in an overall way.

Second, we showed that recognising the general developmental stage of students can help teachers adjust their teaching methods so they stimulate all students in such a way that they can progress. These teaching methods are the topic of the next chapter. Enforcing school rules may be a good instrument to prevent the morally indifferent from doing bad things, while habituation, i.e. giving students opportunities to practise the virtues themselves under teacher guidance, is a method that can help them to internalise what they already 'know' is good. Listening to music, reading books, attending plays, films and concerts can have a beneficial effect on self-controlled children whose feelings and judgments are not completely in line with each other. Conducting dialogues with students and teaching about the good life is, finally, suitable for those who already love what is good and have acquired good habits. Further instruction helps them to acquire knowledge of *why* an act is virtuous, after they already know *how* to act virtuously.

Objectives reached

At the end of this chapter, you should have clear ideas about:

• the differences between the Character Development Ladder and Kohlberg's cognitive developmental approach;

- the components of virtues, and how these components change as a person develops morally;
- the difference between the four stages of character development: moral indifference, emerging self-control, self-control and virtue;
- what to look for when you want to recognise the stage of students' character development.

Questions for reflection

- What level of character development do you think most primary and secondary school students are at? And what about adults? Do you think that children and adults can be at the same stage?
- Do you think that people's moral development can ever be finished? If so, why?
- Can the Character Development Ladder rebut Kohlberg's critique that moral education is often relativistic?
- What do you think of the suggestion that the emotion of 'shame' is crucial for character development?

5 Classroom-based approaches to character education

Summary

This chapter explores how character education can be taught in schools through classroom-based strategies. We explain a number of tried and tested teaching approaches: from a formal taught course in character education based on Jerome Bruner's spiral curriculum model, to ideas for teaching character through and across a wide range of curriculum subjects, including the statutory Religious Education (RE), Citizenship Education and Personal Social Health Education (PSHE). We describe taught and caught educational approaches to character education including the Jubilee Centre's Secondary Programme of Study (Jubilee Centre, 2014a) based on four stages of moral development, and we demonstrate how the subject can be made more intentional, explicit and planned both in and beyond the classroom. We think it important, when considering the approaches to character education described below, that they are not seen as 'off the shelf' activities that can simply be applied in any school without any consideration for the context or the learners. The chapter aims instead to provide some inspiration and examples that will encourage readers to adapt the suggested approaches to their own particular subjects and needs.

A taught course in character education

One approach to character education is to teach it as a discrete subject perhaps once or, in the case of the University of Birmingham School, twice a week – it could replace the Citizenship or PSHE slot. Before laying out what a taught course in character education might consist of, it is important to inject a word of caution: any taught course in character can only hope to offer the vaguest of outlines about what is required or recommended to live a life of virtue, or in the building of character. As Aristotle observed, building character is a most inexact and messy 'science'. The emphasis has to be on the students owning the issues raised, colouring, detailing and reshaping them with the unique stories of their own lives.

To do this, the best curriculum model to adopt in designing a taught course may be the Spiral Curriculum model, set out by Jerome Bruner in his *Process of Education* (Harvard, 1960). As Figure 5.1 suggests, the spiral curriculum model

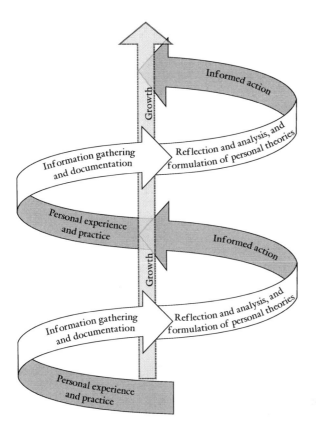

Figure 5.1 Spiral curriculum model.

Originally published in Compton, L., & Davis, N. (2010). The impact of and key elements for a successful virtual early field experience. *Contemporary Issues in Technology and Teacher Education*, *10*(3). Retrieved from http://www.citejournal.org/vol10/iss3/general/article1.cfm

moves students through phases of personal experience and practice, information gathering and documentation, reflection, analysis and internalisation, and informed action, then round again, as if moving up a spiral. This enables students to see previous learning and experience in a new light, and look at new learning from the perspective of previous experience. The purpose of such an approach is growth in knowledge, judgement and skill in practice. It is an experiential curriculum model, with an emphasis on personal engagement, ideas, reflection, refinement and internalisation, or habituation.

Pedagogy

The spiral curriculum model reconceptualises the role of teachers and places important demands on them. Within this context, the teacher is to become a wise and sensitive guide, responsive to the needs, strengths and weaknesses of their individual students. It allows for a more personalised approach to development. Any taught course needs to include a combination of pedagogical approaches that reflect the differing elements of Aristotle's approach to moral education. Some approaches need to be shaped in deductive and conceptual terms, with students coming to understand the structure of a virtue, then thinking through how these principles apply to their lives, and how they can use those realities to practise the virtue or virtues in question. Other approaches need to be more inductive, beginning with specific issues, working towards the realities of the students' lives, and then on to the underlying principles. Both are necessary and both can be harmonised. Amongst the challenges teachers have faced in character education to date is the development of a mutually intelligible discourse – many students simply do not have the language of character education, let alone the concepts; they are not what we have called 'virtue literate', a concept that we explain more fully in the next chapter. A taught course is the best means of redressing this problem.

In September 2014, the Jubilee Centre launched its first attempt at thinking through a discrete taught course in character education, known as the 'Secondary Programme of Study' (2014a). The Programme of Study contains three broad approaches to character education.

Approach 1

This focuses on building Virtue Knowledge, Virtue Reasoning and Virtue Practice for some classically recognised virtues. This forms the more conceptual part of a taught course, and is found in the teaching of specific virtues, e.g. the virtue of courage, or the virtue of self-control, etc. It sets out the framework or 'bare bones' anatomy of specific virtues. Whilst this part is more conceptual and deductive, there are plenty of opportunities here for application.

Each specific virtue is broken down into three sections, and each section explores how to exercise the virtue in question.

- *Section 1:* Virtue Knowledge
- *Section 2:* Virtue Reasoning
- *Section 3:* Virtue Practice

Virtue Knowledge is about acquiring and understanding the somewhat technical language and concepts associated with virtue. Here, students learn the following features for each virtue:

- what those who have this virtue can do particularly well;
- the benefits of enacting this specific virtue;
- which situations may be appropriate for the enacting of this virtue;
- which emotions, desires or feelings may be alerting one to the need to practise this particular virtue;
- how to think through and construct dilemmas and scenarios which illuminate how the virtue might best enacted.

But knowing *about* virtue is not sufficient for *being* virtuous – in other words, it may not necessarily change behaviour for the better. Students may, for instance, know what courage is in general, and how it is required when one experiences the emotions of fear or overconfidence, but this need not necessarily *make* them courageous in the situations that call for it. A taught course needs to move students from knowing what a virtue is to practical knowledge of how and when it should be implemented. This requires an education in virtue reasoning, where the material in the Virtue Reasoning phase of the taught course becomes relevant.

Virtue Reasoning is about making reasoned judgements about when and how to act well. This includes the ability to explain differences in moral situations, such as moral dilemmas. This emphasis on acquiring judgement is reflective, and allows for each individual to make their own decisions about how best to give expression to the virtues in situations that are pertinent to them. Virtue reasoning, for example, is about taking our understanding of courage and thinking through how best to give expression to it when we find ourselves in relevant situations.

Here, students learn the following features for each virtue:

- Their basic dispositions and inclinations in the light of this virtue – are there patterns to their emotions and desires when in this situation? When and how well have they practised this virtue in the past?
- The circumstances, options and choices for practising this specific virtue. When can they practise this virtue in the near future?
- Where the *Golden Mean* lies for them and which actions will allow them to best express this in self-identified scenarios; which actions will look like falling short in the virtue; which actions will look like over-shooting the virtue?

Virtue Practice: Both of the above components – Virtue Knowledge and Virtue Reasoning – are linked to the promotion of Virtue Practice. Students may, for instance, acquire some cognitive understanding of the desirable virtue to display in certain circumstances, but they may be unable to translate this knowledge and reasoning into virtuous action on a consistent basis. Virtuous practice therefore enables expression of virtue in desirable, recognisable and observable attitudes, behaviours and actions. Self-examination makes up an important component of virtue practice, which demands that students be courageous in situations that they identify as calling for that virtue; virtue practice also demands that students are able to examine how courageous they really are when they are actually in the situation that called for it, and how they might continue to build on their strengths and shortcomings in relation to the virtue. They will also understand how their emotions alert them to how well they are practising the virtue.

Approach 2

The second approach in the Jubilee Centre Programme of Study for the taught course is to furnish the students with the tools to build virtues that are neither mentioned nor developed in the Programme of Study. This offers scope to apply Approach 1 above to the very unique and specific circumstances of students' individual lives or contexts. Students, for instance, are invited to build their own understanding of virtues like gratitude and compassion and how best to exercise these in their lives. This makes for some interesting applications.

They are encouraged to identify the virtues that they need to cultivate in order to flourish once they enter the world of work. Those aspiring to journalism, for instance, may wish to cultivate the virtue of truthfulness; those aspiring to medicine, the virtues of compassion and care; those aspiring to teaching, patience and humility and so on. This enables students to practise the conceptual and practical tools required to continue the project of growing in virtue beyond the time they leave formal education.

Using the various templates should also enable individual subject teachers to explore growth in specific virtues through their subjects. It allows for a more individualised approach to the cultivation of virtue, situated within genuine issues with which students must grapple. How, for instance, could Physical Education become a context for exploring and practising the virtue of courage? Or how could a study in English of *The Grapes of Wrath* by Steinbeck help us to explore and practise the virtue of compassion? Or how might the pursuit and enjoyment of music help to grow in virtue overall, as Aristotle most definitely thinks it has the potential to do?

Approach 2 would also be particularly useful to schools wishing to prioritise the development of specific virtues as a 'whole school' focus. Schools may, for instance, feel they wish to develop greater self-control, resilience and calm in their students, especially in the face of substance abuse or stress issues; or they may wish to tackle virtues connected with justice and self-control, raising the social awareness of their students. Good schools know the needs of their students well. Faith schools, in particular, may wish to explore how the revelation around which their community is shaped integrates, builds upon, extends and deepens (or indeed unravels) the concepts set out in this particular exercise of emotion, reason, action and self-knowledge. How, for instance, might a Catholic school make sense of the golden mean for generosity, when the story of the Prodigal Son speaks of the wasteful and lavish love of the father? Or how can one prevent forgiveness becoming overly indulgent, or 'cheap', when Jesus commands his followers to forgive 'seventy times seven'?

Approach 3

The third pedagogical approach to a taught course is to focus on issues that elicit a call to act virtuously. This forms the more applied, inductive part of the course. It is primarily about how we bring our knowledge, reasoning and practice about virtues to bear on specific issues that call for their exercise. Many of these specific issues arise out of what we may recognise as the PSHE curriculum. Here we address issues such as: *Why do good people do bad things? How do we develop resilience, and how can we best handle stress?* We each react differently to situations or moral issues; each moral situation will call for the exercise of a virtue, or a cluster of virtues; and this will vary from person to person – as will the way in which we are called to practise them. The moral virtues that we practise – or fail to practise – will have performance and civic implications. Thinking through how to practise and develop virtues in the performance and civic domains forms an important part of Approach 3, moving out beyond the moral agent to the wider society.

Aristotelian elements

As indicated in Chapter 2, any neo-Aristotelian taught course must contain certain discernible elements central to Aristotle's ethical theory. At the centre of this approach is the cultivation of virtue. Figure 5.2 shows what a virtue is, on Aristotle's reading.

This is perhaps easier to understand if we look at how we come to acquire and practise 'virtues' – we and our students are no doubt already doing this to varying degrees. Put at its crudest, the way to build character consciously and systematically goes something like this:

- First, we have to recognise that we are in a moral situation. A moral situation is one that calls for us to do something we ought to do. To do 'that thing that we ought to do' requires the exercise of a virtue.
- Second, this situation triggers emotions, desires or feelings in us. Sometimes, these can be very strong; on other occasions, they may be very weak. We have to be able to specify and identify the emotion or desire triggered in us by the situation.
- Third, we need to identify the virtue(s) that can cultivate those specific emotion(s) that help us realise the good in our situation. We 'realise the good' through words, actions and deeds – by doing the right thing, at the right time, in the right way, and for the right reasons – and hopefully with the right consequences. Stages one to three are covered by *Virtue Knowledge*.
- Fourth, we need to think through our options and to weigh up the morally relevant features of a situation: how we can practise, or give expression to, the virtue(s) that corresponds to the emotion(s), or desire(s) that are stimulating us, or failing to stimulate us. This is where *Virtue Reasoning* comes

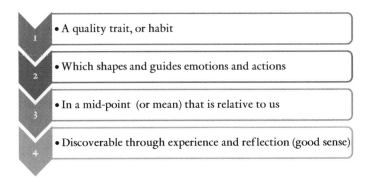

1 • A quality trait, or habit

2 • Which shapes and guides emotions and actions

3 • In a mid-point (or mean) that is relative to us

4 • Discoverable through experience and reflection (good sense)

Figure 5.2 An Aristotelian reading of virtue.

in. These practices need to tread a careful path between 'overdoing it' and 'underdoing it', trying to give the very best expression to acting in a way consistent with *the golden mean* – the ideal, most reasonable, morally good, set of actions, given the circumstances. These practices will educate and shape our emotions – rather than eradicate them.

- Fifth, we need to act, to learn by doing, by getting involved in service learning, or social action, or some other small-scale moral project. Then we need to reflect on how well we handled the situation, looking at where we might be strong, and where we still might need to grow, or to practise the virtue. We need to look at our emotions, desires, pleasures and pains, and of course, the quality of our actions – which together point to our fumbling and clumsy attempts at becoming better people. This is where the *Virtue Practice* comes in.

Even if Aristotle may need some updating, including him in our contemporary ethical discourse should make for some interesting and fruitful pedagogical chemistry.

Evaluating character development

Aristotle suggests some basic tools or frameworks that enable us to reflect on how far we are growing in the life of virtue. These tools are necessarily inexact, but useful nevertheless, because growing in virtue is both an objective and a subjective experience. It is *objective*, because some desires and actions are clearly off-limits for the life of virtue, and will erode character, rather than build it. We can reason reliably to some positions, e.g. that taking more than our fair share of cake is unfair if there are others at the table who would still like some. Moreover, we can *perceive* virtue and vice in others, and that virtue or vice is real. It is also *subjective*, because only the subject can say with any confidence what is *really* happening to them emotionally. Only they are able to say whether it pained them to do the right thing, or whether they actually enjoyed engaging in virtuous activity. Only they can *really* know if they were pained at offering their little brother some cake to even things out, or if it pleased them to do so; or, if it pleased them to deny their little brother cake as an act of spite, unjustly denying him what was rightfully his! Similarly, any self-reporting will be bedevilled by the so called 'self-biases' that lead subjects to view themselves in the most positive if unrealistic light. We will look at all these evaluation and measurement issues in more detail in Chapter 7.

Building character takes practice; and practice presupposes that we make mistakes, but are constantly prepared to learn from them. This is a healthy and realistic attitude to becoming a better person. Growing in virtue not only takes maturity but also a commitment to grow in virtue, which is itself the first sign of ethical maturity. We all have to be prepared to get it wrong, to be frank (with ourselves) about our mistakes and think through how we can better educate our emotions and consider our actions more carefully when similar situations arise. Being frank with ourselves does not require us to publicise our emotions to others or to disclose information that could damage us or those associated with us beyond reasonable limits. It is simply a call for us to reflect more deeply on the issues and to learn from them. Whilst it may only have the status of 'folk wisdom' amongst professional teachers, teachers do know instinctively that the more mature their students are in outlook and attitude, the better they are able to cope with the challenges and pleasures of school life. We see 'maturity' as coterminous with 'character' – and the mature among us can admit their mistakes and learn from them.

Evaluating and assessing a taught course in character education

We set out below the basic stages in the Programme of Study that Aristotle uses to reflect on how we are building or strengthening our character, rather than engaging in actions that erode and undermine it. According to Aristotle, those in the initial stages (the Person A and Person B categories) are unable or unwilling to be persuaded that building their character is a worthwhile pursuit. Those who exhibit the characteristics of a Person A, for instance, are simply not yet sufficiently ethically mature – or free enough from psychological, biological or environmental factors – to contemplate acting well in terms of some particular virtues. Those defined as Persons B are not persuaded by the call to virtue, and would prefer to shape their lives around ends that could ultimately erode character, rather than build it. For both, patience and compassion are no doubt required; they may need time, ethical and spiritual maturity, psychological balance, healing, the effect of significant life events and a range of positive influences (not least compassionate, ethically mature people) to help them move beyond these stages and to commit to a more worthwhile, ethical life.

Once we move beyond the Person A and Person B categories, we have various stages of moral development and their associated characteristics.

Here we give an overview of those stages in terms of the hallmarks or characteristics of the Person A and Person B individuals, and the subsequent Stages, 1 to 4, that provide a framework for reflecting on our own moral development:

'Person A' – 'Not ready for this yet': *I am not yet free enough to commit to growth in the life of virtue.*

- I may have had traumatic experiences or major personal difficulties surrounding this virtue. These historic experiences and circumstances prevent or constrain me from acting differently. I may, for instance, have an addiction, over which I have no control.
- I may have been socialised into a culture or environment that has generated bad habits – I may, for instance, have been taught that stealing from others is a good thing, or that one should always give in to stronger forces; or that being rude and offensive to others is commendable.

- I may simply be unwell. It may, for instance, be no good talking to me about self-control when it comes to drink, as I am an alcoholic. I need sympathy and therapy, not a life of virtue.

'Person B' – 'Not buying into this yet': *I am not convinced that the life of virtue is really what it's all about, or that building one's character is in any way commendable. I would much rather shape my life around the pursuit of fame, pleasure, money and power, whatever the cost. The Aristotelian ethical project simply does not speak to me at any stage.*

- I can frankly admit that my actions are motivated purely by the pursuit of wealth, status, pleasure, power or self-aggrandisement. I see nothing at all wrong with this. Anything that threatens to stand in my way on the way to these goals needs to be eliminated. I want much more money than I need; I want it to impress my magnificence upon others; I want it for influence and power; and I want to be feted and celebrated wherever I go. I am happy to give up any pretence of 'building character'. I don't just want self-preservation, I want emphatic self-assertion: I'm basically out entirely for myself in the most selfish ways possible, and I'm not afraid to admit it.
- I simply cannot see the point in living an ethically sound life.

Aristotle does not think much can be done with such attitudes as those found in Person A and Person B types. He might prescribe extrinsic positive and negative reinforcement strategies. Failing that, critical shaping events on lives lived in such ways may become educative and pedagogic, forcing a rethink. Perhaps it may be best to delay the conversation about virtue until a later stage in the lives of such individuals, when they have more material to reflect on.

For the sake of argument, let us all assume that students can begin their self-reflection from the following stage, which we will call Stage 1. We think it fair to assume that we are all more or less committed to growth in the life of virtue, and to building our character, rather than the reverse.

Here, then, are the stages of moral development – corresponding broadly but not exactly with the Character Development Ladder explained in Chapter 4. In the four stages outlined below, the last has been divided into two sub-stages (a and b). Stage 4a is full virtue without extensive reflection, and 4b is full virtue with extensive reflection. The division of Stage 4 into two parts should enable teachers to make more accurate evaluations of how their students are progressing.

Stage 1: *I am open to the idea of acquiring this virtue; I am committed in principle to this idea but I am as yet unconvinced by some aspects.*

- I may for instance be unsure about how the virtue in question builds character or leads to a flourishing life.
- I am a little inept in applying the principles of the virtuous life and character building to specific cases.

- However, I am interested in virtuous action for its own sake, and would really like to lead this kind of life.
- I let my emotions get the better of me on many occasions – I even let them cloud my judgement.

Aristotle would suggest that you need encouragement to move on from this stage. Acquire and internalise knowledge about which acts are virtuous and which are not; and don't be afraid to experience a sense of personal disappointment at failing to have acted correctly – this can often be a strong motivator to future virtuous action.

Stage 2: *I am committed to building this virtue but my emotions carry me away. Despite knowing the right thing to do, my emotions push me into acting in ways I know to be character eroding.*

- I know the right thing to do and wish to do it simply because it is the right thing to do. I'm not looking for applause and I don't have self-interested motives.
- However, I let my desires and emotions carry me away; sometimes these emotions erode the principles I know to be good and worthwhile.
- When I succumb to my more powerful emotions, I sometimes experience a sense of remorse and regret.

To move to the next stage, Aristotle might suggest that you overlay your bad habits with some good habits. If, for instance, you want to develop the virtue of self-control, you might turn off the television and go for a run instead; or if you want to improve your study concentration, turn off all distractions and commit to study for a specific period of time without shifting from your desk. Habituating yourself to act in this way will strengthen the particular virtues you are trying to work on. You can also think through how you might feel if you behave badly or do things you'd rather not admit to yourself. You can let the prospect of personal disappointment prevent you from acting like this. Never be afraid to listen to your regrets – remember, the wise person listens to them and learns from them; the fool suppresses or ignores them. From these regrets, you can identify new resolutions to live by. You can acquire the habit of acting rightly so as to triumph over bad acts.

Stage 3: *I can practise this virtue, but only through gritted teeth. It pains me to do the right thing.*

- I know how to give expression to the virtues in given situations.
- I can perform virtuous actions habitually, more or less.
- I know what needs to be done; however, I don't always do it.
- My emotions occasionally carry me away, and do not run in line with what I know to be right.

- And I am not really that clear about how and why certain sorts of acts might express various virtues, or even why I should be virtuous at all in this situation.

According to Aristotle, to move on from this stage, students need to keep looking for opportunities to perform virtuous, character building acts such that they become habitual. Ensure that, wherever possible, you expose yourself to the very best in art, music, literature, politics and sport – this might inspire you to get a better grip on your emotions, especially when they conflict with what you know to be the right actions.

Stage 4a: *I am committed to becoming a better person in respect of this virtue; I've got a pretty good grip of myself and am consistently able to bring my emotions into line with my reasoning; but I'm not really sure why.*

- I can do the right thing simply for the sake of doing the right thing.
- I know which acts are virtuous and build character, and which acts erode or destroy it.
- I know how to enact these virtuous acts in many differing circumstances in my life.
- I have acquired habits of virtuous action in certain domains.
- I have acquired habits of virtuous emotion – it gives me pleasure and joy to do the right thing, and it pains me not to do the right thing when confronted with situations that call for a moral response.
- However, I don't really understand why virtuous acts are actually virtuous.

According to Aristotle, those at this stage need to build their character. Using virtue reasoning, you need to think through acts that show particular character traits and determine whether that character trait is a virtue. You need also to understand how this fits with a happy, flourishing life. If you keep acting well, you will think well; and, if you think well, you will act well.

Stage 4b: *I feel the right way about the right things, at the right time and in the right way. I act it out rightly and, I know why.*

- This stage includes the characteristics set out in Stage 4a, but the chief difference is that those in Stage 4b are able to *explain why* some actions are more virtuous than others. This provides a basis for commending certain courses of action – and inaction) – in others. It is perhaps best if we assume that this may become more refined with maturity, even if we already see signs of this stage in our students.

At the end of each chapter in the Programme of Study, there is a self-reflection framework corresponding to Stages 1 to 4 above and tailored to the virtue under discussion. Teachers, parents and students can use this framework as a guide for ensuring that students get the most out of their self-reflection.

Growth into self-knowledge and ethically responsible adulthood is necessarily a rough and ready business. Aristotle has given a suggestive framework, with which students and teachers can begin to make some sense of the confusion. We believe that this framework is best applied by means of a taught course.

Teaching character through curriculum subjects

In conjunction with the discrete taught course we have laid out above, character can be 'taught' through and within all curriculum subjects (Jubilee Centre, 2014b). Physical Education (PE), Personal Social Health Education (PSHE) and Citizenship Education teachers might not find such a proposition challenging; after all, teaching about the virtue of compassion is integral to good citizenship education, while fair play is integral to PE and temperance integral to PSHE. However, what about teachers of other core curriculum subjects, such as science and English? Although the links might be less obvious at first, the content of these subjects, as well as others, can be excellent vehicles for character education. For example, English teachers can draw on a long history of great literature as a rich source to initiate discussions with students about the character strengths and weaknesses of the heroes and heroines. Science teachers must be mindful of the moral virtues of integrity and trustworthiness when conducting experiments, as well as a host of intellectual virtues, such as critical thinking and enquiry.

It is not just through the subject content that character virtues can be discussed and developed – the pedagogical practices that teachers employ are also important. Teachers should encourage students to discuss and debate issues of morality, ethics and character that come up in their subjects in a critically reflective – as opposed to a didactic – way. Furthermore, they can offer real life opportunities linked to the subject to test the character virtues of students. For example, a community service activity in citizenship is a good opportunity to undertake beneficial service, and performing a musical concert is a good opportunity to demonstrate courage. The important point here is that character education should not be confined to the classroom, it can also be undertaken through the whole school, as well as out of school activities that link to various subjects, as we show in the next chapter.

The teaching of virtues is implicit throughout both the primary and secondary curriculums and can be embedded into the lesson content without too much adjustment. In many cases, only minor modifications to the lesson plans are needed to make the teaching of virtues an explicit learning outcome of any particular activity. In the section below, we explore nine statutory secondary school curriculum subjects, and we make suggestions for how to teach character education through and within each of them. Following this, we explore in more detail two non-statutory subjects – PSHE and RE – which might traditionally be considered to have a natural affinity to character education. If character education is to become an intentional, planned, organised and reflective part of all schooling, then the onus is on all teachers to seek out opportunities in their own subjects, such as those detailed below, to educate the virtues. In doing so, they will gain an understanding that character education can and should complement (and indeed lead to) increased attainment in the subjects.

Citizenship education

Good citizens need to possess good character virtues and their development should therefore be an ambition of citizenship education. Citizenship is a curricular area offering opportunity for the explicit teaching of virtue knowledge, reasoning and practice, as well as being a virtue in itself. As a discrete subject, there exists a wealth of curriculum opportunities to explore what is expected of the 'good citizen'. There is more to citizenship than simply knowing about systems, structures and underpinning democratic principles, and Aristotle believed that a good society had to be built on the foundations of ethically good characters. For Aristotle, trying to impart political principles without prior attention to the characters of the people who are meant to put them into practice, is putting the cart before the horse. At its very best, citizenship education has a valuable contribution to make in shaping and forming those 'good characters'. The 'virtue of citizenship' is particularly well expressed in community spirited action, be it with respect to the local or global community. For example, so-called *Service Learning* programmes are often integrated into citizenship education since these encourage young people not only to be civically aware and active, but also, importantly, to reflect critically on their civic engagement. Likewise, citizenship education encourages young people to be active citizens through taking part in volunteering and youth social action programmes. We discuss this in the next chapter, where we also give some case studies.

The citizenship education curriculum content lends itself to educating the virtues of political and public service, including tolerance and justice, among others. Teaching about political literacy and involvement in the political process can be considered in terms of what it means to undertake service for the benefit of others.

The virtues of mutual respect and tolerance are implicit in approaches to explaining human rights, and setting them in the context of human flourishing allows students the chance to explain why we cannot have total freedom without constraint. Likewise, the virtue of justice is inextricably linked to democratic citizenship. When students study criminal and civil systems, they explore the interaction of a variety of virtues, and they debate the involvement of emotions and other factors contributing to citizens' moral actions. They contemplate difficulties faced by jurors and legal advocates in remaining objective and assessing problems when determining guilt and innocence. Service is also a key component of the development of good citizenship. It can be taught explicitly through looking at public institutions and voluntary groups, and can be implicitly developed through encouraging students to engage actively in their own voluntary work.

Computer Science

A key question for Computer Science teachers to ask their students is '*How can we use technology more wisely*'? We believe that a focus on character in lessons should be a priority and contribute to the development of young digital citizens who use technology for positive ends such as cyber-citizenship, rather than negative activities such as trolling, cyber-bullying or online plagiarism. This means that computer science classes should concentrate not only on the knowledge and skills associated with programming, but also on ethical issues associated with emerging digital technologies and the Internet.

A focus on character virtues could be particularly useful for lessons about how to use the Internet wisely. In cyberspace, there are often no rules identifying the right thing to do when faced with an ethical dilemma. Likewise, owing to the nature of the technology, it is often hard to predict the consequences of any particular course of action. Therefore, the onus is on teachers to encourage their students to consider the compassionate or honest action in any particular situation. For example, students need to question if, for example, their Facebook message is likely to cause offence to someone else, or if they are in danger of plagiarising when they are referring to other people's work they have found online. Recent research conducted by the Jubilee Centre for Character and Virtues at the University of Birmingham has shown that 11 to 14-year-olds in England think that the Internet is largely unregulated and that rules about what is right and wrong are often opaque (Harrison, 2014). Participants in the studies state that their teachers might enforce rules in the classroom, but these are often broken when they are at home, alone and online in their bedrooms. Website giants such as Facebook, Instagram and Twitter find it hard (or are sometimes unwilling) to regulate personal profiles or impose rules regarding their use. Furthermore, even when the rules are understood, the young people reported that they might bypass them by going online anonymously.

This research also shows that many 11 to 14-year-olds are unaware of the consequences of some of their online actions (Harrison, 2014). For example, due to the lack of visual clues and feedback from the recipient, they are often unaware that the messages they have sent are upsetting people. Furthermore, because the journey of any particular online communication is so unpredictable, messages that were intended for one individual can quickly spread around a whole school, with significant unintended consequences. This is why many teachers report having to deal with fallouts from supposedly private emails, or 'sexting' posts that have been transmitted across the school.

Computer Science lessons are ideal for developing learning strategies to educate more digitally wise young citizens who are able to 'self-police' their technology-related activities. A reconceptualised computer science curriculum would require teachers to provide time and tools for their students to reflect on and learn from their online interactions. This could also include basic Netiquette with its civic virtues of respect, responsibility and consideration. Writing in the New Yorker

(10 June, 2013) about his new book *Emily Post's Manners in a Digital World: Living Well Online*, Daniel Post Senning remarks that:

> Ultimately, we are talking about traditional social norms – being friendly, thoughtful, considerate, sincere, respectful – and how we carry those with us when we enter the world of social media and mobile devices.

The teaching tools to support such an approach could be hosted on websites, such as structured online reflection blogs, or online moral dilemma games, where students have to practise making difficult ethical decisions. Such tools would help young people to develop the capacity to acquire online practical wisdom – or good sense – and choose the compassionate, honest or courageous action, even when no-one is watching.

Design and technology

How can the designing of graphics and images or the production of materials become a vehicle for teaching virtue? Traditional craftsmen, such as stonemasons and cabinetmakers, would have had an emphatic answer to this: cultivating a refined aesthetic sensibility requires creativity, imagination, self-discipline, ingenuity and resourcefulness, amongst many other virtues.

There are plenty of opportunities through the design and technology curriculum to explore and practise the virtues. As the subject is largely practice-based, students are obliged to solve design problems with a limited range of materials and skills – meaning that they have to be resourceful and self-disciplined. Resourcefulness and creativity can be taught through learning activities and schemes that require students to produce designs or solutions within severe constraints. Limiting choice in this way leads students to discover the scope of the material on hand. The focus on actual practice not only hopefully brings the ultimate reward of competence but also teaches the associated virtue of perseverance: stick with it and you will improve. Finally, insight and empathy are also essential to successful design – if designers want others to buy and use their designs, it is worth their while to study what people are really like and how they behave.

English and English Literature

English and English Literature are subjects directly, deeply and widely concerned with notions of virtue and, in particular, the development of virtue literacy in students – an idea we explore in greater depth in Chapter 6. It would be possible to find a literary text that explored any of the virtues, be they moral, performance, civic or intellectual. Many great stories explore several virtues and as such, make an excellent vehicle for observations of characters' practical wisdom when competing virtues clash. For example, a discussion of *Othello* will focus on issues of trust, honesty, respect, compassion and leadership; it will consider the damaging effects of a lack of empathy in human relations; and it will consider the cultural role of dramatic tragedy as an exploration of personal and civic virtues in the contrasting societies. A discussion of George Orwell's *1984* will focus on issues of citizenship, social justice, communication, respect, courage, trust and resilience.

In English, the content does not have to be limited to literature. Persuasive speech-writing might be studied through examples such as Martin Luther King's 1963 speech at the Lincoln Memorial, which addresses issues of social justice, tolerance and hope, and by the study of communication through rhetoric and leadership – once again, Aristotle pioneers this approach in chapters 5 and 6 of his *Rhetoric*, where he explores the relationship between ethics and rhetoric. Imaginative writing is an intellectual exercise in creativity, rooted in an empathic understanding of other people and the moral, civic and performance issues they face. In short, because English concerns itself with communication, debate, discussion and reflection on what it is to be a human being living in a social context in relationship with other human beings, it is probably the most fitting subject through which to study almost all the virtues.

Geography

Geography can inspire students with a curiosity and wonder of the physical and human dimensions of our planet – and as such can be an excellent catalyst for asking students to reflect more deeply about the place of character and virtue in human flourishing. Awe, wonder and amazement at the beauty of the natural world and its vastness can all be developed and cultivated through a sensitive pursuit of Geography. Not only should it broaden the intellectual horizons of students, it should also deepen and refine their moral outlook. This could apply to the implications of the wise stewardship of the environment and to sustainable development.

Curriculum content can be a great vehicle for exploring the virtues mentioned above as well as many others. For example, compassion could be a focus when exploring the quality of life and proneness to natural disasters in less economically developed regions by encouraging students to reflect on local living conditions in a diary. Empathy and respect could be elicited when encountering and understanding very different lives in other parts of the world. A decision-making exercise could be used as an opportunity for students to empathise with the opinions of a range of stakeholders – for instance, local residents, businesses, environmentalists and politicians. Civic virtues of community awareness and neighbourliness can be explored when introducing the concept of sustainable development. The environment, more generally, is also an opportunity to explore those virtues associated with sustainability – a continuous thread that runs through the Geography curriculum, in both physical and human geography topics, and one repeatedly stressed in the many BBC broadcasts by Sir David Attenborough.

Hursthouse (2007), amongst others, provides new interpretations of traditional virtues and applies these to how humans might best relate to nature. Important sustainability virtues for Hursthouse include prudence, practical wisdom, compassion, benevolence, unselfishness, honesty, patience and far-sightedness. These can be contrasted with vices that are often cited as the causes of unsustainability such as greed, self-indulgence, short sightedness, cruelty, pride and vanity.

Sandler (2007) also promotes what he calls the *environmental virtues* – among which might be included awe, discernment, compassion, self-control, cooperativeness, delayed gratification and solidarity. These virtues help ensure that that scientific discovery and progress is undertaken reflectively and in harmony with the natural world.

History

Like English, History provides an excellent stimulus for exploring the achievements and follies of humanity. Stories from history are relevant to broader human interests and personal ethical development, even if they are not central to the theory and methodology of the subject itself. Historical narratives of key events can bring students into discussions about the very central questions about how we should live – questions with which the greatest minds in history have grappled.

The history curriculum can be used as a vehicle for the education of character through a variety of complementary approaches. These include exploring controversial character traits of key figures from history, looking in particular at sympathetic and unsympathetic views of their biographies. For example, what character virtues did Churchill display during the First World War and, importantly, how did he act when these virtues came into conflict? Other approaches could explore the tensions between public morality and private vice in the lives of iconic figures in the past, relations between rulers and the ruled, the powerful and the powerless and the redressing of perceived injustices.

The subject can also provide good ground for ethical debate, critical reflection and observation. Teachers can provide students with examples of key historical events that contain differing views on the issues. These 'worldviews' can be considered alongside the complexities and pressures of reporting truthfulness when reporting history. Likewise, teachers can reconstruct debates about ethical dilemmas in history, which will allow students to understand their complex and often intractable nature.

Mathematics

The links between Mathematics and character education are not immediately apparent. However, a more in-depth view shows possibilities for education in some of the core moral and other types of virtues, including intellectual virtues. The exacting nature of Mathematics challenges students to develop patience, studiousness and humility. Integrity is also required in the analysis and use of statistics. Perhaps more than any other, the subject requires the performance virtues of real determination, grit and perseverance in the face of problems that may at first sight appear impossible.

Besides the practice of Maths itself, the subject content can potentially be directed at the discovery, discussion and development of virtues in young people. For example, when teaching about graphs – using death rates and world poverty statistics as examples could be designed to lead to debate and discussions amongst students about the virtues of fairness, justice and compassion. Students also learn how to use questionnaires and to create surveys and analyse data, encouraging the development of curiosity and resourcefulness.

Science

At its most fundamental level, science has a deep concern for empirical truth; it is also important that scientific knowledge is used wisely within an ethical framework, rather than for vicious ends. The means of acquiring scientific knowledge are therefore related to wider ethical issues and questions about what is right for society – including social justice – as well as for the natural environment, as already discussed above.

There is a great deal of opportunity to teach character and virtues through both scientific practice as well as through analysis and critique of scientific issues. Intellectual virtues, such as critical thinking in the evaluation of data stand out, along with the moral virtues of honesty and integrity, for instance in measurement and accurate reporting of experimental results. Ethical issues connected with compassion in relation to human benefits arise with animal experimentation. The practice of science can also enhance the development of performance virtues, including creativity. Examples include the lateral thinking required to construct experiments, such as the way Stanley Milgram used a fake electric shock study to measure obedience, or how Erwin Schrödinger devised the famous cat paradox to explain quantum mechanics.

Science also has a clear role in the development of some key civic virtues, such as social justice, which one could potentially explore through ethical issues arising during clinical trials of drugs, such as how that information is used, and who benefits physically, and financially from such trials. This in turn raises ethical issues relating to honesty and integrity in the non-reporting of unfavourable clinical trials or the incentivisation of doctors to prescribe specific drugs through lavish conference expenses and speaking fees.

Physical education

Many schools will point to the playing fields when asked where the character of their students is most likely to be formed. Physical Education has been an important element of curriculums throughout history not only for its health and wellbeing properties – *mens sana in corpore sano* – but also because it provides a specific context for the development of character. This is why it is one of the few subjects where the word 'character' is actually mentioned in the national curriculum guidelines. The guidelines state that the purpose of study is to provide opportunities to compete in sport and other activities in order to build character and help embed values such as fairness and respect. (See also Jubilee Centre, 2014b)

Initially, Physical Education might seem to highlight performance virtues, such as teamwork, problem solving, leadership and self-discipline, but these can be supported by intellectual virtues such as cooperation, communication and reflection. Moreover, Physical Education also provides an opportunity to develop moral virtues, such as humility, fairness and courage. Honesty can equally be expressed in accurate self-evaluation and sportsmanship, and compassion and kindness in handling victory and defeat. A focus on these moral virtues can help ensure a balance between the development of performance and civic virtues.

The ability to explore and develop the virtues discussed above rests on the ability of teachers to see themselves as not just technically good sports coaches, but also as character coaches. This includes an awareness of how the teacher or coach is modelling the virtues themselves, how these are communicated to students and the ways in which they facilitate opportunities for discussion and reflection. This gives students the chance to discuss not only how they won or lost a game, but what they learned about themselves and their teammates in the process.

Non-statutory subjects: PSHE and RE

Alongside the statutory curriculum subjects, all schools in England are also required to teach Religious Education at all key stages. Secondary schools must also provide sex and relationship education in key Stages 3 and 4. These areas are normally taught through the two subjects, Personal Social Health Education (PSHE) and Religious Education (RE). Given the traditional role of PSHE and RE in cultivating character, we give these two subjects lengthier consideration below.

Personal Social Health Education

PSHE is perhaps, alongside Citizenship Education, one of the most natural vehicles for character education, since it is at its very core concerned with human flourishing and wellbeing. It provides dedicated space in the curriculum for students to learn about virtues and their acquisition, as well as how to live well as human beings and as members of a community and society. Life experiences can be explored through the prism of virtue in the PSHE lesson and pupils can then apply these refined understandings to their own lives.

Whilst PSHE education remains a non-statutory subject and there is no prescribed curriculum, all schools must make some provision for PSHE, which The Department of Education considers a necessary and important part of all pupils' education. The National Curriculum framework states that:

> Every state-funded school must offer a curriculum whichpromotes the spiritual, moral, cultural, mental and physical development of pupils at the school and of society' and 'prepares pupils at the school for the opportunities, responsibilities and experiences of later life.

Schools generally meet these requirements through their PSHE provision, but there is also a clear link to a more schoolwide, cross-curricular and holistic vision of character education, as we discuss in the next chapter. In fact, the links between the PSHE content commonly taught in schools and character education are so close that the character education programme of study developed by the Jubilee Centre (2014a) encompasses much of the PSHE programme. The introduction to the Programme of Study states that:

> The concepts and approaches set out here could be used to recast PSHE within character education terms, looking at the ways the issues and challenges dealt with in PSHE could best be met by growth in virtue and ethical maturity.

A brief look through the titles of the schemes of work encompassed in the Programme of Study shows how this aspiration might play out in practice. For example, there are sessions on issues such as substance misuse, mental health and coping with stress, which emphasise such virtues as tolerance, temperance, compassion and resilience.

We believe that PSHE has a four-fold task when it comes to character education. First, it should teach directly all of the virtues across the four domains – moral, intellectual, civic and performance. Although there is no curriculum common to all schools, themes commonly covered in PSHE make this task relatively easy. For example, lessons on relationships will have a natural link to the moral virtue of compassion; lessons on ethical consumption have a link to the civic virtue of citizenship; performance virtues such as grit and resilience are relevant to issues such as mental health and wellbeing; and intellectual virtues such as critical thinking are embedded in the whole content. A balanced PSHE curriculum will ensure that all four types of virtues are duly represented, as in the Programme of Study, so as to ensure it is not biased towards any one of them. We think it essential that moral virtue forms a significant component of any PSHE programme, otherwise we have a Machiavellian situation where a focus on performance virtues (such as resilience) without a connection to the greater human good might produce resilient and emotionally sophisticated but unscrupulous individuals.

The second task is to teach awareness of the processes involved in the acquisition of virtue, such as becoming aware of associated emotions, subjecting thought to rational scrutiny and developing an understanding of agency over our actions. The core task here is to provide learners with opportunities to reflect on their own actions, thus making the subject real and relevant. So, pupils should be required to consider how their virtues and indeed vices play out in their everyday lives, rather than just consider abstract examples. Schools often use a variety of methods to encourage such personal awareness, including Think-Pair-Share (TPS) activities and personal reflection logs. They could also use new technologies such as film blogs and Twitter feeds for this purpose.

Third, it should help students to acquire through practice new ways of feeling, thinking and acting. Again, the emphasis is on moving from the feeling and thinking to actually doing and being. PSHE should be a place where students not only gain knowledge about important issues – many of which relate to the ideal of flourishing – but also modify their behaviour if required. So, they can find out why smoking or drugs can be harmful, and they can actually demonstrate the virtue of temperance when faced with a peer pressure situation on having to make a choice about whether or not to take drugs.

Finally, PSHE should teach pupils how to acquire and practise the meta-virtue of *phronesis* – good sense or practical wisdom. This is where a spiral curriculum – such as that emphasised in the character education Programme of Study – really comes into its own. As we have seen, a spiral curriculum model moves students through phases of personal experience and reflection with the aim of them moving up the spiral. As they progress upwards, the learning includes information gathering and documentation, analysis, internalisation and informed action. The ideal is for students to consider all learning from the perspective of personal experience. This leads to a growth not only in knowledge, but also ideally in wise practice. Using such an approach, they can recognise that there are no fixed outcomes, as the journey of growth is never complete. Instead, pupils are encouraged to develop good sense, through informed judgement about their actions in different life experiences.

An example of a school that places a strong emphasis on character education taught through PSHE is Kings Langley School in Hertfordshire. To demonstrate the importance and commitment to PSHE, they have doubled the amount of time given to the lessons, while halving the normal class size, so as to ensure that the character related themes addressed can be explored in smaller and more intimate groups. The smaller group sizes and increased time allow for challenging topics to be properly considered. All students have resilience lessons as part of their PSHE programme. The lessons are based on the Penn Resilience Programme (PRP): an evidence-based approach to teaching young people critical life skills. The programme is designed to enable young people to flourish and thrive. All teachers attend special resilience training sessions to learn how to deliver the programme.

Religious Education

Religious Studies can be explored in two main ways to build character: first, through the process of learning *about* religions, and second, by learning *from* religions. In learning about the great religions that have animated and engaged humanity, students can develop a keen sense of respect for others and sensitivity towards what is important for them. This is a civilising quality in itself. Such a respect and sensitivity can also, with guidance, cultivate the virtue of humility: if the gods of whom the great religions speak are indeed incomprehensible, then students could learn to be humble in the face of so many differences in belief. Moreover, students of Religious Studies could also become alert to the false claims that some make regarding religions, especially by those who abuse religion for purposes that are overtly political. This clarity of mind can help to build resilience and encourage students to be constructively critical of those both within and outside various religious traditions. Such study certainly informs the guiding virtue of 'good sense'. Regardless of a student's own position on the religion studied, they should be able to articulate the claims of that religion, and the grounds upon which such claims have been and are being made, and they should strive to do so with a deeper understanding than most adherents of the religion. As John Stuart Mill (1989: 38) observed: 'he who knows only his own side of the case knows little of that'. This practice cultivates the virtues of fairness, integrity and intellectual honesty.

The ways in which students can learn *from* rather than simply *about* religions through the pursuit of Religious Studies can however be even more fruitful. Within the Judeo-Christian tradition, for example, the Decalogue and the Beatitudes should provide extremely rich material for reflection and guidance, as should any number of Jesus' parables, especially the Prodigal Son, in addition to his scathing critiques of religious hypocrisy. Moreover, the Wisdom Tradition contained in the Scriptures can provide a sounding board for discussion. Texts such as Ecclesiastes, with its challenge of 'vanity of vanities, all is vanity', and other books within the Wisdom Tradition, such as the Book of Wisdom and Proverbs, have all played a central role in shaping human reflection and action. The Book of Job grapples with questions about the nature of God, existence and humanity's response to suffering. Indeed, a foundation in such texts would not only build character, but also provide a solid basis for accessing the great books of literature. Such a pursuit can potentially broaden rather than narrow the mind, and raise rather than lower the mental horizons of the students.

Issues such as self-awareness, relationships, and rights and responsibilities should all provide material for reflection and personal application. Such approaches are, of course, not restricted to the Judeo-Christian tradition, but are also central to all of the great world religions. Great religious texts – and great religious leaders, prophets and gurus – have all wrestled with such central questions as the need to grow in self-knowledge, build strong relationships, and live in a responsible, reflective and considerate way. Judicious 'exposure' to the best that has been thought and said can lead directly to personal application – or rejection – of such considerations. The most relevant themes include global issues and an interfaith dialogue, which have potential for cultivating open and responsible character development.

Taking this further, character education in Religious Studies could also involve learning from those who have learned from religion, by looking at and reflecting on the quality of their lives, as we already suggested with respect to English and History. Within the Judeo-Christian tradition, individuals such as Jean Vanier, Oscar Romero and Leonard Cheshire all shine out with religiously-inspired action. This also links to the very important pedagogical approach of learning from exemplars through role modelling. Students should be invited to select and explore inspiring religious individuals and explain the qualities they see in them, and the reasons why they find them so challenging, if not attractive. This could provide material for enjoyable tasks, such as 'imitating a great religious figure' for a day and reflecting on it.

Of all the curriculum subjects, Religious Studies is arguably the subject that lends itself most naturally to the formation of character, not least since the great world religions have been involved in this very enterprise for millennia.

Conclusion

In this chapter we have explored how character education can be taught in schools through classroom-based strategies across the curriculum, including but by no means limited to RE, Citizenship Education and PSHE. There are in fact many opportunities to introduce and illustrate virtues in both the sciences and arts, including the important area of computer science and online communication. In addition, we explained the Jubilee Centre's Programme of Study (2014a) based on an Aristotelian approach of the development of virtue knowledge, virtue reasoning and virtue practice as an example of how character education can be made more explicit, intentional and planned. We hope that the subject examples we have given will inspire innovative practice among teacher readers.

Objectives reached

By the end of this chapter you should have clear ideas about:

- the relevance of Bruner's Spiral Curriculum Model to character education where the teacher is a wise and sensitive guide;
- the Jubilee Centre's three approaches in its Programme of Study for character education;
- what it means to build Virtue Knowledge, Virtue Reasoning and Virtue Practice;
- Aristotle's conception of virtue;
- the stages of moral development in the taught course;
- ways in which character can be taught across the curriculum, from science and geography to PE and PSHE.

Questions for reflection

- Might character education eventually replace core elements of the current PSHE programme?
- Which subjects do you think lend themselves best to character education?
- Where do you position yourself on the stages of moral development?
- Having read this chapter, do you now regard the cultivation of virtue as more important than before?

6 Whole school approaches to character education

Summary

This chapter explores the application of whole school approaches to character education. We explain the development of 'virtue literacy' in terms of moral sensitivity, moral judgement, moral motivation and moral character through the Jubilee Centre Knightly Virtues Programme (Arthur *et al.*, 2014) using retellings of classic stories. They provide an attractive and potent source for the development of the following eight character virtues: gratitude, courage, humility, service, justice, honesty, love and self-discipline. Most schools see student participation in their many co- and extra-curricular activities as fundamental to the development of their character. Examples include sports, music, debates and school trips. The programmes at King's Leadership Academy in Warrington and Eton College exemplify the strengths of such a comprehensive approach. Students can also benefit from civic engagement activities, such as service or service learning, volunteering and youth social action, many of which entail a 'double benefit'; we provide a case study from East Norfolk Sixth Form College. Partnering with parents on character education can also be very beneficial. They are generally keen for schools to be involved with character education and the moral development of their children using, for instance, character logs. Conscious role modelling by teachers and reflective dialogues can play an important role.

Developing virtue literacy

The construct of 'virtue literacy' relates to the successful *Knightly Virtues* school programme (Arthur *et al.*, 2014). The programme, developed by the Jubilee Centre for Character and Virtues, draws on selected classic stories to teach 9 to 11-year-olds about eight moral character virtues (Carr and Harrison, 2015). Exploring four different stories, the pupils discuss the virtues of the central characters and then relate these to their own lives. The aim of the programme is to develop the virtue literacy of the pupils, defined as knowledge, understanding and application of the language of character.

Although in this instance virtue literacy was developed through stories and primarily in English classes, most subjects offer a good vehicle for the development of virtue literacy in students, as we have shown in the previous chapter. Virtue literacy might be conceived as being developed in two stages. The first is providing opportunities for students to gain a knowledge and understanding of virtue terms, such as courage, honesty, compassion and gratitude. The second stage is encouraging students to apply these terms to real life contexts, most probably demonstrated through writing or speaking about personal experiences. Virtue literacy relates to the so-called 'four component model of moral behaviour' (Rest, 1986), which drew on but made significant departures from Kohlberg's (1981) understandings of moral development discussed in Chapter 4. This model addresses the ways in which moral behaviour occurs, and provides a conceptualisation of successful moral functioning and the capacities it requires. The four components in the model are: moral sensitivity, moral judgement, moral motivation and moral character.

Virtue literacy can be seen to contribute to all of these components, but most significantly to moral sensitivity, which focuses on the ability to identify and discern problematic situations with ethical dimensions. Virtue literacy is the capacity to know and understand the necessary language and virtue concepts required to evaluate morally salient situations. An important component of virtue literacy is the acquisition of virtue language through familiarity and use of virtue terms, as also in the Jubilee Centre Programme of Study already discussed in Chapter 4. Although knowledge of language alone (or indeed at all) is not sufficient for virtuous behaviour, the possession of moral virtue is displayed through reason-responsive conduct. In this way, the acquisition of virtue terms and concepts contributes to one's ability to undertake rational reflection and deliberation. Vasalou (2012) argues on similar grounds that there is a link between the mastery of language and the mastery of virtue.

Students can be introduced to the language of character through educational activities. Developing a deep knowledge and understanding of this language gives them tools to reflect critically on their own character strengths and weaknesses. Being virtue literate therefore contributes to a student's virtue knowledge and ability to apply virtue reasoning, and ideally leads on to virtuous practice. It also equips students with a language for critical reflection on their virtuous practice, which in turn contributes to the development of practical wisdom or good sense.

The question then is how best to develop virtue literacy in schools? Many schools display pictures of character virtues in their corridors and classrooms. However, the display of such images is not enough, as it is unlikely that students will internalise the virtues by some form of osmosis. Furthermore, most virtue concepts are complex and often only become real to them when applied to personal experiences. Explanation and context is often required to make them come alive and be seen as more than simply words on a page or a wall. Many schools emphasise the virtues through structured assemblies and other whole school activities, which will help students understand their importance. However, such approaches might also be deemed insufficient and at times too 'preachy'. Top down and largely one-way approaches could actually inhibit students' desire and/or ability to engage with the virtue terms and apply them to their own contexts. By extension, virtue terms cannot be absorbed through a form of rote learning, as the very life and soul of these virtues is likely to be lost – and such an approach may even do more harm than good.

The acquisition of virtue literacy requires learning activities, ideally linked to the curriculum, that enable students to discover and develop a personal under-standing of the different virtues. The use of stories and literature adopts such an approach and was advocated by Aristotle himself. He believed that stories have a power to illuminate morality and other aspects of human motivation, such as feeling and agency, in a way that natural or social scientific sources of knowledge and insight are not necessarily equipped to do. Since Aristotle viewed the devel-opment of emotions and motivation as crucial to the cultivation of moral virtues, he gave exposure to narratives – including plays – a large role in the education of character.

Stories offer several advantages for the development of virtue literacy in students. Many stories are not black and white, and good stories feature com-plex characters whose actions are not wholly good or evil, as we observed in the section on English Literature in the last chapter. The 'grey areas' in these stories offer ample opportunity for skilled teachers to open up debates in which stu-dents discuss what the 'right' thing would be for the characters to do. Complex moral dilemmas contained in stories make an excellent vehicle for debates about the golden mean of any particular virtue, as well as the wise decision when any two particular virtues collide. Stories offer a safe space for students to project their own virtues onto the characters and come to their own moral decisions about what would be the right or wrong action in any given situation. It is also a 'safe' way for students to consider and discuss virtues and moral dilemmas without feeling any pressure to reveal personal information about themselves and their lives.

We can draw evidence of the success of stories as an educational tool for the development of virtue literacy from the aforementioned *Knightly Virtues* pro-gramme. Four stories, *Gareth and Lynette*, *El Cid*, *Don Quixote* and *The Merchant of Venice*, formed the basis of this programme. A before and after trial conducted on the programme demonstrated that these stories provided an attractive and potent source for the development of the following eight character virtues: grati-tude, courage, humility, service, justice, honesty, love and self-discipline. The sto-ries contained in the *Knightly Virtues* were carefully re-written to highlight these eight virtues. In addition, each student who experienced the programme was provided with a personal journal, which encouraged them to make the initial link between the stories and the virtues, and then to make the link between the vir-tues and their own lives. The programme was careful to indicate that virtue terms should not be considered 'stand-alone' or 'unrelated', but mutually supportive and interrelated. The controlled trial demonstrated that those students who had experienced the programme not only had a greater knowledge and understand-ing of the eight virtues, but were also better able to apply them to their own lives than the control group.

Co- and extra-curricular activities

Student participation in the many extra-curricular activities run by most schools is fundamental to the development of students' characters. Most schools see these activities as just as important as the formal curriculum and recognise their value by calling them co-curricular, as opposed to extra-curricular.

Some of the popular extra-curricular activities that schools run are associated with the curriculum subjects discussed in the previous chapter – such as sporting matches and music concerts. There are also many other popular character-building activities not directly related to the curriculum; debating clubs are a good example. The aim of debating is to develop confidence and courage through the communication of ideas in adversarial environments. Likewise, environment clubs aim at the exploration and expression of core virtues associated with sustainability. Other popular examples include art and drama clubs, activities such as radio and publishing connected to the media, and pursuits linked to established organisations, such as faith groups, the Duke of Edinburgh and the military.

Co- or extra-curricular activities are considered beneficial for the development of character virtues in students for a number of reasons. Primarily, they are a chance to introduce students to real-life opportunities that test their characters. Such activities often involve trying out new experiences. The students might succeed or fail at any particular activity, but important learning about character takes place regardless of the outcome. Learning through experience is vital to the development of practical wisdom or good sense.

Virtues nurtured in classroom environments can be tested further in different settings. For example, courage can be tested by asking a student to speak in front of their peers in school, but further tested by speaking at a public engagement in the community. Likewise, students might perhaps learn as much if not more from undertaking a service activity in the local community than one run in school. This is why school trips, overnight events and outdoor activities provide a great basis for the building of character and the cultivation of practical wisdom.

Participation in the activity is not sufficient to ensure that learning about character takes place. Activities require careful facilitation by teachers to ensure that they are successful vehicles for building character. The role of the teacher is to initiate opportunities for the students to reflect on their virtues before, during and after participation in a one-off or series of extra-curricular activities. Reflection strategies should be embedded into the activities as they are integral to the development of self-knowledge. Reflection could be carried out before the activity takes place to set personal character development goals. Reflection during an activity could involve teachers and others adopting the role of a 'character coach' (Jubilee Centre, 2015a) and directing questions at students that encourage them to think about the virtues they are displaying. Post-activity reflection is also important as it enables students to think about what they have learnt from their participation and what they might do differently next time.

Reflection activities initiated by the teacher might be more or less formal in nature. Examples of formal reflection strategies include character logs, passports or journals where students record their character development journey in writing as they progress. These tools might be highly structured and involve students identifying at the outset particular character virtues they hope to develop through the activity and keeping a record of their progress towards achieving these goals. Informal reflection activities might include more casual discussions between students and teachers during the activity, or peer-to-peer reflection sessions built into the activity programme.

Case study: King's Leadership Academy, Warrington

King's Leadership Academy was the overall winner of the Department for Education Character Awards in 2015. A large part of this success was due to how the school integrated co-curricular activities into the more traditional school day. The school places considerable emphasis on ensuring that an ethical spirit and a strong values system permeates everything it does. The school prioritises character education, which is taught through a structured programme of character and leadership development. It has a longer school day (7:45 am–4:30 pm), smaller class sizes (24 or less) and a large enrichment programme of accredited awards. The school teaches the academic core in the morning and in the afternoon they teach the creative and physical subjects most aligned to character development. These are taught by qualified teachers backed up by external experts known for their excellence in their profession. Individual sports are given priority, so no student can hide and all have a chance to shine.

For example, every child at King's completes an accredited 18-week programme of Sword Fencing every year led by an Olympic fencing coach. Drama and music are taught by experts from the national theatre, whilst accredited programmes in First Aid, lifesaving and outdoor survival are undertaken annually. The school also runs a bespoke cadet programme called the 'King's Officer Troop'. A programme of public speaking, designed to develop confidence, is also built into the core and creative curriculums. Access to these co-curricular character development programmes is seen as an entitlement for all students. All the activities that the students undertake during their time at school and that contribute to their character development are recorded in a personal character passport. The passport is also designed for students to reflect on the wider key skills developed through any given experience.

Case study: Eton College

Eton College was founded by King Henry VI in 1440. It is an all-boys boarding school with 1,300 pupils on the roll, aged from 13 to 18 years, and with a sixth form of more than 500 boys. The school seeks to foster self-confidence, enthusiasm, perseverance and integrity. The school regards the character development of all students as an integral part of its mission. One of the most visible areas of the school where character development takes place is the phenomenal number of extra-curricular activities on offer to the students. In fact, there are so many extra-curricular opportunities at Eton that it is almost impossible for students to avoid undertaking activities that are going to be character building. For example, there are nearly 6,000 sports matches every year (many of which are organised by the students themselves); every week the boys invite well-known speakers to speak at school societies and on average there is a play performed every two weeks. In all these activities, the students are encouraged to go outside their comfort zone and attempt things such as taking on challenging parts in a play. They are expected to take risks, and normally gain a sense of pride through this achievement. In addition, all lower sixth students do social service or the Combined Cadet Force (CCF) and many students gain at least the Silver Duke of Edinburgh Award.

Within each of these activities, the focus is on what the student can learn about character as much as on the activity itself. For example, in sport the students are taught that winning is not everything, but that participating fully and enjoying the game is the most important thing. The school has a director of coaching, whose role is not about making the teams better, but is focussed on 'coaching the coaches' to get the most out of the students. The school wants all sports coaches to see themselves as 'character instructors'. A strong emphasis is placed on humility, playing fair and good sportsmanship. Sports masters are encouraged to ask questions like 'Did you enjoy the game?' 'What did you learn?' and 'How did you play?', rather than 'Did you win?' The Head of Games also thinks that sport gives the students a chance to 'learn how to fail' successfully.

Civic engagement: service learning, youth social action and volunteering

There is a range of experiences in which young people participate both inside and outside schools that develop character and can be classified under the umbrella heading of 'civic engagement'. These include service or service learning, volunteering and youth social action.

An integral feature of civic engagement experiences is that many have what is commonly termed a 'double benefit'. They are an effective and meaningful way for students to develop character virtues while often bringing more direct and immediate benefits to the school's community (whether local, national and/or global). This double benefit is central to a longer-term view of character development since by taking action students make an important contribution to society, while at the same time building core virtues and capacities essential to human and societal flourishing. The double benefit is illustrated by the IWill Ambassador programme (see www.iwill.org.uk/iwill-ambassadors). Every year 50 10 to 20-year-olds are selected to be Ambassadors. They have all not only given their time, energy and talents to make a difference to their communities, but also recognised the character virtues they demonstrated as well as developed in doing so. The Ambassadors include young people who have taken part in campaigns, fundraised, been mentors, set up social enterprises and volunteered, amongst many other beneficial activities. The Ambassadors talk passionately about the difference their work has made to their communities, but also about the significant impact it has had on them personally. Examples include Rebecca Brunskill, who explains that 'there are real benefits to giving up spare time to help someone else and the benefits are not only to the person being helped, but to the volunteer as well' and Rhiannon Sweeny, who comments 'I'm passionate about helping others, and I'm glad I'm able to make a difference to my community – it has made me the person I am today.'

Those who take part in civic engagement activities, as well as those who facilitate them often celebrate the transformational possibilities they bring – both for the students themselves as well as their communities. A recent study (Arthur *et al.*, 2015c) showed that a majority of the largest youth social action providers in the United Kingdom identify the primary aim of their charity as the development of character. These organisations see the development of virtues such as compassion, resilience, courage and social justice as central to their goals and vision. Similarly, character development can be viewed as a core element of civic engagement programmes run by schools (sometimes in partnership with charitable organisations). The opportunities force students to think about their relationship with others, as well as their own sense of purpose. A sense of purpose is often cited as one of the core outcomes of civic engagement programmes, as participation enhances moral virtues associated with flourishing.

Schools are ideal places to introduce young people to the advantages of being civically engaged. The introduction to such activities often takes place from as early as reception class when students are encouraged to participate in fundraising activities. Opportunities exist throughout their time at school and often involve increasing responsibility as students move up through the school. For example, it is common for students to take part in reading partners or peer mentoring programmes where they support other students younger than themselves. Although many schools limit their activities to within the school gates, they hope that students will develop a 'thirst' to seek out opportunities to make a difference further afield. Another approach to expanding opportunities is for the school to partner with a local or national charity such as the National Citizens Service, or a local faith group to run programmes that encourage active citizenship beyond the school gate.

A strength that schools bring to their student civic engagement activities is the opportunity to embed the experience within an educational learning context. It is the educational process of taking part in the experience as much as the experience itself that helps to ensure character development. The key is for schools to stress the benefits of building in some opportunities for personal reflection to the activities. Honest reflection on activities such as fundraising, mentoring or volunteering in the community requires students to think deeply about various aspects of their civic action – including times when difficulties have arisen or when the action has not met its intended outcomes. Structured reflection opportunities, either verbal or written, help make civic engagement activities a 'safe space to fail', and ensure that the experiences are both educational and involve learning about oneself.

Lessons from service learning programmes can be drawn on. The key to service learning is not simply the act of service itself, but the educational experience wrapped around it. This includes encouraging students to take ownership of the experience by having a say over what they do as well as how they do it. Reflections may not necessarily be entirely positive as students should be encouraged to reflect critically on their experiences and what they learned about themselves. They should be encouraged to make recommendations for how they might act differently next time. Reflection is intrinsic to supporting students to understand their own personal growth gained through taking part in active citizenship activities. This process might be considered beneficial to the development of practical wisdom, since knowledge gained is transferable to other situations.

Case study: East Norfolk Sixth Form College

There are 1,750 students in East Norfolk Sixth Form College and the college's vision is that all students and staff are civically engaged in the community. One of the college's seven strategic objectives is 'we will strive to make a positive impact within our community.' The school employs a Director of Progression and Employability who helps with careers guidance and also co-ordinates volunteering placements. Volunteering and work experience are treated equally. Students are encouraged to apply for projects via the schools 'Moodle' website where all opportunities are listed, and a tracking device keeps records of these placements.

Examples of Youth Social Action projects that the students have participated in recently, include:

- Up to 100 students a year work in the James Paget University Hospital on the meal times volunteering programme.
- Students volunteer on yearlong placements with the St John's Ambulance, at a local memory club for elderly people with Alzheimer's, in a young person's playgroup and at a care home.
- Student volunteer short-term experiences include a local primary school to design a new logo, and with the Borough Council to advise on how to make Great Yarmouth a more attractive place to live and work.
- Peer mentoring – part of the '5 ways to well-being programme' – students volunteer to be peer mentors, primarily for students with learning difficulties or mental health issues.

The school reports that the experiences have a significant and lasting effect on the character of the students involved. They grow in confidence and aspiration and gain an awareness of broader issues, as well as how to make a difference. The Head teacher of the school states 'this is not about fundraising or working in charity shops, this is about young people giving up their time and their talents to serve others.'

Partnering with parents on character education

As we have stated throughout this book, parents should be considered the primary architects of their sons' and/or daughters' characters. However, we also argue that this should be done in partnership with schools and other influential organisations and individuals with whom children come into contact as they grow up. As the distinguished character educator Thomas Lickona (1996) observed, 'schools that reach out to families and include them in character-building efforts greatly enhance their chances for success with students'. It stands to reason that such an alliance is crucial to the success of both effective schooling and parenting; it is difficult to nurture virtues such as honesty, compassion and courage in schools if these are neglected in the home – or of course vice-versa. However, the challenge is, as ever, how such a partnership on character development might be formed and maintained. Although educational policy has increasingly advocated a closer partnership between teachers and parents, the results of this partnership tend to be a greater emphasis on teachers communicating to parents the educational progress of their sons/daughters through meetings and reports. This includes communication between teachers and parents about ways that attainment can be enhanced through, for example, homework. Few schools take the extra more courageous step to seek an active and genuine partnership with parents on the very important business of character development. This point is significant, as perhaps one of the most important respects in which teachers and parents might usefully seek to work together – namely, on the education and formation of the moral values and character of young people – is also precisely one of the most sensitive and contentious.

There are several reasons why a parent/teacher partnership on character education is considered challenging. First, some teachers and parents might have different priorities for the character development of young people, and these could come into conflict. For example, a parent might be keen that their child wins at all costs on the sports field, whilst the teacher is keen to encourage fair play and honesty over the final result. A second challenge is a perceived tension or conflict between school and home values, making teachers nervous about promoting beliefs or perspectives to which parents might object. A final challenge is more practical in nature – how might a real and genuine partnership be achieved? How can teachers go beyond functional communications about behaviour or homework, and develop a meaningful dialogue with parents built on long term character development goals?

Despite the challenges outlined above, it seems that parents are keen for schools to be involved with character education and the moral development of their children. A poll carried out by Populus (Jubilee Centre, 2013a) found very strong support among parents for the idea that schools should be promoting character development alongside academic study. Of those parents surveyed, 87 percent felt that schools should focus on character development as well as academic study, not simply academic study alone; and 84 percent thought that teachers should encourage good morals and values in students. Perhaps the most striking result is that 95 percent of parents felt that it is possible for schools to teach students values and to shape their character in a positive sense through lessons and dedicated projects or exercises at school. This reinforces the case for formal character education provision.

Some enlightened schools have adopted strategies for serious practical cooperation between teachers and parents to help students acquire core character virtues that contribute to flourishing. For example, character logs are becoming increasingly popular, where both parents and teachers initiate discussions and comment on the development of an agreed set of character virtues. These logs may be a practical step towards parents and teachers sharing the process of enhancing the virtues in young people and making observations on their progress. Some schools include a section on character in the end of year reports or during parent/teacher meetings – after all, many parent/teacher communications are in fact about character virtues, even if these are implied rather than explicit. One school makes them explicit by ensuring that all personal tutors write a letter home at the end of each term about the character of the student and invites parents' comments and observations.

We can draw a good example of a home/school partnership on character education from the *Knightly Virtues* programme. In this literature-based programme discussed above, the parents were invited to share or contribute to the learning experiences of their children. Each student participating was given a personal project journal including the stories and character education learning activities. The students were encouraged to take their journals home so that parents could read the stories with their sons/daughters as well as take an active role in the completion of some of the activities and exercises. Parents were also asked to offer some comment in the journal – at a mid-point as well as at the conclusion of the programme. Analysis of these entries showed that the majority of parents were pleased that their sons and daughters were reading stories such as The Merchant of Venice and Don Quixote, and welcomed the opportunity to (re)discover these stories alongside their children. The comments also suggested that the programme was a good basis for stimulating rich conversations at home (as well as in school) about the salient moral concerns in these narratives. Furthermore, the students themselves were touched by such parental approval and enthusiasm for the programme and the issues it explored. This example demonstrated the possibility of encouraging cooperation and partnership between teachers and parents on character education through structured programmes.

Role modelling

Compared with other approaches to moral education, character education is unique in unambiguously advocating role modelling as a fundamental 'method' to help students develop character traits, such as courage or fairness. The central idea is that children develop virtues through a process of observing educators and the consequences of their actions. For Thomas Lickona (1991: 118), 'the most important moral lesson in the character curriculum' is the idea teachers can only cultivate children's character if they display it themselves. Virtue is first 'caught', we might say, and only later 'taught'. It will not come as a surprise that several character education-based handbooks and websites offer a repertoire of teaching materials on how to be a good role model.

But why give tips on how to be a good role model? Is this not something that all teachers automatically do? While it is generally recognised by parents, the wider public and by teachers themselves that teachers should be moral role models to pupils (Sanger & Osguthorpe, 2013); it is not immediately clear what this entails. For example, do pupils actually see teachers as role models? Is role modelling always effective? Research shows that when children are asked about their current role models, typically about 3 percent mention a teacher spontaneously (Sanderse, 2013: 31). This suggests that there is room for improvement. And when can we say that role modelling has been successful? We probably do not want students actually to *imitate* their educators, but what can teachers do to avoid this? The problem is that little thought has been given to the question of how teachers can use role modelling as an explicit and critical teaching method (Kristjánsson, 2006a; Sanderse, 2013). In this section, we will discuss two issues that may help teachers understand what it means to be a role model. We will end with a suggestion about how they can practise becoming better role models.

First, what does it mean to be a role model in terms of character? Being an example can basically mean two things. We can illustrate this by drawing on two ordinary examples. First, take the letter 'a'. We can say that it is an example of a letter, just as the letter 'b', 'c', etc. So, the letter 'a' is as much an example of a letter of the alphabet as the other 25 letters: nothing more, nothing less. There is, however, a second way in which we talk about examples. When we say that 'Muhammad Ali is an example of a boxer', we do not mean that he is a boxer just like any other. We mean that he is a paradigmatic example that shows what 'real' boxing is about.

When we apply this distinction to 'being a moral example', we see that both interpretations are problematic. The problem with saying that teachers are examples in the first sense is that 'modelling virtue' entails nothing more than just being a virtuous teacher. In that case, we lose the specific meaning of modelling. However, when we conclude that teachers should be paradigmatic examples of virtue, we are probably aiming too high. The right mean between these extremes is to say that role models underscore, display or convey the idea of virtue to an observer (Warnick, 2009: 6). Teachers as role models are not just virtuous, but they attract students' attention because they make them notice something about virtue that they had not seen before. For example, this may mean that you, as a role model, are more patient than your colleagues, or that you act courageously in rather intimidating circumstances.

The second question is what you want to achieve by being a virtuous role model. An obvious answer is that you want students to *follow* your example. But what does that mean – that they copy or imitate your behaviour? There is certainly something in this. In the 1960s, Albert Bandura (1963) showed that observing is an extremely powerful learning mechanism that we can see at work in young children, who do not always need reinforcement stimuli to learn. So, children can also learn moral patterns of behaviour vicariously, i.e. without actually practising moral actions themselves or receiving praise or blame (Sanderse, 2013: 35). However, we should avoid treating modelling purely as a non-cognitive form of simple mimicry, as it does not provide students with the means to question teachers' moral authority.

Our solution is that it is the task of teachers to have students *emulate* them. 'Emulation' is the translation of the Greek '*zelos*', which we still recognise in the English 'zeal' (Kristjánsson, 2006a) When a student emulates a teacher, she does not just copy the teacher's behaviour, but goes through a process of recognising what character trait the teacher is modelling, thinking about whether this trait is in fact a virtue, and deliberating about what it means *for her* to exercise this virtue. Students will be more likely to undertake this if teachers work on a meta-level by explaining their actions in words in relation to why and how they teach as they do (Smith, 2001: 11).

Finally, a suggestion about how teachers can go about becoming better role models. In teacher education, role modelling is an important teaching method, as student teachers treat teacher educators as examples of how to teach well. Swennen, Lunenberg and Korthagen (2008) have developed a reflection tool that can also be applied to modelling virtue. This is the MELA-model, which stands for four steps: Modelling, Explaining, Legitimising and Applying. The first step is to think about what virtue you, as a teacher, want to model, and why modelling this trait suits you as a person. The second step is to explain to yourself (and others) how you put this virtue into action. How can people tell that you are modelling this virtue? What will they notice? The third step is to legitimise your chosen virtue. Why did you pick this one? For example, did you model 'respect' because there is a problem in your classroom, as students are not respectful towards each other? What do you want to achieve? The fourth step is to think about how you can enable students to apply the virtue you model. How can you make sure that students recognise your virtuous behaviour and are stimulated to apply this virtue in their own lives? Going through these steps can help teachers to connect their moral ideals with their actual behaviour in the classroom.

Dialogue

Advocates of 'critical thinking' have sometimes criticised character education for being a conservative attempt to impose religious values on children. Admittedly, there are character education programmes that go in this direction. However, we have already made it clear that this is not the kind of critical character education we have in mind. A thread running through this book is precisely that the exercise of moral virtue is guided by reason, and that the development of the intellectual virtue of good sense is implied in the cultivation of one's emotions. Moreover, the section on role modelling in this chapter explained that the process of acquiring virtue does not have to be a mindless process. Quite the contrary: it is better understood as a critical practice that encourages children to deliberate about which character traits teachers are modelling, and how they can acquire these virtues for themselves. There are, however, other practices that virtue ethics can offer in educating children's capacity for moral reasoning, one of which is conducting dialogues.

Readers may wonder how just talking about virtue can help students to be more virtuous. Ancient Greek philosophers such as Socrates and Plato assumed that when people have a proper understanding of the nature of, for example, 'friendship' or 'courage', they are also able to be a good friend and do courageous things: *knowing* what is good leads to *being* good. We agree with Aristotle that, for most of us, this connection between knowledge and action is by no means self-evident. Children need to be brought up in good habits too, so that they feel the right things while passing moral judgments. In the absence of this process of habituation, we are only 'taking refuge in argument' (Aristotle, 1985: 40 [1105b12-14]) in arguing and learning about what it means to lead a virtuous life. This is unrelated to our practical attempts to lead a good life. So, on the account we have developed in this book, dialogues can stimulate moral reasoning, but, crucially, they only contribute to the overall development of our character if they have been preceded by and are accompanied by an education of the emotions.

Now that we have established the place of dialogue within a comprehensive programme of teaching character education in schools, we can turn to the question of how teachers can go about conducting dialogues with students in their classrooms? There are many options: almost all contemporary approaches to moral and philosophical education – such as Noddings' care ethics, Kohlberg's cognitive development, Lipman's Philosophy for Children (P4C), and Nelson's Socratic method – have recommended 'dialogue' as a key method for the education of students in moral and intellectual virtues. However, they have different ideas about the purpose and proper method of conducting dialogue. For example, (the early) Kohlberg wanted teachers to discuss hypothetical moral dilemmas so students would be confronted with higher levels of moral reasoning, enabling them to move on to the post-conventional stage. For Noddings, on the other hand, the subject of a dialogue mattered less than the encounter that teachers and students have through a conversation.

This overview raises the question of what kind of dialogue might contribute to teaching character education in schools, or, put differently, what the typical character education take on dialogue is? One interesting recent suggestion, which has the advantage of being grounded in Aristotle's own writings, is that dialogue is first of all a matter of children having 'character friendships' with their classmates. Kristjánsson (2014c: 343) writes that 'it is precisely by being inducted into friendships and striving to perfect them that we become capable of reassessing, reinforcing, revitalising, and, if necessary, restructuring our broad moral schemas.' While we may agree that friendship is 'perhaps the most important school of virtue' (p. 343), it does not help teachers who want to know how they can instigate and manage a character-building conversation in the classroom. So we have to look elsewhere for help.

We are looking for a form of dialogue that stimulates the development of children's good sense, which, as readers know by now, cannot develop independently from the moral virtues (see Chapter 4). Good sense has two functions. It has the *action-guiding* function of helping people put their virtues into practice in the concrete circumstances of everyday life, and it has the *virtue-specifying* task that helps us notice something new in each situation and to improve our understanding of the virtues (Sanderse, 2015: 6–8). If dialogues are to contribute to the development of good sense, they will have to help people perform these two tasks or functions better. This means two things.

First of all, dialogues that develop good sense will have a practically oriented, deliberative dimension. The central question of the dialogue is: 'Knowing what virtue is, what should be done in this situation?' This part is concerned with students who more or less know what moral principles are at stake in a given situation but who do not know yet how to act. They analyse and interpret the details of their situation, and deliberate together about what should be done. These would have to be moral problems or dilemmas that students are about to face.

Second, dialogues conducive to good sense will have a more theoretically oriented, reflective aspect. The leading question during this part of the dialogue is: 'What is apparently virtuous, having acted in the way I did?' This question aims at arriving at a better understanding of virtue by reflecting on experiences in situations encountered before. For example, a student might say at one point that a punishment was 'unfair'. When a teacher thinks the time is right to start a dialogue about this, it will be about whether his classmates agree with his view or not, and what they apparently presuppose about fairness when they pass such judgments.

This deliberative aspect of dialogues is also advocated by the Philosophy for Children (P4C) movement developed by Mathew Lipman (1980) and others. The reflective aspect is typical of the 'Socratic method' developed in Germany by Leonard Nelson (1970). It is not by accident that these two methods are considered to be 'two very influential philosophical methods in Europe and elsewhere which have inspired both those who work with children and those who work with adults' (McCall 2009, chap. 6). Both are used in schools, and both have developed several practical methods for classroom discussion, which can be consulted in textbooks and online.

Conclusion

In this chapter we have highlighted whole school approaches to character education, citing some examples of best practice and noting that most schools see student participation in their many co- and extra-curricular activities as fundamental to the development of their character. We have also discussed the double benefits of civic engagement activities such as service or service learning, volunteering and youth social action. We have shown that there is widespread support among parents for school involvement in character education and opportunities for partnership – for example through a parental role in the Jubilee Centre Knightly Virtues programme.

We think that conscious role modelling by teachers is undervalued and needs to be developed not only professionally but also in training colleges as an aspect of the study of character education.

We believe that reflective dialogues can play an important role in the development of virtues in young people.

Objectives reached

By the end of this chapter you should have clear ideas about:

- the nature of virtue literacy and how it is fostered by the *Knightly Virtues* Programme;
- the role of co- and extra-curricular activities in character education;
- the importance of incorporating reflection into these activities;
- the way that the case studies show how character education can be embedded across a school;
- how civic engagement can bring a double benefit;
- the importance of schools partnering with parents on character education;
- how teachers can best become role models;
- how various forms of dialogue can be used in character education.

Questions for reflection

- Which co- and extra-curricular activities do you think are most effective for building character?
- Do you agree that it is important to incorporate a reflective component into such activities?
- What do you consider the best ways of schools partnering with parents on character education?
- Do you think that consideration should be given in teacher education to their role as moral exemplars?
- Which form of dialogue do you think best applies to character education?

7 How can we measure virtue and evaluate programmes of character education?

Summary

This chapter addresses the challenge of measuring and evaluating the effects of character education programmes, with special reference to an Aristotelian approach and to young moral learners. Ideally, we need evidence of both (1) improvement in virtue literacy, (2) improvement in moral behaviour, and, most crucially, (3) some indication that (2) is in fact linked to (1). We discuss the strengths and limitations of self-reporting instruments and advocate a triangulation methodology where such reports can be crosschecked with reports from significant others and other more objective measures. So, we have peer reports, self-reports and behavioural data. The Jubilee Centre conducted such a study of the moral virtues of 14–15-year-olds in the UK using neo-Kohlbergian Defining Instrument Tests on moral dilemmas as a third resource, with encouraging results. We look at the work of Catherine Fallona on the moral virtues that teachers express in their relations with students and a more recent smartphone app for giving feedback on virtuous actions. We also consider implicit measures, some aiming to tap into unconscious processes of evaluation shaped by past experiences and others based on vocabulary analysis. We also consider the claim that neuro-scientific measures will ultimately replace implicit tests and, indeed, all the other measures of virtue. We conclude that a proper instrument to measure moral virtue needs to be an eclectic patchwork and offer the possibility of triangulation.

Introduction

To recap, in previous chapters we have taken a firm stand on some of the controversies surrounding character education. We have argued that the question of whether it is the role of schools to educate character is misleading because character will always be formed at school through role modelling and emotional contagion. The question is simply whether this is done well or badly, systematically or haphazardly. We have also shown the taught-versus-caught dichotomy to be illusory. Ideally, character should be *both* taught and caught; and in the preceding chapter, we suggested various methods by which this can be done in educationally sound ways.

Yet, a worry looms. Although considerable anecdotal evidence exists for the effectiveness of character education programmes, there are no widely agreed-upon instruments to measure progress in this area. In an ideal world of Aristotelian character education, we would have instruments that:

- track objective moral features, such as moral virtues in students and school ethos, and do not rely on mere self-reporting;
- are faithful to the theoretical and methodological assumptions of Aristotelian character education;
- have transformative as well as research-based aims, i.e. can measure and monitor progress;
- are simple and easy to use and satisfy demand from schools for a pre-and-post test for implementing character education initiatives;
- fit, conceptually and linguistically, into the culture of UK schooling;
- provide information of use to head teachers, teachers and parents about the moral landscape of their school.

In this chapter, we explain why such instruments have been difficult to come by. More specifically, we take you on a rollercoaster ride of the problems of measuring character and possible ways to solve them. Given the current state of play, our main conclusion in this chapter is that a proper instrument to measure (Aristotelian) virtue needs to be eclectic and offer the possibility of triangulation. It is further suggested that a mixed-method instrument combining self-reports, other-reports and potentially more objective measures – in particular, dilemma tests – may be the best available option at the moment.

Two methodological problems

When character educationists start to suggest interventions aimed at cultivating character in schools, such as the ones we spelled out in the previous chapter, these have to compete with other suggestions of non-Aristotelian provenance about what schools can do to promote pro-social ends. The standard requirement is that they offer pre-tests and post-tests of the success of implementation, ideally conducted via a randomised controlled trial – the platinum bar of school-based research. Here the demand will be to measure students' virtues before and after the proposed implementation and to demonstrate that the moral character of those who undertook it has truly improved, compared to a control group. However, here we stumble upon exactly the problem around which this chapter revolves: *How do we measure (Aristotelian) virtue in people in general and in young moral learners in particular?*

This general problem actually comprises two more specific problems that are both concerned with the way in which character and virtue are defined on an Aristotelian conception of character education (as explained in Chapter 2).

First, Aristotelian virtue ethics is, as was explained in Chapter 3, a type of moral naturalism. Moral naturalists are realists about morality; they believe that such moral properties as honesty or wickedness constitute objective features of the natural world and of human selves inhabiting that world. For natural-ists, statements about 'moral facts' are true if they correspond to this natural reality, but false if they do not. The great majority of existing instruments to measure moral character are, however, simple self-reporting questionnaires – for instance, the positive psychological VIA-instruments for youth and adults (Peterson & Seligman, 2004). We say more about self-reports later in this chapter. Let us simply note that self-reported measures typically ground their rationale in anti-realism about the human self, according to which the self is the same as self-concept, defined as the set of beliefs we attribute to the self (Kristjánsson, 2010). Moral realists complain about possible response biases in such measures caused by self-fabulations, self-confirmation tendencies and social desirability norms. The fact that you indicate you are honest in a self-report does not make you honest, for you might just be saying this to please the researcher who you think is looking for honest respondents. Nor does truly believing that you are honest make you honest, for you might be self-deceived. Nor even do reports of your honesty by parents, teachers and friends make you honest, for they might all be mistaken about who you really are deep down. So, we urgently need to find some more *objective* ways to measure honesty, if we want, say, to gauge the effectiveness of an honesty-cultivating intervention in character education.

Second, Aristotelian character education is supposed to cultivate a host of different virtues of the moral, performative and intellectual kind, and help them interact with one another in a well-rounded way. Moreover, each moral virtue is seen to comprise various components, having to do with cognition, emotion, motivation and behaviour. The measurement problem would be much less thorny if neither of these strict demands were made. For example, Paul Tough (2013) produces convincing evidence from the KIPP schools in the USA, which foreground performance virtues, such as resilience, grit and self-confidence, showing both how these particular virtues can be boosted individually and their dramatically positive effect on one specific variable: getting into college. Unfortunately, this is not a measure of the all-round cultivation of character in an Aristotelian conception, as we have no idea about the moral development of the students. They could, for all we know, be resilient and confident egotists.

Regarding the component-side of the second problem, we do have reliable evidence showing progress with regard to *specific* components of moral virtue, such as moral *cognition* (e.g. virtue literacy – see previous chapter and Arthur *et al.*, 2014) and virtuous-looking *behaviour* (Berkowitz & Bier, 2006). Indeed, quite a lot of the positive evidence of the impact of character education interventions, especially from the USA, is derived from research into (a) observable classroom behaviour or general school ethos, rather than (b) moral virtue in individual students – or, more specifically, research based on (a) without providing evidence for the claim that (a) is best explained as the result of (b). This is insufficient to demonstrate progress in virtue on an Aristotelian understanding.

For that we need, ideally, evidence of both (1) improvement in virtue literacy; (2) improvement in behaviour; and (3) most crucially, some indication – gained, for instance, by tapping into students' emotions and motivations – that (2) is in fact linked to (1).

It could be argued, in response, that if observed behavioural changes follow immediately on the heels of the invocation of a programme of character education – aimed at changing states of character – then an inference to the best possible explanation would ascribe those behavioural changes to changes in character (Curren, 2014). However, without further evidence, we would still not know if those character changes were stable and consistent across domains, as Aristotelian virtue should be, or simply domain-specific to the particular school environment. So the problem remains.

Self-reporting instruments

The briefest of Web searches demonstrates that the commonest tools to measure virtue in students and adults are self-reporting instruments. The most widely used of those seems to be the set developed by positive psychologists as part of their VIA-project to chart and measure universal character strengths and virtues.

The (6) general moral virtues and their (24) operationalisable manifestations, famously identified by positive psychologists, were allegedly derived through a variety of considerations: some conceptual, such as being measurable, trait-like, distinctive, non-exclusive of others, valued as ends; and some historical like being ubiquitous and morally valued across cultures, being recommended by the world's most influential religious and philosophical traditions, being embodied in certain identifiable historic moral exemplars (Peterson & Seligman, 2004: 21–28). As the proposed 'social science equivalent of virtue ethics' (2004: 89), the VIA classification is meant to be 'grounded in a long philosophical tradition' (2004: 9) harking back, *inter alia*, to Aristotle.

The most tangible methods devised by positive psychologists for measurement purposes are self-report surveys: the VIA Inventory of Strengths (VIA-IS) and – more relevantly for present concerns – the VIA Inventory of Strengths for Youth (VIA-Youth), developed for the 10–17 age group. As VIA-Youth is already widely used, data on the distribution and relevant correlates of the character strengths of young people are rapidly accumulating. One significant finding is that youth possess – or take themselves to possess – all the same strengths as adults. Nevertheless, some strengths are more common among youth: hope, teamwork and zest (Park & Peterson, 2009) – thus supporting Aristotle's insight that young people do possess character strengths of their own. Shorter versions of the instruments have now been developed as the original ones take considerable time to complete.

The exclusive reliance of the VIA-Model on self-evaluated traits is worrisome, however. It is widely known that, in addition to well-known social desirability and self-confirmation biases, self-reports often involve hefty doses of self-serving spin. Wilful deceptions of others as well as unwilful self-deceptions pose a threat to outcome validity, as we pointed out at the beginning of this chapter. It seems to us that positive psychologists are singularly cavalier about those concerns. Having said that, what people think about themselves does make up *part* of what they truly are, and we may thus have good reason to give *some* credence to self-reports in measurements of virtue, especially if those can be corroborated by other more objective types of evidence.

We have more specific concerns about the current state of VIA-research, however. First, the original codification of the data that was supposed to underlie the 6-virtues-24-strengths taxonomy remains unavailable for scrutiny. Second, and more generally, personality psychologists Noftle, Schnitker and Robins (2011) argue that the taxonomy on offer in positive psychology is under-theorised, under-conceptualised, under-researched and in all likelihood redundant with respect to the Big-Five Model. Extant research has failed to replicate the theoretical structure of VIA's Big-Six. Even positive psychologists themselves have in the past produced factor analyses that yield three, four or five, rather than six, basic factors. Further confirmatory analyses suggest that none of the theoretical models purporting to present the structure of the character strengths provide a good fit to the data. These criticisms have not fallen on deaf ears within the positive psychology community, and psychologist Bob McGrath has recently been entrusted with the task of undertaking a major revision of the VIA classificatory system (McGrath, 2014).

Triangulation

'Triangulation' is a term used to indicate that more than a single method is used in a study, with a view to crosschecking data from multiple sources to search for regularities in the research material. We raised concerns earlier about the subjectivity of self-reports. It does improve matters somewhat that in triangulation studies of, for instance, the Big-Five Model, reports from significant others (peers, parents, friends) have been found to correlate significantly with self-reports (McCrae, 2009: 150). Nevertheless, as already noted, the fact that not only I, but also my friends and family, consider me to be honest is not sufficient evidence to prove that I really am honest.

Having said that, there is something quintessentially Aristotelian about crosschecking the validity of self-reports by asking friends – at least if they are 'character friends' (as distinct from friends for utility or pleasure). In true character friendship – the only 'complete' friendship – *A* loves *B* (1) for *B*'s own sake, (2) for what *B* really is and (3) because *B* has a virtuous character. Because moral virtue is an objective merit and, once gained, an enduring one, character friendships tend to be stable and lifelong, come rain or shine. In general, we are able to observe others better than ourselves; thus character friends can become our second selves, often knowing us better than we do ourselves (Aristotle, 1985: 209–216). This is an excellent potential source for triangulation. The downside is, however, that in order to know if a friend is really a character friend – and can be relied upon to help us solve the measurement problem – we need to be able to measure her character, but that is precisely the problem at issue. We might thus find ourselves caught up in a methodological vicious circle.

At the Jubilee Centre for Character and Virtues, we decided to draw upon the triangulation method in a study of the moral virtues of 14–15-year-olds in the UK. First, we asked the teachers of those pupils to tell us what they considered to be their students' most prominent character strengths and weaknesses (as a group, not individually, which would be difficult for ethical reasons). Second, we compared those answers to the strengths and weaknesses that the students self-evaluated collectively, in the short version of the VIA-Youth, as their top and bottom assets. Third, we compared those scores to more objective findings, derived from another (moral-dilemma based) part of the mixed-method instrument (Arthur *et al.*, 2015b) – to which we turn in the next section.

Moral dilemma tests

Rather than remaining satisfied with eliciting self-evaluations of virtue, an Aristotelian approach would ideally explore how people do in fact react – attitudinally, emotionally, behaviourally – to morally-charged situations. Could this perhaps be done by exposing them to scenarios involving moral dilemmas and recording their responses? We do not have to look far for the mother of all dilemma testing: Lawrence Kohlberg's famous cognitive development approach that we explored in Chapter 4. Clearly, Kohlberg's dilemmas were not meant to ascertain the respondents' degree of Aristotelian virtue, but rather how developed they are cognitively as Kantian agents. It seems, however, not so far-fetched to conceive of dilemma tests that would attempt to home in on the virtues.

Concerns about self-transparency obviously do remain. How do we know if the answer to a question given in an online test tracking virtuous responses accurately reflects how the respondent would truly react in such a situation? In other words, if the answer reveals the possession of or lack of a praiseworthy *trait*? Nevertheless, dilemma tests – especially those done under relative time constraints – seem to offer the sort of critical distance from mere navel-gazing that self-reports about perceived virtue do not.

We at the Jubilee Centre for Character and Virtues have found ourselves drawn to tests devised by so-called neo-Kohlbergian moral psychologists, who are indebted to Kohlberg but also depart substantially from his assumptions and methods. They have designed instruments that are, in our view, worthy of serious consideration for Aristotelian character educationists.

Kohlberg's student, James Rest, started to work on a so-called Defining Issue Test (DIT) in the early 1970s as a paper-and-pencil alternative to Kohlberg's semi-structured interview measure. The test was gradually developed further by Rest and his colleagues, Narvaez, Bebeau and Thoma (1999), and is now in widespread use. Similar to Kohlberg's test, the DIT presents respondents with moral dilemmas. They then have to decide what the protagonist ought to do in the story, and why? Finally, respondents are asked to rank the four items that best reflect their view about how to solve the dilemma (Thoma, 2006: 68).

In order to get a grip on the theory behind the DIT, two assumptions need to be made explicit. The first is the so-called *Four Component Model* of moral functioning, according to which (successful) moral functioning is the result of four relatively independent processes: moral sensitivity, moral judgement, moral motivation and moral character. Originally, the DIT was meant to measure only moral judgement. However, moral judgement is supposed to operate at different levels from more or less context-independent 'bedrock schemas' that activate tacit understandings of moral rightness (onto which the DIT is meant to latch), through thicker 'intermediate concepts', to ultra-thick surface-level 'codes of conduct'.

The second main assumption is that of *schema theory*. While difficult to summarise briefly, schemas are understood as tightly woven networks of tacit knowledge, residing in long-term memory and organised around particular life events, helping individuals to facilitate and react to new information (Narvaez, 2005; Thoma, 2006). Based upon large-sample analyses, neo-Kohlbergians argue that the DIT measures three developmentally ordered schemas: personal interest, norm-maintenance and a post-conventional schema. The DIT has thus been recast as a schema-activation measure, the idea being that the sentence fragments provided as options in the DIT give sufficient information to trigger a moral schema, but not too much (by over-determining the response).

An adolescent version of the DIT has recently been developed: The Adolescent Intermediate Concepts Measure.[1] It may sound odd, given where DIT-research is coming from (and given Kohlberg's own scepticism about virtues), but the instrument is actually virtue-based. The idea is that the AD-icm does not activate bedrock schemas like the DIT, but rather intermediate concepts. To search for such concepts, the neo-Kohlbergians in question came up with seven prototypical virtues around which the seven dilemmas in the AD-icm revolve (fairness, responsibility, loyalty, self-discipline, honesty, courage and respect). After each story, respondents are asked to rate a set of action choices and the three best and the two worst choices. Finally, respondents are asked to rate the justification items on a 5-point-scale from 'strongly believing this is a good reason' to 'strongly believing this is a bad reason'. The authors of the AD-icm do recognise the historic tension between virtue-based and cognitive developmental models of moral education. However, they believe that by focusing on intermediate concepts, they have created a measure of adolescent moral thinking that is congruent with adult thinking measured via the DIT, and that captures the development of virtues in aspiring moral learners.

This feature makes instruments like the DIT and AD-icm in many ways appealing for Aristotelian character educationists, but there is a frustrating drawback. At its inception, the notion of 'schema' was clearly defined within cognitive psychology and conceptually limited. The original idea in neo-Kohlbergianism was thus that the DIT only measures moral judgement schemas. This assumption still holds sway among post-Kohlbergians such as Thoma (2006) who represent the 'Kohlbergian' rationalist part of the label rather than the 'neo' part. Schema theory, however, gradually became more inclusive, incorporating the construction of the moral personality as a whole. On Narvaez's broad interpretation of schemas, the measures in question will be taken to evoke grand moral schemas, covering more or less the whole of moral functioning. What is more, in her view, 'the moral habits of virtue theory are social cognitive schemas whose chronic accessibility favours automatic activation' (Lapsley & Narvaez, 2006: 268). In other words, moral schemas are basically the same as Aristotelian *traits* and DIT/ AD-icm begins to look like a promising measure of expected moral *performance* in general. Whereas Narvaez's broad interpretation of schema theory will resonate well with Aristotelians, Thoma's narrow one will do so to a much lesser extent.

One feature of a broad Aristotelian conception of moral trait that dilemma methods will, however, fail to elicit is the perception of moral salience. Rather than checking if respondents notice a morally salient issue in their environment, dilemmas present them with situations that have already been singled out by the researcher and accorded significance, only inquiring what would be a good choice in *that* pre-defined situation. In other words, dilemmas are externally structured and authored, and they do not allow the same sort of reflective interplay between the reader and the text as more detailed flesh-and-blood stories.

Despite this shortcoming, and although the jury is still out, more generally, on whether the narrow or broad interpretation of moral schemas is more appropriate in the case of DIT/AD-icm, researchers in the Jubilee Centre decided to use a shortened version of the AD-icm as part of a triangulation process to home in on the virtues of 14–15-year-olds. The results of the AD-icm were compared with results from the short version of the VIA-Youth measure, and also with teachers' assessments of pupils' virtues (Arthur *et al.*, 2015b). This was, to the best of our knowledge, the first time that the findings of dilemma tests have been compared systematically to findings from a validated self-reporting measure. Steve Thoma advised the Jubilee Centre team on how to reduce the number of dilemmas in the AD-icm from seven to three, and to de-Americanise its language, without destroying its psychometric properties. The eventual decision was to focus on courage, self-discipline and honesty, as those virtues allowed for obvious comparisons with constructs from the VIA-Youth. While it is outside the remit of the present chapter to report on the findings of this research, they are readily available online. We strongly encourage readers to study these findings as this was the biggest research project into virtue development among UK adolescents ever undertaken (Arthur *et al.*, 2015b).

Observations

If a tree is best known by its fruit, then surely virtue must be about actual moral performance, rather than having the right feelings or giving good answers in dilemma tests, and thus be measurable (in part at least) through observable behaviour? Despite the common Aristotelian refrain that virtue is not *just* about behaviour, we should not forget Aristotle's own insistence that 'Olympic prizes are not for the finest and strongest, but for contestants, since it is only these who win; so also in life [only] the fine and good people who act correctly win the prize' (1985: 20). The implication of those words seems to be that attempts at virtue development would be futile if they did not manifest in the form of explicit changes in conduct.

Consider here one notable systematic attempt to observe Aristotelian virtues in a school context, not only among students but teachers. Catherine Fallona's (2000) aim was to draw attention to the moral virtues that teachers express in their relations with students. She focused on a list of Aristotelian virtues, including bravery, wit, generosity and justice, and used a qualitative interpretative method of 'focused observations' (including field notes and videotaping) to 'identify teacher behaviour that was reflective of virtue' (2000: 688). Her method prompted her to distinguish between more and less 'visible' virtues. Identifying the less visible ones 'requires a high degree of interpretation' (2000: 690), in Fallona's view, where observations are not sufficient, but input from teachers (through interviews) is also needed. Notice, however, that even for her choice of virtues, Fallona decided to focus her observations on the 'action virtues' from Aristotle's *Nicomachean Ethics* rather than the 'emotion virtues' (e.g. compassion) listed in the *Rhetoric*. That may tell us something about how limiting the method of using only virtue observations will turn out to be.

There is no reason to completely discard the option of observing behavioural changes, for instance by simply counting instances of serious bullying or knife crime in the school yard before and after a character education intervention. After all, all head teachers will celebrate a reduction of violence in their schools – by whatever mechanism that happens. The problem, however, is that without being able to penetrate into the minds of the students and elicit their *reasons* for acting, we do not know if an Aristotelian virtue 'schema' has been activated or not. Have disruptive students perhaps simply learnt new ways of not being found out? Observing emotion virtues presents an even deeper problem. Take anger, which can either be an instantiation of an Aristotelian virtue or a vice, depending on the context and the reasons for it. Suppose we observed fewer instances of student anger being demonstrated in the school in the wake of a character education intervention. Should we interpret that as an enhancement of the virtue of 'mildness of temper' – or as a proliferation of the deficiency-extreme of 'insensitivity to committed offences'?

Compounding the above-mentioned theoretical issues are more mundane practical concerns. Observations, which typically need to be longitudinal, are labour- and-time consuming and difficult to administer. For example, the multifaceted observation methods listed by Lyseight-Jones (1998: 37–38), of examining children's work and behaviour over extended periods of time in class, assemblies and at play, by taking photographs and using video and audio recordings, may only be feasible in long-term ethnographic studies. Even in such studies, however, researchers – if they are interested in moral character – are faced with the interpretative task of getting under the skin of the children and coding what the recorded behaviour really means in terms of virtue and its development. Perhaps the best hope of success here lies in action research conducted by the children's teachers themselves (Sanderse, 2016), who will know them more intimately than any external researcher.

There is some indication that the constraints of time and space may be transcended by applying a technology already widely used by young people, namely smartphones. Schueller (2014) thus describes a smartphone app called NOVA (Networked Virtue Assessment), which works such that when User 1 observes the virtues of kindness, gratitude or forgiveness in User 2, User 1 records that in her smartphone. That triggers a message in User 2's phone where she is asked about the intention and emotion behind this virtuous act. Simultaneously, the app takes a 'snapshot' of the situation with 38 sensors from both the smartphone devices, recording, *inter alia,* time, location and any ambient noises. Schueller notes that this method, which is still at the trial stage, would be ideal for use in schools. In the present context, NOVA carries promise for character educators, not only because it may help overcome some of the practical problems that mar observational studies, but also because it assumes that a realistic assessment of virtue will involve triangulation of data from a number of different sources: in this case, peer reports, self-reports and behavioural data.

Implicit testing and biological measures

For Aristotelian character educationists, paradigmatic moral virtues either *are* emotions (such as compassion) or *incorporate* emotions (such as courage, which incorporates a regulated quantity of fear). Given the lack of self-transparency that typically characterises people's engagement with their emotional lives, would it not be ideal to find a measure of moral virtue that somehow tracked emotional reactions directly without the medium of potentially biased rationalisations? So-called *implicit measures* are supposed to do just that. They aim to tap into introspectively unidentified, unconscious processes of evaluation, shaped by past experiences, which typically act as automatic triggers of emotional reactions – including moral reactions. Implicit measures work on the assumption that cognitive primings can reveal truths about who we really are: truths, however, which remain irredeemably below the waterline of conscious thought. Various ingenious tests have been developed to operationalise this assumption. One of the most famous is the 'implicit association test' where respondents are asked to match, in rapid succession, sets of words on two sides of a computer screen – where on one side will be words like 'white', 'black' and 'coloured', or proper names such as my own and some other people's, and on the other side are positive or negative adjectives.

Somewhat surprisingly, we found only one study that directly focuses on moral virtue via an implicit measure designed along the above lines (Perugini & Leone

2009). This study examined the subjects' implicit moral self-concept through an implicit association test and compared this with their explicit (self-reported) moral self-concept. When the subjects in the study believed it was over, they were rewarded, as promised, with a free lottery ticket. Some, however, received two as if 'by mistake'. It turned out that the implicit moral self-concept was a better predictor than the self-reported one of which subjects actually handed back the second ticket to the researchers. While this was a single small study conducted in a single country, the implication seems to be that we may be able to know more about the virtue of (actual) honesty by using implicit testing than other more standard methods. Closely related to the association tests are implicit measures that analyse subjects' eye movement as they track moral options given to them on a computer screen. Fiedler, Glöckner, Nicklisch and Dickert (2013) have, for instance, found differences in social value orientation being reflected through stable differences in patterns of information search and preferences for specific types of information, as revealed by eye-tracking data. It must be noted that although there is considerable excitement about implicit measures in current social psychology, the method has its critics. Debates rage in psychological circles about whether responses on implicit measures actually reflect stable representations in long-term memory or are simply fluid constructions generated on the spot (Payne & Gawronski, 2010).

Although it is still at an early stage of development, a different sort of implicit testing, which could be called *vocabulary analysis*, has attracted considerable attention. This method draws on new technologies, enabling extensive scanning of online texts and self-expressions. Kern and colleagues (2014) examined Big-Five personality traits and online word expressions using millions of status updates from almost 70,000 Facebook users who had also signed up for the application *MyPersonality*, which allows access to their Facebook profiles. By systematically analysing the vocabulary (both single words and word groups) used in those updates, the researchers identified the vocabulary features most positively or negatively correlated with each Big-Five factor. Consequently, it becomes possible to predict a person's Big-Five profile without any Big-Five measure ever having been completed.

The problem with applying this method to measurements of virtue is that no established benchmarks exist in this area (such as the Big-Five in personality research). Frimer *et al.*, (2012) suggest a way of circumventing the problem by using established paragons of virtue and vice (in this case chosen by a group of 102 social scientists from a list of the world's most influential people published in *Time Magazine*) as benchmarks, people like Martin Luther King on the upper end of the scale and Hitler at the lower. Frimer and colleagues work on the assumption that, in subtle ways, people reveal their private thoughts and desires when they speak, and the more they care about *x*, the more they will use words that describe *x*. They then use text-analysis software to count up the number of 'agency' versus 'communion' words in extant interviews and speeches. This method, when applied to selected texts by the exemplars chosen, seems to distinguish well between the Martin Luther Kings and the Hitlers of this world, with people one would expect to score somewhere in the middle also falling in the middle.

There is considerable optimism about this new method of linguistic analysis, so much so that prominent psychologist Martin Seligman, a famous former devotee of questionnaires, has been heard remarking informally in a recent conference that the era of questionnaire research for self-reporting may soon be over (cf. also Snow's 2014 equally revolutionary speculations about future uses of 'big data' to track moral virtue). Some concerns remain, however, about the accuracy of potential texts chosen for analysis. As Kern *et al.*, (2014) freely acknowledge, sites such as Facebook and Twitter reflect identity-and-reputation management: one presents the face that one wants others to see. They seem to be fairly optimistic, however, that relevant expressions and omissions in the natural language used in Facebook updates over a long period of time is less susceptible to self-reporting biases than manipulated responses in more transparent self-reporting questionnaires.

Some critics of implicit testing say that it is in the end nothing but a poor substitute of biological, especially neuro-scientific, measures and that those will ultimately replace both implicit tests and, indeed, all the other measures of virtue that have been canvassed so far – thus, ultimately solving once and for all the measurement problem. Some brain research has already produced salutary findings for questions of measuring virtue. More than a decade ago, Greene *et al.*, (2001) showed through an fMRI investigation that areas of the brain associated with emotion become significantly more active when respondents are presented with moral dilemmas than non-moral ones. A more recent finding indicates that although subjects predict that they will be extremely upset by blatant racial acts or comments, they actually exhibit little emotional distress when this occurs, as evidenced by emotional brain activity in an MRI-scan (Kawakami, Dunn, Karmali & Dovidio, 2009). Before we gain insight into the biological substructures that process moral virtue and underlie manifest behaviour, the benchmarking problem must obviously be solved first. Additionally, MRI-scans still offer only a crude measure of brain activity. They may tell us, for example, whether *any* emotional activity is taking place and what its reactions times are, but not precisely what *sort* of activity: i.e. not, say, which potential emotional virtue has or has not been evoked.

Concluding remarks

The progress of character education is hampered by the problem of how to measure moral virtue. In this chapter, we have offered a number of observations on this messy theme. By doing so, we hope to have deepened the discourse and laid a foundation for future work in this area. Given the current state of play, our main conclusion is that a proper instrument to measure moral virtue needs to be an eclectic aggregation and to offer the possibility of triangulation. We have suggested how a mixed-method instrument combining self-reports, other-reports and more objective measures such as dilemma tests, may be our best bet at the moment. The triangulated instrument used in our work with UK adolescents is available on the Web (Arthur *et al.*, 2015b), and we have also been working on an Evaluation Handbook which could be used directly by schools without our assistance. Producing a 'simple' instrument that is still triangulated is a tall order, however, and we must bear in mind that what is gained in simplicity may easily be lost in specificity.

In an ideal research world of unlimited time and resources, we can imagine the possibility of drawing up, step by step, a complex picture of students' broad moral traits by homing in separately on each of the components of Aristotelian virtue, for example gauging *perception of moral salience* by letting them analyse a novel, a poem or a film and identify the moral issues that it elicits, gauging *moral emotion and desire* through an implicit-measure test, gauging *moral self-concept* through a self-reporting questionnaire, gauging *moral understanding/reasoning* through a deep interview, gauging *moral motivation* through dilemma testing, gauging *moral behaviour* and general character-related *school ethos* through a longitudinal observational study, and then corroborating the findings of the study through detailed *peer reports* (parents, friends, teachers) over an extended period of time. As current research resources in the actual world will scarcely allow for such an extensive measurement project, we need to make do with less ambitious instruments. Most significantly, we need to enlist the aid of teachers – who generally know their students best – to design such instruments and help us carry out research in this exciting area.

Objectives reached

At the end of this chapter, you should have clear ideas about:

- the specific features of (Aristotelian) character education that complicate efforts at measuring impact;
- the pros and cons of self-reporting measures;
- the ways in which dilemma testing may be considered more objective that mere self-reporting;
- some exciting cutting-edge work in the area of virtue measurement;
- the benefits of triangulated instruments.

Questions for reflection

- Do we really need to be able to measure virtue? Why is anecdotal evidence not enough?
- Find VIA tests of character virtues or Big-Five tests of personality on the Web and fill them in. Subsequently ask yourself: Was I fully honest in reporting about myself?
- What are the pros and cons of using observations of student behaviour to track their virtues?

- Will brain scans ever be able to tell us the whole truth about the moral virtues that people possess?
- Do the words people choose in their Facebook or Twitter statuses reveal significant truths about who they are deep down?

Note

1   Hereafter referred to as AD-icm, see Thoma *et al.* (2013).

8 Character education books, papers and resources

This chapter contains a selection of recommended books, papers and resources on character education. The materials have been organised into the following four categories:

1 **Papers**
   Recent academic papers published in peer-reviewed journals about different aspects of Aristotelian character education.

2 **Books**
   Recent books, published in both the UK and internationally, on character education. Theoretical and practical books are included in this section.

3 **Teaching resources**
   Free character education teaching resources that can be adopted and adapted by teachers and other educational professionals. Many of the resources can be downloaded for free from www.jubileecentre.ac.uk.

4 **Research reports**
   Research reports on the impact of character education on students, teachers and schools.

1. Academic papers on character education

Paper	Author(s)	Description	Reference
Levels of virtue literacy in Catholic, Church of England and non-faith schools in England.	James Arthur, Tom Harrison, Ian Davidson	This article reports on an innovative empirical research project, using a quasi-experimental trial, in which 9 to 11-year-olds learned about character and virtues through the exploration of four classic stories. The overall aim of the programme was to enhance virtue literacy. Virtue literacy is defined as the knowledge, understanding and application of virtue language, and is viewed as being integral to the development of character.	Arthur, J, Harrison, T. Davison, I. (2015d). Levels of virtue literacy in Catholic, Church of England and non-faith schools in England: A research report. *International Studies in Catholic Education*, 7(2), 178–200.
Personal character and tomorrow's citizens: Student expectations of their teachers	James Arthur	Research evidence from UK primary and secondary schools suggests that students expect teachers to engage in character development and values education and that this assists in their holistic learning. This article is based on a major UK research study, which indicates that explicit and implicit attention to values in schools is positively welcomed by students. Students of all ages believe that the teacher can make a difference in contributing to their personal moral development.	Arthur, J. (2011). Personal character and tomorrow's citizens: Student expectations of their teachers. *International Journal of Educational Research*, 50(3), 184–189.
The re-emergence of character Education in British education policy	James Arthur	Character education is a specific approach to morals or values education, which is consistently linked with citizenship education. But how is it possible for a heterogeneous society that disagrees about basic values to reach a consensus on what constitutes character education? This article explores how character education has returned to the agenda of British education policy, having been largely neglected since the 1960s in response to unsatisfactory attempts at character education going back to the nineteenth century.	Arthur, J. (2005). The re-emergence of character education in British education policy. *British Journal of Educational Studies*, 53(3), 239–254.

(continued)

Paper	Author(s)	Description	Reference
There is something about Aristotle: The pros and cons of Aristotelianism in contemporary moral education	Kristjan Kristjánsson	The aim of this article is to pinpoint some of the features that do – or should – make Aristotelianism attractive to current moral educators. At the same time, it also identifies theoretical and practical shortcomings that contemporary Aristotelians have been overly cavalier about.	Kristjánsson, K. (2014b). There is something about Aristotle: The pros and cons of Aristotelianism in contemporary moral education. *Journal of Philosophy of Education*, 48(1).
Ten myths about character, virtue and virtue education – and three well-founded misgivings	Kristjan Kristjánsson	Initiatives to cultivate character and virtue in moral education at school continue to provoke sceptical responses. Most of those echo familiar misgivings about the notions of character, virtue and education in virtue – as unclear, redundant, old-fashioned, religious, paternalistic, anti-democratic, conservative, individualistic, relativist and situation-dependent. The paper exposes these misgivings as 'myths', while at the same time acknowledging three better-founded historical, methodological and practical concerns about the notions in question.	Kristjánsson, K. (2013b). Ten myths about character, virtue and virtue education – and three well-founded misgivings, *British Journal of Educational Studies*, 61(3), 2013.
Character in learning for life: A virtue-ethical rationale for recent research on moral and values education	James Arthur, David Carr	This article has three broad aims. First, to draw attention to what is probably the largest empirical study of moral, values and character education in the United Kingdom to the present date. The second is to outline – in a way sufficient for present purposes – a plausible, conceptual or theoretical case for placing a particular virtue. The third is to suggest a number of practical ways in which character education might be developed or pursued in formal or informal school curricula, or in the wider community.	Arthur, J., & Carr, D. (2013). Character in learning for life: A virtue-ethical rationale for recent research on moral and values education. *Journal of Beliefs & Values*, 34(1), 26–35.

Title	Author	Description	Reference
After Kohlberg: Some implications of an ethics of virtue for the theory of moral education and development	David Carr	This paper argues that a basically Kohlbergian approach to thinking about moral education is difficult – if not impossible – to sustain in the face of this neo-Aristotelian critique; however, it attempts to explore the possibilities of an alternative virtue-theoretical basis for understanding the nature of moral life and education.	Carr, D. (1996). After Kohlberg: Some implications of an ethics of virtue for the theory of moral education and development. *Studies in Philosophy and Education*, 15(4), 353–370.
Towards a new era of education in theory and practice	David Walker, Kristjan Kristjánsson, Michael Roberts	The authors use a Bourdieuean framework of 'legitimating principles' and the 'symbolic capital' of dominant 'discursive themes' to explore (a) the genealogy of and (b) the current state of the discourse on 'character education' (understood broadly as any approach to moral education that foregrounds the cultivation of moral character and moral virtue).	Walker, D., Roberts, M., Kristjánsson, K. (2015) Towards a new era of education in theory and practice. *Educational Review*, 67(1), 79–96.
Eleven principles of effective character education	Thomas Lickona	This paper sets out 11 principles to guide schools as they plan their character education initiative.	Lickona, T. (1996). Eleven principles of effective character education. *Journal of Moral Education*, 25(1), 93–100.
Aristotle's educational politics and the Aristotelian renaissance in philosophy of education	Randall Curren	This paper assesses the historical meaning and contemporary significance of Aristotle's educational ideas. It begins with a broad characterisation of the project of Aristotle's *Nicomachean Ethics* and *Politics*, which he calls 'political science' (*hē politikē epistémé*), and the central place of education in his vision of statesmanship. It proceeds through a series of topics fundamental to his educational ideas, culminating in the account of education in *Politics* VIII. A concluding section appraises the uses to which Aristotelian ideas are currently put in philosophy of education, identifying some confusions in the influential literature of 'practices'.	Curren, R. (2010). Aristotle's educational politics and the Aristotelian renaissance in philosophy of education. *Oxford Review of Education*, 36(5), 543–559.

2. Books on character education

Book	Author(s)	Description	Reference
Education with Character: The moral economy of schooling	James Arthur	An introduction to character education within the British context by exploring its meanings, understandings, and rationale, through the perspective of academic disciplines. The author examines character education from a philosophical, religious, psychological, political, social and economic perspective to offer a more detailed understanding of character education and what it can offer.	Arthur, J. (2003). *Education with Character*. London: Routledge.
Aristotelian Character Education	Kristján Kristjánsson	This book provides a reconstruction of Aristotelian character education, shedding new light on what moral character really is, and how it can be highlighted, measured, nurtured and taught in current schooling. Arguing that many recent approaches to character education understand character in exclusively amoral, instrumentalist terms, the author proposes a coherent, plausible and up-to-date concept, retaining the overall structure of Aristotelian character education.	Kristjánsson, K. (2015). *Aristotelian Character Education*. London: Routledge.
Educating Character through Stories	David Carr and Tom Harrison	This book explores how character might be educated through stories. The book draws on the experience of developing and trialling the Knightly Virtues programme. It provides a comprehensive philosophy behind the programme, as well as practical lessons learnt from implementing it in schools.	Carr, D. and Harrison, T. (2015) *Educating Character through Stories*. Exeter: Imprint Academic.

Title	Author	Description	Reference
Intelligent Virtue	Julia Annas	Intelligent Virtue presents a distinctive new account of virtue and happiness as central ethical ideas. Annas argues that exercising a virtue involves practical reasoning of a kind which can illuminatingly be compared to the kind of reasoning we find in someone exercising a practical skill. Rather than asking at the start how virtues relate to rules, principles, maximizing, happiness or a final end, we should look at the way in which the acquisition and exercise of virtue can be seen to be in many ways like the acquisition and exercise of more mundane activities, such as farming, building or playing the piano.	Annas, J. (2011). *Intelligent Virtue*. Oxford University Press.
Citizens of Character: New directions in character and values education	James Arthur (ed)	The contributors discuss why character education is considered valuable, what character education is taken to mean, and identify and test hypotheses about various influences (schools, families, communities, employers) on the development of character through reporting on our research in UK schools, universities and businesses.	Arthur, J. (2010b) *Citizens of Character: New directions in character and values education.* Exeter: Imprint Academic.
Of Good Character: Exploration of virtues and values in 3–25 year olds	James Arthur	This book presents a substantial body of empirical evidence about what parents, teachers and pupils are thinking and doing in the area of character education.	Arthur, J. (2010a) *Of Good Character: Exploration of virtues and values in 3–25 year olds.* Exeter: Imprint Academic.
The Road to Character	David Brooks	A popular book by a New York Times journalist exploring the difference between résumé and eulogy virtues.	Brooks, D. (2015) *The Road to Character.* New York: Allen Lane.
Virtues and Vices in Positive Psychology: A philosophical critique	Kristján Kristjánsson	A provocative book will excite anyone interested in cutting-edge research on positive psychology and on the virtues that lie at the intersection of psychology, philosophy of mind, moral philosophy, education, and daily life.	Kristjánsson, K. (2013). *Virtues and Vices in Positive Psychology.* Cambridge University Press.

(continued)

Book	Author(s)	Description	Reference
Learning to Ride Elephants: Teaching happiness and wellbeing in schools	Ian Morris	There has recently been an explosion of interest in positive psychology and the teaching of well-being and 'happiness' in the PSHE world in schools, and many teachers are looking for clear information about how to implement these potentially life-changing ideas in the classroom. This book provides an introduction to the theory of positive psychology and a practical guide on how to implement the theory in (primary and secondary) schools.	Morris, I. (2015) *Learning to Ride Elephants: Teaching happiness and wellbeing in schools.* London: Continuum International Publishing.
Educating for Character: How our schools can teach respect and responsibility	Thomas Lickona	In this book, Lickona, a professor of education at the State University of New York, addresses the controversial topic of 'values' education and its place in today's classrooms. In a well-balanced presentation distilling his decades of experience, Lickona suggests practical approaches that have been developed by several programmes of moral education.	Lickona, T. (1991) *Educating for Character: How our schools can teach respect and responsibility.* New York: Bantam Books.
Building Character in Schools: Practical ways to bring moral instruction to life	Kevin Ryan and Karen Bohlin	Ryan and Bohlin provide a blueprint for educators who wish to translate a personal commitment to character education into a schoolwide vision and effort. They outline the principles and strategies of effective character education and explain what schools must do to teach students the habits and dispositions that lead to responsible adulthood – from developing a curriculum that reinforces good character development, to strengthening links with parents. A useful resource section includes sample lessons, programme guidelines, and a parents' list of ways to promote character in their children.	Ryan, K. and Bohlin, K. (1999). *Building Character in Schools.* San Francisco: Jossey-Bass.

Title	Author(s)	Description	Reference
Character Education: A neo-Aristotelian approach to the philosophy, psychology and education of virtue	Wouter Sanderse	Many teachers want to contribute to children's moral development, but this desire has not always resulted in a profound grasp of what 'moral education' really means, why it would be desirable and how it can best be achieved. This book confronts these questions by examining what Aristotelian virtue ethics can illuminate about moral education.	Sanderse, W. (2012) *Character Education: A neo-Aristotelian approach to the philosophy, psychology and education of virtue*. Eburon Uitgeverij.
Character Compass: How powerful school culture can point students toward success	Scott Seider	In *Character Compass*, Seider offers portraits of three high-performing urban schools in Boston, Massachusetts, that have made character development central to their mission of supporting student success, yet define character in three very different ways. One school focuses on students' moral character development, another emphasises civic character development, and the third prioritises performance character development. Drawing on surveys, interviews, field notes, and student achievement data, Character Compass highlights the unique effects of these distinctive approaches to character development, as well as the implications for parents, educators, and policymakers committed to fostering powerful school culture in their own school communities.	Seider, S. (2012) *Character Compass: How powerful school culture can point students toward success.* Cambridge: Harvard Education Press.
Handbook of Moral and Character Education	Larry P. Nucci, Darcia Narvaez and Tobias Krettenauer (Eds)	The purpose of this *Handbook* is to replace the ideological rhetoric that infects the moral education field with a comprehensive, research-oriented volume that includes the extensive changes that have occurred over the last fifteen years. Coverage includes the latest applications of developmental and cognitive psychology to moral and character education from pre-school to college settings.	Nucci, L. P., Krettenauer, T. and Narváez, D. (eds) (2008) *Handbook of Moral and Character Education*. London: Routledge.
The Moral Child: Nurturing children's natural moral growth	William Damon	Drawing on the best professional research and thinking, the author charts pragmatic, workable approaches to foster basic virtues such as honesty, responsibility, kindness, and fairness – methods that can make an invaluable difference throughout children's lives.	Damon, W. (2008) *The Moral Child: Nurturing children's natural moral growth.* New York: Simon and Schuster.

3. Character education teaching resources

Resource	Description	Available from
A Framework for Character Education in Schools	The Jubilee Centre for Character and Virtues' position on Character Education is set out in the document 'A Framework for Character Education in Schools'. It calls for all schools to be explicit about how they develop the character virtues of their students and for parents, policymakers and employees to recognise the important role teachers play in making and shaping the character of young people.	http://jubileecentre.ac.uk/userfiles/jubileecentre/pdf/other-centre-papers/Framework.pdf
Statement on Character and Youth Social Action	A short statement developed by an influential group of experts on how youth social action develops character virtues in young people.	http://www.jubileecentre.ac.uk/userfiles/jubileecentre/pdf/StatementSocialAction.pdf
The Knightly Virtues Programme	This educational programme seeks to provide 9 to 11-year-olds with the chance to explore creatively great stories of knights and heroes and the virtues to which they aspired. Drawing from timeless historical and literary narratives, this programme is tailored towards encouraging pupils to enjoy reading about inspiring people, whilst helping them to consider their own virtues of character.	http://www.jubileecentre.ac.uk/1576/projects/previous-work/knightly-virtues
Schools of Character	This publication showcases seven schools (including two primary schools) that make character education a conscious part of their day-to-day practice through a variety of approaches. The case studies presented are designed to highlight the most pertinent features of character education in each of the schools and aim to provide inspiration, as well as examples, for other schools seeking to develop their character education provision.	http://www.jubileecentre.ac.uk/userfiles/jubileecentre/pdf/character-education/SchoolsOfCharacterPDF.pdf

Title	Description	Link
Teaching Character through the Curriculum	This publication demonstrates how character might be taught through fourteen secondary school curriculum subjects. The link between character virtues and the pedagogical practices and content of each subject are also explored. For each subject, the virtues that might be considered most closely linked to it are emphasised and learning and teaching activities that develop character virtues in the classroom, across the whole school and in the community are suggested.	http://www.jubileecentre.ac.uk/userfiles/jubileecentre/pdf/Teaching_Character_Through_The_Curriculum1.pdf
Inspire/Aspire Awards	A programme run by Character Scotland for schools focused on developing values in young people through designing and developing posters about their character.	http://www.inspire-aspire.org.uk/
Becoming Value-able	A set of nine teaching activities developed by Learning for Life that will enable young people to discover what values are and why they are important. The back of the booklet contains all the resources you need to carry out the activities.	http://www.jubileecentre.ac.uk/userfiles/jubileecentre/pdf/previousresearch/Becoming_value-able.pdf
Character Building	Who are you? Who do you want to be? A teaching resource developed by Learning for Life that will enable young people to discover what character is needed to be successful in life as well as a successful member of society.	http://www.jubileecentre.ac.uk/userfiles/jubileecentre/pdf/previousresearch/Character_Building.pdf
Character Education Programme of Study – Primary and Secondary	The Jubilee Centre has developed character education programmes of study for primary and secondary schools, providing a taught programme for Reception through to Year 11 (it is recommended schools adapt these). Within the programmes a series of lesson plans are provided for teaching moral, civic, performance and intellectual virtues at each stage. The course allows flexibility to suit individual school/teacher approaches. Teacher's notes and accompanying PowerPoint presentations are also provided for each series of lessons.	*Primary:* http://jubileecentre.ac.uk/1635/character-education *Secondary:* http://jubileecentre.ac.uk/1636/character-education

4. Research reports on character education

Report	Lead author/ organisation	Description	Available from
Character Education in UK Schools: Research Report	James Arthur The Jubilee Centre for Character and Virtues	The research project described in this report represents one of the most extensive studies of character education ever undertaken, including over 10,000 students and 255 teachers in schools across England, Scotland, Northern Ireland and Wales. The research explored the formation of character in students in 68 UK schools and investigated how teachers view their role in developing good character and virtue in students.	http://www.jubileecentre.ac.uk/userfiles/jubileecentre/pdf/Research%20Reports/Character_Education_in_UK_Schools.pdf
The Good Teacher	James Arthur The Jubilee Centre for Character and Virtues	The report sets out new research, focusing on the virtues that good teachers might need and the role these virtues play in teaching. The research was conducted with 546 novice and experienced teachers.	http://www.jubileecentre.ac.uk/userfiles/jubileecentre/pdf/Research%20Reports/The_Good_Teacher_Understanding_Virtues_in_Practice.pdf
Character Nation	Jonathan Birdwell DEMOS	This report provides a series of policy recommendations for governments to ensure that character development is embedded across the education system.	http://www.demos.co.uk/publications/character-nation
Character and Resilience Manifesto	APPG on Social Mobility	A report from the All Party Parliamentary Group on Social Mobility on the importance of character and resilience for social mobility.	http://www.centreforum.org/assets/pubs/character-and-resilience.pdf
Character Education: The role of Youth Social Action Organisations (YSAOs)	Generation Change	A report describing the benefit of Youth Social Action Organisations across the country with reference to teaching character in schools in terms of positive relationships, role models and supporting empowerment in young people.	http://www.jubileecentre.ac.uk/userfiles/jubileecentre/pdf/character-education/generation-change_character-educaiton.pdf

9 Primary and secondary sample lessons

Summary

This chapter contains some sample lessons drawn from the Primary and Secondary Programmes of Study developed by the Jubilee Centre for Character and Virtues (Jubilee Centre, 2015a; Jubilee Centre, 2014a). These Programmes of Study provide a guide to building character through the means of a taught course. It is a direct response to the issues set out in the Jubilee Centre's A Framework for Character Education in Schools (see Appendix A). There it is argued that character education is not only 'caught' through the ethos and values of a school, but that 'taught' sessions also have an important role to play in the shaping of character. These taught sessions focus on both the theoretical and the practical aspects of acquiring virtue; they are most meaningfully situated in the context of a whole school approach to character education.

Underlying the Framework (Jubilee Centre, 2013b) are at least two distinctive hallmarks of the Jubilee Centre's approach to character education. The first hallmark is that character education is about acting well, and thinking well, about developing good 'moral' sense, or practical wisdom, in the differing circumstances of students' lives. This marks a refreshing, grounded and realistic approach to the cultivation of virtue. It steers us away from the notion that character education is exclusively theoretical and abstract; it also challenges the notion that character education is about imposing a monomaniacal, mechanical uniformity on others. Perhaps even more helpfully, this accent on cultivating 'good sense' frees us from the egregious claim that character can be built by an instruction manual, or text that seeks to provide cases for every eventuality. Rather, we are given tools and practices that will enable us to experience the freedom in the moral life that is akin to what freedom of the keyboard is for the accomplished pianist. The second hallmark of the Centre's approach is that engagement and dialogue with tradition is healthy and unavoidable. This also is refreshing and realistic: it would be absurd to suggest that relative beginners in the moral life have reached a stage of maturity where they are experienced and competent enough to decide, understand, or even recognise without assistance what is involved in the sometimes very tricky business of making decisions that enable human flourishing. These Programmes of Study, then, hope to respond to these concerns and to assist students in the building of their character, in guiding them towards flourishing and fulfilling lives.

Secondary lesson plans

Below are four lesson plans drawn from the Character Education Programme of Study. The lessons are provided as samples and the full programme is available from www.jubileecentre.ac.uk. The following four lessons are detailed below.

> *Lesson 1: The Emotions*
> *Lesson 2: Good Sense*
> *Lesson 3: Using the Tools of Virtue*
> *Lesson 4: The Virtue of Courage*

Sample lesson 1: the emotions

Some good books that explain the emotion system clearly are:

- *Emotional Intelligence* by Daniel Goleman
- *A User's Guide to the Brain* by John Ratey
- *Emotional Rollercoaster* by Claudia Hammond
- *Intelligent Virtue* by Julia Annas (in which the relationship between emotions and virtue is clearly explained)

Session 1: understanding the emotions (performance virtue)[1]

1. How do you feel? How do you know?

- Ask students to write down how they feel (in a word) and how they know they feel that way. Ask them how one other person in the room feels and how they know. They should concentrate on verbal and non-verbal signals, as well as physiological signs like pulse, temperature (sweating, etc.).
- Feedback ideas.

2. Recognising emotions

- Give students the opportunity to see if they are able to recognise more complex emotions, using more limited information. There are some good, free, online tests of emotional recognition, e.g. http://greatergood.berkeley.edu/ei_quiz/ and http://kgajos.eecs.harvard.edu/mite/ (available February 2015). It is worth noting that the teenage brain is at a stage of development where emotional recognition is harder.
- Discuss why it is important that we are able to read the emotional state of others accurately: What benefits might this ability bring us? How can an ability to read emotions enable us to develop virtues and character?

3. The causes of emotions: why we feel the way we feel

- Emotions are present for a reason. Give students the slide with a number of different emotions on it and ask them to identify the causes of those emotions: they can be specific (e.g. Liverpool winning the Premiership causing joy) or generic (believing they have been insulted causing anger).
- Feedback and discuss. Try to identify the root causes of particular emotions, rather than individual, specific causes. Perhaps discuss how it is possible for two people to be in the same situation and yet each feels different emotions.

4. How does the system work?

- The basic idea is that emotions are responses to real or perceived stimuli in our environment (e.g. a real threat might be a lion; a perceived threat might be a group of teenagers – both may result in our feeling fear). The response is physiological and psychological. Emotions fit into two main groups: approach emotions and avoid emotions. Approach emotions are experienced when we perceive we are safe and there is something good in our environment; avoid emotions are experienced when we perceive we are under threat and there is something harmful in our environment.
- Ask students to work in small groups to devise a way of bringing the emotion system to life. This could be using a diagram of a machine that works the same way the emotion system works, or even using people in the room to act as components in the system.

Session 2: managing the system (performance virtue)

1. Managing our emotions

- Give the statement 'you can choose how you feel' to the students. Ask them whether they agree or disagree with it, and why? There is the famous quote from Aristotle on anger on the following slide.
- There are some good examples of the idea of managing emotions on the internet:

  https://www.youtube.com/watch?v=2qnsCssTU1s   [available   02/15] (James Kingston, urban free climber)
  https://www.youtube.com/watch?v=pFkRbUKy19g   [available   02/15] (angry birds and controlling anger)

- Get students to discuss the strategies they have seen in the stimulus for managing emotions. Ask them to talk about any strategies they use to manage the way they feel.
- Feedback.

2. Emotions zones

- Show students the emotions zones circular diagram and explain how it works.

- The green line is the positive-negative energy line; the purple line is the high-low energy line. The green line corresponds to the release of serotonin: high serotonin means positive emotion. The purple line corresponds to adrenaline: high adrenaline means high energy.
- The two lines create four emotions zones: Survival (high + negative, e.g. anger), Burnout (low + negative e.g. sadness), Performance (high + positive e.g. excitement) and Recovery (low + positive e.g. contentment) and they get stronger as they move outward from the centre point: therefore, top left is the highest and most negative energy. We will find ourselves in particular zones depending on what is happening around us and in our minds. We can move ourselves between zones by engaging in particular thinking or activities.
- Give students the list of 20 emotions and ask them to place these emotions in the right zone.
- Give feedback on where they placed different emotions and notice any disagreement/incorrect placement. The zone will be correct/incorrect; e.g. anxiety is a survival emotion, not a burnout emotion, but the position in the zone will vary because the intensity with which people feel anxiety is subjective.

3. Positive action to manage emotion

- Give students the list of 10 ideas for managing our emotions and moving between zones. Ask them to identify which of these techniques they already use, or would use to manage their emotions.
- Ask students to plan to test out at least one new strategy for managing emotions in between lessons.

Session 3: using emotions to help us decide (the moral virtues)

1. How are emotions involved when we choose between right and wrong?

- Ask students to think about the last time either they did something they now regret and know was wrong, or that they believe was the right thing to do. Looking back, was emotion involved in their decision at all? When they decide between right and wrong normally, is there any emotion present?

Emotions move us towards things we think are beneficial, and away from things we think are harmful. Emotions therefore generate desires, which may be said to be in tension with what is in our interests, or what is good. This is sometimes referred to as the choice of Hercules: the choice between the pleasant life and the virtuous life.

Aristotle would say that the virtuous life is the pleasant life because being virtuous is intrinsically rewarding. Immanuel Kant said that moral decisions should be rational, rather than emotional, whereas David Hume said that moral decisions are emotional, not rational.

Psychologist Jonathan Haidt, is a leading researcher in the role of the emotions in moral decision making. He has constructed ingenious stories, which from a rational perspective appear morally sound (because no harm is done), but from a moral perspective seem deeply offensive or wrong. There are some examples on the slides (best used with KS4/5 students).

- Ask students whether they think emotions should influence our moral decision making.
- Show them the cute slide. Ask them if they could harm any of the individuals in the slide.
- Show them the less cute slide and ask them again.
- Can students think of any REASONS why we might need to harm any of the cute individuals (e.g. chemotherapy for a sick child) and protect any of the less cute individuals?
- Use the Haidt stories to explore the role of emotions in moral decision making (best used with KS4/5).
- Ask students to discuss whether moral decisions are emotional, rational or a mixture of both. If they are a mixture, what role does each play in formulating a choice?

2. Good Sense: choosing using more than just emotion

There are plenty of examples from film, literature and popular culture where emotion may have clouded a person's judgment. One such is Zinedine Zidane's head-butt on Marco Materazzi in the 2006 football World Cup Final. An interesting case study on this topic is the case of Jon-Jaques Clinton, whose conviction for the murder of his wife Dawn was overturned in 2012, when the judge decided that he had been too emotional to be in control of his actions. This case set a precedent in British law, which allowed for guilt to be lessened or even eliminated if there is sufficient emotional provocation.

- Choose a piece of stimulus and ask students whether emotion (in the stimulus) clouded judgment and led to a poor response, or provided motivation to act in the right way.
- Emotional decisions are often referred to as 'heat of the moment' decisions and could be depicted in red, whereas rational/intellectual decisions are often referred to as 'cool, calm and collected' and could be depicted in blue.
- Provide students with a range of scenarios where emotion is likely to be present. Ask students in small groups to speculate on what a red, emotional decision would look like, and what a blue, rational decision would look like.
- Ask the students to come up with practical strategies to enable them to make moral decisions, which are not just emotional, but are guided by reason too.
- Ask the students to think about the seven principal virtues: Courage, Justice, Honesty, Compassion, Self-discipline, Gratitude and Humility. Do any of them seem more red than blue, or vice versa? In order to be courageous, do we need to be more emotional, more rational, or a mixture of both?

Session 4: using emotions to help us engage (the civic virtues)

1. Using emotion to make a difference in the world

- The key idea in this lesson is to show how our emotional responses are clues to our moral reaction to situations and that they can move us to enhancing the world.
- Provide students with some stimulus: a good example is Michael Buerk's original BBC News report on the famine in Ethiopia, which provoked Bob Geldof to set up BandAid and LiveAid: it is on Youtube. There is also an amusing Ricky Gervais video from Comic Relief 2007, which plays with the idea of how emotion is exploited to get us to donate to charity.
- Ask students the following questions: what do you feel in response to this? What does your emotion tell you about your values, and what does it tell you about your thinking response (e.g. Bob Geldof's anger at the famine in Ethiopia tells us about his values surrounding human life and equality and his thoughts about the injustice of the situation and his perceptions of harm). There are some prompts on the slides and an explanation of the link between certain thoughts and certain feelings/emotions.

2. Emotions, practical intelligence and virtue

- Our emotional response to a situation tells us about our values and about what we think of the situation. Emotions powerfully propel us to act. Ask students to speculate on how a strong emotional response to the stimulus in Part 1 of the lesson, could have led to a poor response to the situation.
- Practical intelligence and the virtues can help us harness the energy of an emotional response and temper it into a constructive and meaningful response to a situation. Give students a situation that should provoke an emotional response, e.g. someone takes something of yours without asking, or someone you care about is harmed by someone you dislike. Ask students to work through the practical reasoning questions and then the virtue questions. Do these questions help the students to identify a good course of action?

3. The role of empathy

- Another important angle is the role of empathy.
- Ask students to identify how empathy can help us to respond constructively to the issues in our communities.

There are two good RSA Animate videos: a very short explanation of the difference between empathy and sympathy https://www.youtube.com/watch?v=1Evwgu369Jw and a longer video explaining how empathy is the beginning of positive social change: https://www.youtube.com/watch?v=BG46IwVfSu8 [both available 02/15].

4. Planning to make social change

- Get students into small groups. Ask them to identify things in their world that annoy them or make them unhappy and which they would like to change. Ask them to discuss their emotional response and explore it in depth: this will provide their motivation for action.
- Now ask the students to use practical intelligence and virtues to plan the things they can do to change the situation that makes them irritated/annoyed/sad/angry. It's important that students select something in their immediate environment, so that they can see the impact that their actions can have on something tangible.

5. Making social change

- Ask students to act on what they have talked about and be prepared to discuss the outcomes in their next lesson.

Session 5: reflection

Why are emotions important to virtue?
  Ask students to reflect upon and discuss the following questions.

1 What have you learned about your emotions?
2 How have you become more emotionally skilful?
3 What have you learned about choosing between right and wrong?
4 How have you used your emotions to improve your immediate environment?

Sample lesson 2: an intelligent virtue – good sense

Session 1: virtue knowledge

Good sense

The virtue of 'good sense' forms part of every other virtue. It moulds, informs and transforms our basic desires, emotions, instincts and impulses into morally good decisions. These decisions strengthen our virtues and tackle our vices. 'Good sense' is like a lighthouse that illuminates what we have to do to realise or practise the virtues. It is a moral compass that steers us towards the more virtuous decisions, and away from the less virtuous ones. It takes a lifetime of practice, experience and reflection to calibrate this compass correctly.

  Developing and acting with 'good sense' gives us freedom – being thoughtful and vigilant about what we are doing, why we are doing it and what we hope to achieve for ourselves and others through doing it. On this reading, to be 'free', means to have the freedom that the practised musician, artist or sportsman enjoys: they have all the basic and advanced movements – quite literally at their fingertips – and are able to weave them together almost intuitively, like second nature, as they respond to the demands of a situation. This is what 'good sense' does – it pulls together and balances out all the necessary virtues to cope with what the situation demands.

Living with 'good sense' sets out the ways and means of realising the good in the down to earth, concrete realities of any given situation. When it is well practised, it enables suppleness in the face of the complexities of the ethical life. It is the essence of a life well lived.

1. What can those who have this virtue do particularly well?

The person who lives with good sense is able to order their lives well.

- They know what the point and purpose of human life is (to flourish as a human being, rather than to wither; to build character, rather than to erode or destroy it).
- Those with 'good sense' know how to suit their actions to that very goal. All that the person with good sense does will turn out well.
- To live with good sense is to be able to direct all human action to the goal of human flourishing, or happiness.

Good sense directs emotions and actions to their proper goal, or end. This direction is first of all a work of reason and moral intuition, or perception. It requires:

- Foresight to realise what is and is not required to do this. This foresight is based upon a remembrance of past experience and a correct estimate of the present conditions and circumstances. It enables us to direct our actions to their goal, thoughtfully.

Perhaps the best way to think of 'good sense' is to think through what 'bad sense' might look like.

It is bad sense, for example, to live unfairly, or exploitatively, to live and act with cowardice, or rashness, or to live an overly indulgent lifestyle. Acting in such ways will not count as flourishing as a human, neither will it make us genuinely happy.

Those with good sense are able to decide or determine which act or acts will attain the goal of human flourishing in any situation. The chief act of this virtue is to command.

TASK 1

- Put the above definition of 'good sense' into your own words.
- When have you had to act with 'good sense'?

Discuss.

- Think of a person from real life, or literature who you think has demonstrated particularly 'bad sense'. Explain your answer in a short paragraph.

2. What are the benefits of acting out this virtue?

As we develop the habit of acting well, we will develop the habits of thinking well, or of perceiving what is required, or demanded by the situation and the circumstances we are in.

Without good sense we will target goals that fail to satisfy, or find ourselves trapped by unbecoming desires and satisfactions. Without 'good sense' there is no virtue. Living without 'good sense' can make us timorous, small-minded, selfish, anxious and not to mention foolish. It is 'bad sense' to be unfair, cowardly or overly indulgent.

Living with 'good sense' enables us to live vigorously and decisively, with vitality and a touch of moral nobility.

TASK 2

- Define 'timorous'.
- Talk about a person who you think has displayed particularly noble moral qualities. Explain what those qualities were, and how they acted with good sense.

3. When might I have to practise this virtue?

Whenever we are called to practise any virtue at all, the virtue of good sense will form part of that other virtue. It assists us in perceiving what kind of response the situation calls for, and how to reconcile the virtues, if and when they collide, or point towards contradictory actions. It forms the deliberation and evaluation part of every other virtue.

For example:

- Adam borrows £50 from Baruch. The virtue of justice demands that each person gets what they deserve. Justice demands, therefore, that Baruch reimburses Adam to the tune of £50.

But how and when shall it be paid back?

- If Adam lacked good sense, then he would never pay it back. He would simply not have the foresight or resolution to set aside the appropriate funds. Instead, he might delay the reimbursement until he had inherited some money, or go for an easy gain by gambling at the races.
- If Adam lacked good sense, he may also pressurise himself to pay it back too quickly, on terms that were personally disadvantageous.
- Alternatively, if Adam had good sense, then he would be able to reimburse according to his means, as soon as possible and within an agreed timeframe. He may, for instance, deposit £5 a week in a bank, with a view to paying the loan back as soon as possible. And, having determined that this is the just thing to do (which indeed it is), he would see his actions through until

Baruch is reimbursed. It is also worth mentioning that Adam would have had the 'good sense' only to borrow what he could afford to pay back, and for things that were worth having.

TASK 3

- Show how 'good sense' can be used to help Adam decide whether he should borrow the money in the first place. What sorts of things will he need to consider?

4. Which desires or emotions may be alerting me to practise this virtue?

Every desire, emotion, or passion is an invitation to practise 'good sense'. It is good sense that moulds, transforms, and educates the emotions towards morally right actions.

For example:

My emotions, instincts, impulses and desires tell me that:

- I am angry because I sense unfairness is at work here. But, I want to be a fair person, giving each what they deserve; I don't want to be harsh and cruel in doing this, neither do I want to be a 'push over'. Acting with good sense will temper my anger and guide me in how to be fair in the situation.
- I am afraid because I sense danger is at work here. But I want to be a brave person, overcoming the internal and external obstacles to my being a fair person; I want to overcome my fears and do the right thing, without being reckless. I don't want to be a coward, nor do I want to be foolhardy, or rash. Acting with good sense will temper my fear and guide me to be brave in whatever situation I am in.
- I am craving because I sense my appetite for food, knowledge, material objects (e.g. shoes or video games) and pleasure need fulfilling. But I want to live with self-control – I don't want to consume more than my share, or use others as a means to experiencing pleasure. But I also don't want to starve to death. Acting with good sense will transform my instinctual cravings, guiding me to make decisions that will lead me to strengthen self-control in whatever situation I am in.
- It helps us to weigh up the situation, the activity that is required in the situation and then make a decision that we can carry out to realise the good of human flourishing. Good sense guides and educates our emotions towards the roads that lead to this flourishing, to the building up of character, rather than the undermining of it.

TASK 4

- Choose one of the emotions (anger, fear, craving) listed above, or another emotion that you have experienced. Explain how practising the virtue of 'good sense' led you to act reasonably, educating your emotions. How did the situation turn out for you?

TASK 5

- Think of a situation when you have acted with 'bad sense'. Explain it to yourself in a short piece of writing.
- What was the situation?
- What did you do, or say?
- What should you have said, or done to have improved the situation?

Session 2: virtue reasoning

1. What are my basic dispositions and inclinations in relation to this virtue?

TASK 1

Which of the following best sums up your 'bent' in relation to 'good sense'? Check any words you don't understand.

- Am I too hesitant? Am I paralysed in my decision-making, and in acting out the more virtuous action in my situations? Even if I am thorough in informing my decisions, and weighing them up in detail, am I too slow to act in a way that I conclude to be right?
- Am I too impulsive, or rash in my decision-making.

Do I act out what I hastily conclude would be the more virtuous action in situations? Do I neglect to inform my position adequately, or jump to hasty conclusions about what needs to be done?

- Am I inclined to be impressionable, and easily influenced by others?
- Am I inclined to be pertinacious, or stubborn, doggedly sticking to my own views, even in the face of wiser advice?

Look back at the situation you defined in Section 1: Task 5 above. You had to identify a situation when you showed 'bad sense'.

Which of the above inclinations listed above best sums up the way in which you showed 'bad sense'? Were you hesitant, impulsive, impressionable, or stubborn?

2. How do I practise this virtue?

The virtue of good sense forms a part of every other virtue. Without good sense, there is no intentional virtue. These three stages form a part of reflection on every other virtue, and you will see these integrated in the subsequent worksheets on this course.

STEP 1: DELIBERATE:

Inform the decision: What information do you need in order to make a fuller, better-informed decision?

- By drawing upon your memory: What kind of experience can I draw upon when approaching this problem? Which mistakes do I need to learn from? Which situations are similar? What have been my past patterns of behaviour when confronted with such situations? How has my past experience prepared, or shaped me to act virtuously in this situation?
- By drawing upon your understanding: What sorts of things need to be done?
- By aiming high, and aspiring to be a fully flourishing human being: What kind of person do I want to be in this situation? What standards of character do I wish to live up to? Which qualities of character do I want to develop? How can I use this situation as an opportunity to develop those qualities? How can I realise the good in this situation?
- By learning: How do I apply this knowledge to the present situation?

STEP 2: EVALUATE:

Judge the relative merits, or ways of realising the good/moral virtue/human flourishing in the situation: What weight will you give the differing elements of a situation and why? What are the relative merits of the different ways in which the virtue can be expressed, or practised?

- Be thoughtful and sensitive: What are the morally relevant features of the situation? What is of value in the situation, and what is not of value? What kind of virtuous response is the situation calling for?
- Be aware and look around: How am I to give expression in this situation to being the kind of person I aspire to be – a just, brave and self-controlled one?
- Be educable: From whom do I need to take advice? Who will help my understanding of this situation? Can I admit that I don't 'know-it-all', and that I need some help here?
- Be far-sighted: Can I cut a path through this thicket of issues that will lead me to being the kind of person I aspire to be, living more virtuously? In what way shall I act to attain the goals that reason suggests? How will my actions serve my personal good? How will my actions serve the common good? How will my actions serve any other good, e.g. the good of my friends, my family, my school, my classmates, my team?

STEP 3: DECIDE AND DO:

Resolve and Command: What will I do, how and when?

- How can I adapt my actions to the attainment of the goal of life – human flourishing – what is the right human action to realise this?
- What are the present conditions and circumstances that will impact upon my decision, both in terms of opportunities and constraints?
- Where do I need to act with restraint, or caution?
- Where do I need to act with complete freedom, unhindered?

- What is my resolution, or decision?
- How will I go about acting out my thoughts, evaluations and aspirations?

This is summarised in Table 9.1.

Session 3: virtue practice

Should we encounter difficulties in the life of virtue, perhaps the best place to start looking to fix the problem may be examining ourselves in relation to the virtue of 'good sense'. Below is a more detailed guide that sets out how to do this. It helps us to reflect on the quality of our thinking about how best to handle situations that call for a moral response.

Are we inclined to be too hesitant, or too rash, for instance? If too hesitant, then we need to work to tighter deadlines; if too rash, then we need to plan our decision making more thoughtfully.

Task 1

Look back at the scenario where you evaluated yourself as having acted with 'bad sense'. Work through each of the stages in Table 9.2, of deliberation, evaluation and deciding and doing. Show how you could have acted with 'good sense' in that situation. Use the white column as a prompt to your thoughts.

See how the principles set out in Table 9.2 are worked out below.

SCENARIO:

A man living in England is offered a better job in Egypt. Should he accept or refuse?

- His wife has bad asthma, and the climate in England is much better for asthmatics than in Egypt.
- His wife's health is more important than the size of his income.
- But he is concerned that his employers will be disappointed with him and, that if he doesn't take this opportunity, they will withhold further opportunities from him.

Table 9.1 Resolve and command

Deliberations	How have your past experiences helped you to think about this situation?
	How can you apply the 'lessons of life' to this situation?
	What kind of person do you hope to become in this situation?
Evaluation	What are the morally relevant features of the situation and how have you weighted them?
	To whom have you looked for advice, and/or inspiration, and why?
	What might the implications of your decision be, both positively and negatively?
Decision/Action	How will you give expression to the kind of person you hope to become in this situation?
	What will you do?

Table 9.2 A good sense checklist

I understand the moral point and purpose called for by the activity – I know which virtues the situation, or activity is calling me to practise and promote.
I understand how to balance out, or prioritise the clashing virtues.
I understand how to apply the guidelines I have learnt from experience and reflection.
I understand how my actions will be perceived by others. I can specify what my emotions are alerting me to do.
I know how to practise the appropriate virtues to express the moral point of this activity.

	DEFICIENCIES	GOOD SENSE	EXCESSES
	ANXIOUS ABOUT ONE'S JUDGEMENT – TOO TIMID		OVER-CONFIDENCE IN ONE'S JUDGEMENT
DELIBERATION How are you going about your deliberations about what to do in this situation?	HESITATION Dishonest to oneself by omitting relevant details about the past (normally to adopt a 'can't do' stance).	Drawing upon experience Honest engagement with the past – not as we hoped it would be; not falsifying, retouching, displacing, discolouring, omitting, or accenting different aspects of it. Stillness and thoughtfulness	RUSHING INTO DECISIONS Superficial levels of thought Dishonest about oneself by adding in details about the past, or colouring it unduly for specific purposes (normally to adopt a 'I can do anything stance').
EVALUATION OF THE PARTICULARS OF THE SITUATION How much thought are you putting into weighing up the morally relevant features of the situation?	CLOSED-MINDEDNESS; MORAL BLINDNESS; NEGLIGENCE Unable to distinguish good advice from bad advice Setting one's sights too low – on pleasure, wealth, status and power	Open-mindedness to the range of possibilities Able to take advice – especially from friends Quick-wittedness – grasping a situation swiftly Clear-sighted objectivity in unexpected circumstances Foresight: evaluating whether a particular action will lead to the realisation of the goal – regardless of the elements of risk and uncertainty.	'KNOW-IT-ALL' – OVER-CONFIDENT Unable to take advice Cunning – using false ways to good goals; or, good ways to false goals. Insidiousness; guile; craft Unable to see how actions fail to contribute to a life of flourishing; insufficiently interested in the proper goals of human activity to take the means to live with good sense.

DECIDE AND DO How swift are you in enacting your resolutions?	IRRESOLUTENESS	Application of thought into action – nimble-mindedness	RANDOM ACTION; FLITTING ABOUT
	Fickleness; indecisiveness Overly anxious Overly hesitant – waiting for certainties that will never be; inconclusiveness, or a daydreamer, never acting on aspirations. Remissness Unable to take a well-founded risk to act virtuously in a situation that calls for it. Demanding a level of certainty from ethical decision making that is simply impossible.	Deciding for the good, avoiding the pitfalls of injustice, cowardice and intemperance. Energetic promptness Swift performance Alertness Prepared to take a calculated risk, understanding that there are few certainties in ethical decision making: motive/action/consequence	Clinging to false certainties Too rushed, slapdash and risky in action Impulsive and impatient; Acting with utter disregard to the risks of the situation.

What would we advise?

- seek advice from someone;
- use foresight to evaluate the exact degree of danger to his wife;
- use foresight to evaluate the exact degree of danger to his career if he refuses to go;
- if he refuses to go, can he give reasons that his employers might respect?
- He must be cautious not to endanger his whole future by his refusal, or through the way in which he refuses.

OUTCOME:

- He refuses to go to Egypt
- He explains his decision so well to his employers that he retains their respect

As you work through the succeeding resources, be sure to think through the quality of the thinking you do before you practise a virtue.

Use the information in this chapter to:

- Think carefully about the situations that confront you
- Think about the quality of your thoughts

Sample lesson 3: using the tools of virtue

The aim of these sessions is to introduce students to the idea of developing moral reasoning and virtue, and to some of the tools they might use in order to do so. This unit focuses on moral virtue, but could just as easily be used for performance or civic virtues.

The lessons follow a pattern designed to represent a system that students can develop to become more morally skilful. The pattern is as follows:

1   *Notice*: notice something is not as it should be.
2   *Stop*: pause before reacting.
3   *Look*: look at the emotional reactions in the situation (yours and others).
4   *Listen*: giving and taking reasons.
5   *Caterpillar*: think about how what you do now (as a caterpillar) will affect what you become (butterfly).

The sessions are designed around a case study, to be selected by the teacher or the class. By dissecting the case study, the class will be able to see how virtue is developed.

There is a worked example in these lesson ideas: the 1994 film *In the Name of the Father*, which is the story of the Guildford Four, who were falsely imprisoned for the bombing of the Horse and Groom pub in Guildford in 1974.

Some other ideas for case studies are as follows:

- *My Sister's Keeper* (film, with a teenage protagonist).
- Oskar Schindler, *Schindler's List*.
- Joe Simpson/Simon Yates, *Touching the Void*.
- *Atonement*, Ian McEwan (and film version).
- Mark Thomas, political activist: his work on the arms trade chronicled in 'As used on the famous Nelson Mandela' or other activism in 'Mark Thomas Comedy Product' on YouTube.
- Aung San Suu Kyi.
- *Erin Brokovich* (film)
- *Silkwood* (film).
- *Veronica Guerin* (film).
- *Yes Men Fix the World* (film).

Session 1: something is not as it should be

1. Notice

- Recognition of the need to employ virtue often begins with noticing that something is not as it should be and that virtue is needed to respond. Begin with the part of your case study where a character realises that something is not as it should be, that something is not right. *In the Name of the Father* has several key moments of this nature. There are the sequences where the police are interviewing (and torturing) the suspects; there is the moment they are convicted and sentenced in court; there is a sequence where Gerry Conlon realises that he can't side with the IRA terrorist who has confessed to the Guildford bomb and instead decides to work with his father on the campaign for their release; there is the moment where Gareth Peirce, the defence lawyer, discovers the initials of Charlie Burke carved into a park bench.

2. What is not as it should be?

- Looking at your stimulus, ask students to identify the characters that think things are not as it should be. How do the students know this?
- Ask students to speculate on what it is the characters think is not as it should be. Push them to identify as much as they can: e.g. the defendants in *In the Name of the Father* might be thinking 'Innocent people should not be punished'; 'The police should not be corrupt'; 'People shouldn't lie'; 'The courts should protect the innocent'; 'I can't trust authority', etc.
- Ask students to identify their own responses to the situation. What do they think about it and how do they feel?

3. Noticing emotion

- Ask students to observe the emotional responses of as many characters as they can to the realisation that something is not as it should be. The court scenes in *In the Name of the Father* contain a number of emotional responses: from those of the defendants and their families, to those of the police officers at the moment the verdict is announced. Ask students to try to name as many of the emotions as they can and to try to rate the strength of the emotions felt from 0 to 10.

4. Becoming more aware

- Ask students to spend time between lessons noticing (just noticing, rather than both noticing and acting) when things are not as they should be and to make a note of those occasions.

Session 2: something is not as it should be, and I need to pause

1. Rushing in where angels fear to tread

- Looking at your stimulus, and the work done in the previous session, ask the students to look back at the emotional reactions they observed and rated out of 10.
- How many emotions did they score at 8 or above? If the students felt that emotion at that strength in that situation, what would they do? Perhaps use the image or idea of a push or a propeller here: that powerful emotions drive us to respond.
- Ask students to think of a situation of their own where something was not as it should have been, to which they had a powerful emotional response (e.g. someone insults them; they lose something precious belonging to someone else; they make a terrible mistake). This could be hypothetical. If you prefer, use a third party example, such as Zinedine Zidane's response to Marco Materazzi's taunting in the football World Cup final of 2006.
- Ask students to dissect the situation with a rushed, emotional response:
    - What emotion is being felt?
    - What is the emotion propelling me to do?
    - What is said or done?
    - What are the consequences of this?

2. With hindsight

- Ask the students if any of them would have acted differently if they had had the chance. If they could have replayed it, what would they have done?
- Ask students what strategies they already have which enable them to take time to choose well in the moment and act in a way that doesn't lead to regret or shame.

3. The pause button

- Some students might have suggested the idea of a time-out, or some way of pausing before acting. An example of a 'pause button' that can buy us time before responding is mindfulness. Mindfulness of our breathing enables us to calm powerful emotions, which may make it easier to think with more clarity and focus about the situation we are in. There are more detailed instructions on how to teach mindfulness of the breath in lesson 4 of the Building Mental Health slate.

- Ask students to speculate about the benefits and the drawbacks of pausing to decide when the heat is on. Ask them to think of situations they have been in that would have benefited from pausing and situations that might not have. Beware the confirmation bias which makes it harder for us to try new ideas; where we just look for evidence that confirms what we already think, and find reasons to reject things that are new or challenging.

4. Finding pause more easily

- Ask students to spend time between lessons, pausing before reacting. Ask them to try mindfulness of breathing, or to experiment with their own technique for pausing.

Session 3: look: what do emotions tell me?

1. What do emotions tell me?

- Our emotions are a reflection of how we interpret our environment. Some emotions are beyond conscious control (e.g. a startle or disgust reflex), but most emotions result from what we think about what is happening around us or in our own mind.
- Introduce students to some examples of the thoughts reflected by certain emotions (on the slides).
- Using this knowledge, ask the students to look back at the stimulus, to notice the emotions they observe, to name the emotions and to link the emotion to the thought that caused it.

2. Emotions: a window onto what we think is good

- The other information emotions provide us with concerns what we think is the good. Emotions move us away from what we consider harmful, offensive and immoral towards what we consider beneficial, right and good; therefore, our emotional response to a situation tells us what our values are; our vision of how the world should be.
- Ask students to see if they can identify what the emotional responses in the stimulus tell them about what the character(s) think is the good.

3. Using emotions: character analysis

- *In the Name of the Father* depicts three characters who display emotion in contrasting ways. Gerry Conlon[2] is very much at the mercy of his emotions for much of the early part of the story. He is impulsive and does what will make him feel good, rather than being driven along by the good, or by virtue.

The film depicts his early time in prison as alternating between taking drugs to escape from the emotional pain of his situation and being explosively emotional with those who don't see things the way he does. Giuseppe Conlon is much more in control of his emotion. He is calm in contrast to the tempestuousness of his son and his ability to manage his emotion leads him to respond to his situation differently: he launches a campaign to attempt to secure their release and he also avoids conflict with other prisoners and with the prison authorities. He is guided by the good (as witnessed in his refusal to accept an offer of help from a convicted IRA terrorist) and by virtue.

There is a subplot that examines how his virtuous choices have caused him pain (e.g. working in a paint factory to provide for his family, which caused damage to his lungs). Gareth Peirce[3] is very clearly motivated by the good. Emma Thompson's portrayal of her depicts a character with a strong conception of justice and strong emotional responses to injustice, but emotions that are used to achieve actions that support the good (especially the scene where she is offered the chance to look at Gerry Conlon's file and skilfully navigates her emotions to not miss that opportunity).

- Ask students to evaluate how well the characters in the stimulus use their emotions to get them closer to the good. Are they able to manage or control their emotions, or do they lose their temper? What impact does keeping or losing their temper have? Do they use their emotions to get something good for everyone (e.g. justice) or something good just for themselves (e.g. pleasure)?

4. Learning from emotions

- Ask students to spend time in between lessons noticing their emotions, naming their emotions and linking their emotions to the thought that causes them.

Session 4: listen: giving and taking reasons

1. Go beyond emotion: gather reasons

- In moral deliberation, we need to recognise that our emotions propel us to do certain things and our reason (and the reason of others) enables us to check our emotional impulses against what is good or right.
- We know what emotion is telling the character(s) in the stimulus to do, but ask students to identify what they think reason is telling the character(s) to do. For example, in *In the Name of the Father*, it is clear that reason is telling Giuseppe Conlon to respond to the situation in a different way to Gerry Conlon: whereas Giuseppe seems to respect the system and work alongside

it, calmly campaigning for their freedom, Gerry initially seeks to antagonise and work against the system because his reason is telling him to retaliate against the system that has harmed him. Whereas Giuseppe's reasoning is leading him to pursue the good of justice and an end to the imprisonment of the 11 wrongly accused, Gerry's reasoning hasn't got beyond his doing what brings him pleasure or dulling the pain of his imprisonment. They act in different ways because they have each reasoned differently about what will achieve the good.

2. *Giving my own reasons*

- When we act, we need our own reasons to act. But how do we develop these reasons? Ask students to place themselves in the position of one of the characters in the stimulus and ask them to generate an idea of what they would do and what their reasons would be for doing that.
- For contrast, ask students to place themselves in the position of an anti-hero. For example, the police officers in *In the Name of the Father* acted in a way that many would condemn, but they would have had their reasons for acting in that way: ask students to work them out.
- Ask students to try to work out how to decide which reasons are right.

3. *Taking reasons from others*

- Ask students to work out the sources of reasons other than our own desires and thinking (e.g. rules and laws; God or religion; logic and reason; heroes or paragons of virtue).
- Ask students to look at the stimulus and ask if the 'hero' or main character looks beyond themselves for reasons to act. In *In the Name of the Father,* Giuseppe Conlon seems motivated by sources of reasons, such as his duty to his family, moral principles of justice and his faith in God, whereas Gerry does not (initially) look beyond his own desires and reasons.
- Ask students to evaluate how important it is to look to others for reasons to act, especially reasons that disagree with our own.

4. *Learn to give and take*

- In the time between lessons, ask students to practise knowing their own reasons for acting and also, looking for reasons from other sources, especially reasons that disagree with our own.

Session 5: caterpillar

In the children's book *The Very Hungry Caterpillar* by Eric Carle, the caterpillar eats his way through some very colourful food so that he can turn into a beautiful butterfly. The colours of the food emerge on the butterfly's wings at the end of the story. This image could be used for the idea of the development of moral reasoning and virtue: that the things we do have an effect on the person we become.

1. Butterfly

- Ask students to envisage what kind of person they would like to be when it comes to deciding between good and bad, right and wrong: What kind of moral butterfly do they want to be?
- You can use the stimulus here: for example, Gerry Conlon is on a journey of moral becoming. At the start of the story, he is selfish and self-interested, lurching from pleasure to pleasure. He is a disappointment to his father Giuseppe, who is a man of virtue and Gerry is aware of this and feels the shame acutely. Over the course of the story, Gerry becomes morally aware and develops certain virtues, which he continued to display upon his release from prison in the work he did for the wrongly imprisoned.

2. Inspirational butterflies

- Ask students to think of examples of people who exemplify the virtues (Courage, Justice, Honesty, Compassion, Self-discipline, Gratitude, Humility).
- What do these exemplars do that students would need to emulate to make them more virtuous?
- Perhaps use anti-heroes from your stimulus to contrast. The police officers in *In the Name of the Father* are examples of men who have become vicious by believing the wrong reasons for acting, and losing sight of the good that they are trying to uphold.

3. From caterpillar to butterfly

- Ask students to evaluate what they themselves need to do differently in terms of noticing, stopping, looking and listening, which will move them closer to being a virtuous butterfly.

Sample lesson 4: the virtue of courage

This lesson is based upon the interpretation, concepts and approaches set out in Curzer, H.J. (2012) *Aristotle and the Virtues*, pp. 19–64 (OUP).

Session 1: virtue knowledge

1. What can those who have this virtue do particularly well?

Those who are courageous can cope with things that threaten to harm or destroy them. In the face of such threats, they show both firmness of position and boldness of spirit. Courageous people are unduly moved by dangers. They are neither overcome by such dangers, nor do they overestimate their abilities in facing them. Courageous people have trained their emotions so that the levels of fear and confidence that they feel in situations fall into line with what their reason suggests they should feel. They are neither paralysed by inaction, nor reckless with ill-judged action. They fear real dangers in appropriate ways, and are confident about tackling such dangers in appropriate ways.

Those with this virtue feel fear and confidence rightly, and act rightly in situations where they sense risk or impending harm; their actions are for the purpose of achieving a worthwhile good. The courageous person fears and is confident about the right things, in the right way, to the right extent and in the right situations.

TASK 1

- Which emotions does the virtue of courage govern?
- Can courageous people feel fear and confidence?
- How might their fear and confidence differ from those who are less developed in the virtue of courage?

2. What are the benefits of acting out this virtue?

- It will have a positive impact on us: acting courageously is better than acting with cowardice or with bravado and rashness. It is good for us to act courageously, because that's the sort of thing that emotional-rational creatures (us) should do. It is an intrinsically human quality.
- It will have a positive impact on the situation we are in: acting courageously will help us to accomplish fine, noble and worthwhile goals, despite the risk of harm. If we act with cowardice, or rashness, we may fail to have the positive impact on the situation that is morally called for.
- Without the virtue of courage in situations that call for them: failing to act courageously when called to, or more precisely, acting cowardly or with rashness instead, may mean that we suffer harms that we might otherwise not have suffered, had we been courageous. Without courage to check them, the ignorant, or the wicked will prosper!

TASK 2

Think of a time when you acted with courage. Describe the impact your courageous act had on:

- you (did it build your confidence, for example, or challenge your fears?);
- the situation you were in (what good, if any, came of your courageous act?);
- what psychological or physical harm might you have suffered had you not acted courageously?

3. When might I have to practise this virtue?

Practise this virtue in situations that call for courage. Consider these points:

- Will the virtue of courage be able to do something about this situation?
- Will it achieve something worthwhile?
- What do I stand to lose through showing courage?
- What do I stand to lose through not being courageous?

TASK 3

Look at when you identified yourself as having acted courageously in Task 2 above. Explain how your courageous act met the criteria set out above.

4. Which emotions does this virtue govern?

When I experience the emotion defined as 'fear'.
When I experience and identify the emotion or feeling called 'fear', some of the symptoms include:
- Silent trembling
- Going pale
- Cold, as the body's surface temperature is reduced and the warmth rises in the lower digestive tract with the internal heat of that part of the body – we need to go the toilet!
- Fluttering, or pounding heart
- Quavering voice, trembling lip, chattering teeth
- Sweaty palms

Fear is a useful emotion because it alerts us to danger and stimulates us to look for options to resist or escape the danger. This emotion forces us to evaluate whether the principle is really worth suffering harm for. The important point, though, is to overcome having too much, or too little fear when we should be acting rightly.
Points to consider when identifying fear:

- What are the bad things that I fear happening to me by acting, or not acting in this situation? What are the risks to my person?
- What are the grounds of my fears? Should I be (this) afraid?

TASK 4

Identify a situation in which you have experienced the emotion of 'fear'. Look at the signs above. Describe it. How afraid were you?
When I experience the emotion defined as 'over-confidence':

'Confidence' means to have faith in oneself, or in another. It is a useful emotion because it encourages us to act for worthwhile goals. Fear erodes confidence, and confidence overcomes fear.

When I experience and identify the emotion or feeling called 'confidence', some the of the symptoms include:

- feeling 'on the front foot', or bold and positive;
- feeling energised;
- ready for the challenge.

But confidence needs restraining, or grounding on a sure and sound footing. Too much confidence, or over-confidence can lead to rashness, recklessness, and arrogance. It can make us feel invincible without good reason. So, we need to ask ourselves, in whom, or upon what have we placed our confidence, and on what grounds we have placed our confidence in that person, idea, or thing? Confidence is about the belief that something worthwhile can be achieved.

Points to consider on identifying confidence:

- What do I believe I can achieve? Will my actions make a difference to this situation?
- Can I be confident in my own abilities to avoid harm and/or to achieve some worthwhile good (either by how I accept the harm or avoid it)?
- What does over-confidence look like in a person?

TASK 5

Identify and describe a situation in which you experienced the emotion of 'confidence'. What did it feel like 'to be confident'? What was your confidence based upon?

You may find the following a useful means of defining emotions connected to the virtue of courage.

These are direct quotations from the excellent *Emotions: An Essay in Aid of Moral Psychology*, Robert C. Roberts, 2003, Cambridge University Press:

FEAR:

X presents a specific aversive possibility, e.g. dangers, or harms to my personal, physical, social, psychological or spiritual integrity.

Of a [significant] degree of probability, viz, it may happen; it is probable.

May X or its aversive consequences be avoided, i.e. how do I prevent what I fear from happening?

ANXIETY, FRIGHT, DREAD, TERROR, PANIC, HORROR, SPOOK

ANXIETY: X vaguely presents an aversive possibility of some degree of probability; may X or its aversive consequences, whatever they may be, be avoided. I have a vague apprehension of losing money, status or respect.

FRIGHT: X presents an immediate and definite aversive possibility of a high degree of probability; may X or its aversive consequences be avoided right away.

My senses tell me that I am in danger.

DREAD: X is an unavoidable aversive future eventuality; if only X or its aversive consequences could be avoided! The aversive object is inevitably approaching,

e.g. news that I know will be bad (for example, next week's test).

TERROR: X vividly presents an extremely aversive possibility of a very high degree of probability; and I don't know what to do. Paralysing.

PANIC: X vividly presents an extremely aversive possibility of a very high degree of probability; let me do something, just anything.

HORROR: X is strongly aversive because it is grotesquely abnormal; may I escape from X or may X be restored to normalcy. How sensitive am I to what is normal?

SPOOK: By its sinister mysteriousness, X vaguely presents an aversive possibility of some degree of probability; may X or its aversive consequences, whatever they may be, be avoided.

Session 2: virtue reasoning

1. What are my basic dispositions and inclinations in the light of this virtue?

How would you define your basic dispositions and inclinations in the light of fear and confidence?

- Do you feel you tend more towards being overcome by fears in situations that call for courage to achieve something worthwhile?
- Do you feel you tend more towards being overconfident in situations that call for courage to achieve something worthwhile?

TASK 1

- Divide into two groups: those who tend more towards experiencing fear in different situations, and those who tend more towards over-confidence (or 'cockiness'!)
- Discuss the situations in which you encounter those emotions.
- Now, match up in pairs: one from the 'Fear Group', and one from the 'Over-Confidence Group'. As a pair, come up with one practice that can help us to overcome fear, and one practice that can help us to overcome over-confidence.

N.B. According to Aristotle:

- If you tend more towards fear, when faced with the need to be more courageous, then think through ways you can show and practise greater confidence.
- If you tend more towards confidence when faced with situations that call for greater courage, then think through ways you can show greater respect for the real dangers and issues involved in the situation.

Here is some advice from Aristotle on how to educate ourselves to grow in virtue:

> Hence he who aims at the intermediate must first depart from what is the more contrary to it... But we must consider the things towards which we ourselves also are easily carried away; for some of us tend to one thing, some to another; and this will be recognisable from the pleasure and pain we feel. We must drag ourselves away to the contrary extreme; for we shall get into the intermediate state by drawing away from error, as people do in straightening sticks that are bent' (1109a30-b7).

TASK 2

Pool together all the suggestions that the class made in pairs about how to act in a way that overcomes our fears, and how to act in a way that can restrain our over-confidence. Put your suggestions in the appropriate category below. Display it in your workbooks, or classroom.

- Problem: I am afraid of too many things;

Aristotle advises that: I need convincing and training that certain objects are not really dangerous.

- Problem: I am too afraid of failure;

Aristotle advises that: I need convincing and training that certain outcomes are really not so bad.

- Problem: I have too high a level of self-confidence

Aristotle advises that: I need convincing and training that certain objects need to be treated with greater caution, and that certain outcomes are calling me to rethink my approach.

- Problem: I have too high a fear threshold;

Aristotle advises that: I need to think through ways of building my confidence through practising the very things of which I am afraid.

2. Guidelines to handling our fears and over-confidence to act courageously

Aristotle highlights ways in which we can go wrong with respect to the virtue of courage, letting our fears or over-confidence get the better of our actions:

> Of the faults that are committed one consists in fearing what one should not, another in fearing as we should not, another consists in fearing when

we should not, and so on; and so too with respect to the things that inspire confidence. The man, then, who faces and who fears the right things and with the right aim, and in the right way and at the right time, and who feels confidence under the corresponding conditions, is brave.

Aristotle, (1115b15-19) NE III.7

Here are some guidelines on how to think through situations that you identify as triggering fear or confidence, and thus may be a call for you to practise acting more courageously. They should help you to think through whether you are feeling fear and confidence rightly:

FEAR

- Who, or what am I afraid of? Is it the right thing to be afraid of, or the wrong thing? What kind of damage, harm, or injury can it really do to me?
- What is the strength of my fear for this object or situation? Am I too afraid of it – or, not afraid enough?
- What is the situation that is making me afraid?
- Of whom am I afraid, and why?
- For how long should I really be afraid of this?
- Do I fear the right things, the right amount of things, in the right way and to the right amount?

CONFIDENCE

- What am I confident about doing? What are the harms that confidence can avoid, or the good that being confident might achieve?
- What is the strength of my confidence? Is it too little, or too much?
- What are the grounds for my confidence and how reasonable and well-founded are they?
- What is the occasion for my confidence, and why?
- For how long should I have confidence?

TASK 3

Look back at the situations in which you feel you were paralysed with too much fear, or reckless, as a result of too much confidence. Use the criteria above to weigh up whether you feeling fear and over-confidence about the right things, to the right strength, for the right reasons, on the right occasions, and for the right length of time.

3. Courageous role models?

TASK 4

Get into groups of 3.

Person 1 needs to select an example from literature or life of who they think showed particular cowardice. Use the prompts in the 'underdoing it' section to explain how and why they showed excessive cowardice.

Person 2 needs to select an example from literature or life of who they think showed particular courage. Use the prompts in the 'Golden Mean' column to explain why they showed such courage.

Person 3 needs to select an example from literature or life of who they think was particularly over-confident, rash, or cocky. Use the prompts in the 'Overdoing It' section to explain how and why they 'overcooked' the virtue of courage.

Present your answers as a group, and discuss and evaluate them. Ideally, all three people would have been involved in the same scenario.

Underdoing it	Virtue: the golden mean	Overdoing it
The following act or omission would have shown cowardice:	The following act or omission would show courage:	The following act or omission would have shown rashness:
It shows excessive fear because...	It is striving to avoid harm by:	It shows excessive confidence because...
It shows insufficient confidence because...	It is overcoming fear by:	It shows insufficient fear and respect for the true dangers of the situation...
It shows a shirking of courageous acts by...	It is reducing risks of overconfidence and harm by:	It displays hallmarks of ostentation, or bragging, which may lead to significant harm and damage for the individual acting.

Further Points to Consider

- Were your role models acting rightly in situations where there is a risk of some bodily or psychological harm? And, was there a reasonable possibility of avoiding that harm? Was there a possibility of achieving something worthwhile and good?
- Was it really worth taking the risk of physical harm, or damage to confidence, for this particular goal?

- Did the potential gains and the probability of achieving them outweigh the potential losses and the probability of not avoiding them?
- What were the potential gains of acting?
- What were the probable gains? What were the potential losses? What were the probable losses?

4. Scenarios calling for courage

TASK 5

Thinking back:

Talk through a situation that called for you to act courageously. How did you handle it? Here are some suggestions:

- Have you resisted peer pressure?
- Have you spoken out about something that mattered, running against the tide of opinion?
- Have you acted for something worthwhile that could have caused you physical harm?

Thinking forward:

Identify or define a situation that is calling you to act more courageously. Remember, it must be a situation that triggers either 'fear' in you, or 'confidence'.

Use the Virtue Reasoning strategies set out above to work out what a courageous action will look like for you, in your scenario, and what a cowardly or rash one would look like.

Primary lesson plans

Below is a series of lesson plans on the virtue of gratitude for reception to year 6 classes. The lessons are taken from the Primary Character Education Programme of Study (2015a). The lessons below are provided as samples and the full programme is available from www.jubileecentre.ac.uk.

Reception: picture journals – session A

Gratitude is:

- Being thankful for what you have.
- Taking the time to show others that you are grateful.
- Appreciating the generosity of other people.

Description:

Being thankful for what you have and the kindness you receive from others. Taking the time to show others that you are thankful.

Synonyms:

- Saying thank you
- Grateful

Learning objectives:

Children will identify who they are thankful for and describe why.

Suggested resources:

Materials to create a picture brainstorm. For example, 'Gratitude' could be written in the middle of a large sugar paper circle and children's ideas could be written on paper petals.

Script:

Explain to children that today they are going to think about all the things in their lives that they enjoy doing. Who do we enjoy spending time with? What do we enjoy doing most with our time? How do we have fun at weekends? Take a range of answers from children. Explain that it is important to show people how much we enjoy spending time with them and how much we enjoy the things they let us do, like going to the park at the weekends or eating our favourite foods.

Suggested activities:

Give each child a white paper petal (this should be large enough to draw a picture). At tables, children can draw a picture of a person that makes their world a special one – for example, their mum or dad, siblings, aunt, cousin, best friend. Child should label their person and stick it to the centre of the class flower. Gather children on the carpet and ask a few to describe who they have drawn and why they are thankful for them.

Character coaching:

Meaningful praise: Well done – I like the way you have said thank you to that person because they did a kind thing for you.

Guidance: Remember that it is nice to be thankful to people that help you and show you kindness.

Correction: Remember that we should not ignore the kind things that people do for us. It is important to be thankful because it helps everybody get along happily.

Reception: picture journals – session B

Learning objectives:

To be able to identify people that we would like to thank, and to explain why we have chosen them.

Suggested resources:

Prompt cards – teachers may choose their own sentence starters. For example, 'I would like to thank you for…'

Script:

Remind children of this week's focus on being thankful for the things and people around you. In this lesson children will identify two people in school that they would like to say thank you to. Model this exercise for children. For example, by thinking of someone in the school and explaining why you have chosen them. Ask children to offer their two people and explanations.

Suggested activities:

Some children will have chosen friends in the class. Others will have chosen the school receptionist, caretaker, catering team, etc. Give children an opportunity to say thank you to the people they have chosen. If this means leaving the classroom, make sure children are accompanied by an adult. Give children prompt cards with appropriate sentence starters if they require support.

Character coaching:

Meaningful praise: Well done – I like the way you have said thank you to that person because they did a kind thing for you.

Guidance: Saying thank you shows that you have noticed when someone is kind to you. This can help us to make friends.

Correction: Remember that we should not ignore the kind things that people do for us. It is important to be thankful because it helps everybody get along happily.

Year 1: thank you cards – designing

Synonyms:

- Grateful
- Thank you

Learning objectives:

To be aware of someone outside school that we would like to thank. To be able to write a message of gratitude to someone.

Suggested resources:

Pencils and colouring pens/pencils.

Script:

Remind children of the messages they wrote in their previous lesson. Explain to children that today they will be making the front of their cards beautiful. Ask some children to remind the class of the person they are making their card for. What would be the best picture to draw? Steer children towards drawing something relevant. For example, a picture of the person being kind or the child being happy. Remind children that as part of being thankful for the kindness their person showed, they must put lots of effort into drawing a picture on the card. This will help to show the person that they really care.

Suggested activities:

Make sure that children have access to resources to decorate their cards. Gather children on the carpet to discuss how to get the cards to the right people. For example, the child could give the card on the way home from school (e.g. if it is for a lollipop lady) or when they next see the person. Until then they must keep it safe.

Character coaching:

Meaningful praise: Well done – I like the way you have said thank you to that person because they did a kind thing for you.

Guidance: Saying thank you shows that you have noticed when someone is kind to you. This can help us to make friends.

Correction: Remember that we should not ignore the kind things that people do for us. It is important to be thankful because it helps everybody get along happily.

Year 1: thank you cards – writing

Gratitude is:

- Being thankful for what you have.
- Taking the time to show others that you are grateful.
- Appreciating the generosity of other people.

Description:

Being thankful for what you have and the kindness you receive from others. Taking the time to show others that you are thankful.

Synonyms:

- Grateful
- Thank you

Learning objectives:

To be aware of someone outside school, that we would like to thank. To be able to write a message of gratitude to someone.

Suggested resources:

A5 pieces of lined paper. Next week these will be stuck into cards.

Script:

Make a class brainstorm of all the people children are thankful for. Make sure that children explain why they are thankful. Encourage children to think about being thankful – for example being thankful to the lollipop lady for keeping us safe, or to the smiley receptionist who always makes us laugh.

Tell children that today they are going to write inside a card to someone they would like to say thank you to. Write some important words on the whiteboard – 'Dear...', 'Thank you...', etc. Give children an opportunity to think of someone they would like to thank. Ask a couple of children for their sentences to prompt others to think along similar lines.

Suggested activities:

At tables, children write a short message on a piece of A5 lined paper to the person they would like to say thank you to. Make sure children explain why they are saying thank you. Support children with their writing as you would in a literacy lesson, with appropriate differentiation and equipment.

Character coaching:

Meaningful praise: Well done – I like the way you have said thank you to that person because they did a kind thing for you.

Guidance: Saying thank you shows that you have noticed when someone is kind to you. This can help us to make friends.

Correction: Remember that we should not ignore the kind things that people do for us. It is important to be thankful because it helps everybody get along happily.

Year 2: a visit from a school staff member

Gratitude is:

- Being thankful for what you have.
- Taking the time to show others that you are grateful.
- Appreciating the generosity of other people.

Learning objectives:

To increase our gratitude for the school staff by learning more about their work.

Suggested resources:

Ensure that the chosen member of staff, e.g. teacher, cook, administrator, lollipop lady, is fully prepared to talk about their role in the school and in the life of the local community.

Script:

Spend 15 minutes at the beginning of the lesson preparing children for the visit from the core school team. What do they already know about the work of this person? What would they like to know?

Brainstorm some questions. The purpose of this visit is for children to gain a better understanding of all the work that goes on to keep the school running.

Suggested activities:

Ask the member of the school team to introduce him/herself. How long have they been working at the school? Give children an opportunity to ask their questions. Encourage follow up questions. Make sure that children thank their visitor for taking the time to come to the classroom to share their work.

Character coaching:

Meaningful praise: Well done – I like the way you have said thank you to that person because they did a kind thing for you.

Guidance: Saying thank you shows that you have noticed when someone is kind to you. This can help us to make friends.

Correction: Remember that we should not ignore the kind things that people do for us. It is important to be thankful because it helps everybody get along happily.

Year 2: thanking the classroom visitor

Learning objectives:

To understand why we should express our gratitude to a school staff member. To be grateful for what we have and the kindness we receive from others.

Suggested Resources:

Card making materials – card, pencils, pens, art materials.

Script:

'Who visited us last week? Why do they play an important role in the school? Have you seen this person at work in school during the week? What were they doing? What did this mean for you – how has it helped you?' (Teachers may need to support children to understand the work of the visitor in their own experience of school.)

Suggested activities:

The children are going to make a thank you card. You can choose to make one large card with small messages and pictures from children, or a collection of individual cards. Ask the children to write their messages before they start decorating the cards. What would be a nice message for our visitor? What can we say that will tell them how thankful we are for their work in our school? Apply your classroom writing policy to this exercise (e.g. displaying tricky words, writing with pencil, reminders about capital letters, full stops, etc.). Once the children have written a message, give them an opportunity to decorate their cards. Encourage the children to think about a meaningful image – one that resonates with the message they have written. You may find it helpful to model this decision-making process.

Character coaching

Meaningful praise: Well done – I like the way you have said thank you to that person because they did a kind thing for you.

Guidance: Saying thank you shows that you have noticed when someone is kind to you. This can help us to make friends.

Correction: Remember that we should not ignore the kind things that people do for us. It is important to be thankful because it helps everybody get along happily.

Year 3: a visit from a school staff member

Gratitude is:

- being thankful for what you have.
- Taking the time to show others that you are grateful.
- Appreciating the generosity of other people.

Description:

To understand the work of a core member of staff from the school (for example, the caretaker, lollipop lady, receptionist, cook) by asking questions about their work around the school and their role in the community.

Synonyms:

- Grateful
- Thankful

Learning objectives:

To be able to express gratitude for what we have and the kindness we receive from others.

Suggested resources:

Ensure that the member of staff is fully prepared to talk about their role in the school and life in the local community.

Script:

Spend 15 minutes at the beginning of the lesson preparing children for the visit from the core school team. What do they already know about the work of this person? What would they like to know?

Brainstorm some questions. The purpose of this visit is for children to gain a better understanding of all the work that goes on to keep the school running.

Suggested activities:

Ask the member of the school team themselves. How long have they been working at the school? Give children an opportunity to ask their questions.

Encourage follow up questions. Make sure that children thank their visitor for taking the time to come to the classroom to share their work.

Character coaching:

Meaningful praise: Well done – I like the way you expressed your gratitude.

Guidance: Saying thank you shows that you have noticed when someone is kind to you. This is really important for making relationships and communities stronger.

Correction: Remember that we should not ignore the kind things that people do for us. It is important to be thankful because it helps everybody get along happily.

Year 3: thanking the classroom visitor

Learning objectives:

To be able to express gratitude to last week's visitor for their work in the school.
    To know why we should be grateful to people who help us.

Suggested resources:

Writing paper and pencils.

Script:

'Who visited us last week? Why do they play an important role in the school? Have you seen this person at work in school during the week? What were they doing? What did this mean for you – how has it helped you?' (Teachers may need to support children to understand the work of the visitor in their own experience of school.)

Suggested activities:

Write a class letter on the whiteboard thanking the visitor for their visit and their work in the school. Teachers should model good thank you letter writing, demonstrating, in particular, the importance of saying why you are thankful and how their work makes you feel. Take ideas from the class – this must be their letter. Once a draft has been produced on the carpet, give children an opportunity to write a best copy of their letter.

Character coaching:

Meaningful praise: Well done – I like the way you expressed your gratitude.

Guidance: Saying thank you shows that you have noticed when someone is kind to you. This is really important for making relationships and communities stronger.

Correction: Remember that we should not ignore the kind things that people do for us. It is important to be thankful because it helps everybody get along happily.

Year 4: a visit from the school cook

Gratitude is:

- Being thankful for what you have.
- Taking the time to show others that you are grateful.
- Appreciating the generosity of other people.

Synonyms:

- Grateful
- Thankful

Learning objectives:

To learn about the work of a member of staff from the school, for example the caretaker, the lollipop lady, receptionist, or cook.

Suggested resources:

Ensure that the member of staff is fully prepared to talk about their role in the school and life in the local community.

Script:

Spend 15 minutes at the beginning of the lesson preparing children for the visit from the core school team. What do they already know about the work of this person? What would they like to know?

Brainstorm some questions. The purpose of this visit is for children to gain a better understanding of all the work that goes on to keep the school running.

Suggested activities:

Ask the member of the school team to introduce him/herself. How long have they been working at the school? Give children an opportunity to ask their questions. Encourage follow up questions. Make sure that children thank their visitor for taking the time to come to the classroom to share their work.

Character coaching:

Meaningful praise: Well done – I like the way you expressed your gratitude. Did you notice the effect that it had on the staff members? What effect do you think it would have on the school if all of us did this?

Guidance: Saying thank you shows that you have noticed when someone is kind to you. This is really important for making relationships and communities stronger.

Correction: Remember that we should not ignore the kind things that people do for us. It is important to be thankful because it helps everybody get along happily.

Year 4: writing a class thank you letter

Learning objectives:

To be able to express our gratitude to last week's visitor by writing an individual thank you letter explaining why we are grateful for their work, and how this makes us feel.

Suggested resources:

Writing paper and pencils.

Script:

'Who visited us last week? Why do they play an important role in the school? Have you seen this person at work in school during the week? What were they doing? What did this mean for you – how has it helped you?' (Teachers may need to support children to understand the work of the visitor in their own experience of school.)

Suggested activities:

Children will be familiar by now with writing thank you letters. In Year 3 they wrote a class thank you letter to another visitor. Remind children of the objective of this letter – to express their gratitude for the hard work of the visitor and the impact this has on their experience at school. Write some key words on the board as prompts for children; children may use these in their writing. For example, 'grateful', 'thankful', 'feel', 'make a difference', etc. Apply your classroom writing policy to this lesson, for example by giving reminders or writing equipment to pupils. Ensure that once best copies of the letters are complete that children have an opportunity to share their writing and, crucially, give their letter to the school visitor. As there may be many letters, you may choose to display these on a special 'Gratitude' display wall.

Character coaching:

Meaningful praise: Well done – I like the way you expressed your gratitude. What was it like to write the letter and to have it read?

Guidance: Saying thank you shows that you have noticed when someone is kind to you. This is really important for making relationships and communities stronger.

Correction: Remember that we should not ignore the kind things that people do for us. It is important to be thankful because it helps everybody get along happily.

Year 5: where did that come from? – session A

Gratitude is:

- Being thankful for what you have.
- Taking the time to show others that you are grateful.
- Appreciating the generosity of other people.

Description:

Being thankful for what you have and the kindness you receive from others. Taking the time to show others that you are thankful.

Synonyms:

- Grateful
- Thankful

Learning objectives:

To be able to trace the journey of common classroom objects from their origin and think about who provided them and how they get there.

Suggested resources:

A set of common classroom things – for example, an apple, a ruler, a musical instrument; access to the Internet, writing paper and pencils.

Script:

Explain to children that every single item in the classroom has a story to tell. It did not just appear in the classroom from nowhere. Sometimes, lots of people have helped make things that have made their way to the classroom. Today, children are going to investigate who was involved in the 'stories' behind each object, and how. Model this activity to children with an object, for example an apple. Did the apple grow by itself in the classroom? Where do you think it came from? Model searching for its origin using the Internet and an interactive whiteboard. How did it start out in life? Search for pictures of orchards and people planting seedlings. What happened to it next? How did it get from the orchard to the factory where it was cleaned, sorted and bagged? Continue this investigation until you get to the classroom. How many people do you think were involved in making sure we had a delicious break-time snack?

Suggested activities:

Divide the class into small groups and ensure each group has access to a computer with the Internet. Give each group an object or let them choose one themselves and set them to task finding out where, how and who was involved in getting it to the classroom. Make sure that children have access to writing paper and pencils to make notes. They may also want to print some pictures. Explain to children that next week they will be making posters of their object's journey to the classroom and presenting them to the rest of the class.

Year 5: where did that come from? – session B

Learning objectives:

To be able to trace the journey of common classroom objects from their origin and think about who provided them and how they get there.

Suggested resources:

Poster making materials – pens, paper, glue, etc. Children will also need their notes and printouts from the previous lesson.

Script:

This lesson follows on from the previous lesson. Remind children of the task you set them last week. Explain that this week they will be making posters of their object's journey to the classroom. What could they include on their poster? At the end of the lesson they will be presenting their work to the rest of the class.

Suggested activities:

Set children to task creating posters using the information they gathered in the previous lesson. Ensure that everyone stops in time for children to give presentations about the story of their object.

Character coaching:

Meaningful praise: Well done – I like the way you expressed your gratitude. What effect do you think it would have on the people involved in this journey to see your appreciation? What effect do you think it would have if we always showed this much appreciation for the things we take for granted?

Guidance: Remember that it is important to show gratitude to the people that are kind to us or help us.

Who needs your gratitude most today?

Correction: Remember that we should not ignore the kind things that people do for us. It is important to be thankful because it helps everybody get along happily.

Please think how you could express your gratitude to that person in a meaningful way.

Year 6: reflecting on gratitude – session A

Gratitude is:

- Being thankful for what you have.
- Taking the time to show others that you are grateful.
- Appreciating the generosity of other people.

Description:

Being thankful for what you have and the kindness you receive from others. Taking the time to show others that you are thankful.

Synonyms:

- Grateful
- Thankful

Learning objectives:

To be able to answer questions about the good things that have happened in their lives; to reflect on who enabled these good things to happen.

Suggested resources:

Clipboards, with printout of questions, and writing paper for children to take notes.

Script:

This lesson takes place over two sessions. In this first lesson, half of the class will interview the other half about something good that has happened in their lives recently. (In the second lesson, the groups swap around.) Teacher and Teaching Assistant can model the interview process, but first set out some ground rules – what makes a good interviewer? What makes a good interviewee? Run through the key questions that you want children to explore. Tell me about a good thing that has happened recently? Why did this good thing happen? What does this good thing mean to you? What can you do tomorrow to enable more of this good thing? What ways did you or others contribute to this good thing? You may add questions to clarify and build on answers as appropriate.

Suggested activities:

Organise children into pairs. This week one child will be the interviewer and the other the interviewee. Next week they will swap around. Send children to quiet corners of the classroom for this activity. You may want to give children clipboards with the questions and a piece of lined paper for notes. Once pairs have completed the activity, bring everyone to the carpet for the interviewers to share some of their findings.

Character coaching:

Meaningful praise: Thank you for your contribution to the lesson today. You listened really closely when you were interviewing.

Guidance: Remember that it is important to show gratitude to the people that are kind to us or help us.

Who needs your gratitude most today?

Correction: I noticed that you found it hard to listen when you were interviewing. Can you tell me what you think it was like for your interviewee to not be listened to fully? What do you need to do differently next time to listen really well?

Year 6: reflecting on gratitude – session B

Learning objectives:

To be able to answer questions about the good things that have happened in their lives; to reflect on who enabled these good things to happen.

Suggested resources:

Clipboards, printout of questions and writing paper for children to take notes.

Script:

This lesson builds on the previous lesson. See last week's lesson plan for a recap of the circle session. You may use this time to address issues that children had during their interviews last week.

Suggested activities:

In the same pairs as the last week, children should swap roles as interviewer and interviewee. Follow the same format as last week, giving pairs of children time, space and the clipboards to interview their partner. Ensure there is some time for the interviewers to feedback to the whole class at the end of the lesson.

Notes

1   See further *Blame My Brain* by Nicola Morgan (esp. p. 29 and 40 ff.).
2   An article about Gerry Conlon: http://thejusticegap.com/2014/06/days-wish-still-prison-days-wish-dead-2/
3   An article about Gareth Peirce: http://www.theguardian.com/law/2010/oct/12/gareth-peirce-fight-human-rights.

Appendix A

A framework for character education in schools

The document *A Framework for Character Education in Schools* was developed by the Jubilee Centre in consultation with head teachers, parents, academics, employers and young people both in Britain and internationally. It calls for all schools to be explicit about how they develop the character virtues of their students and explains the important role teachers play in making and shaping the character of young people to be properly recognised by parents, policymakers and employees.

Introduction

Developing children's characters is an obligation on us all, not least on parents. Although parents are the primary educators of character, empirical research shows they want *all* adults who have contact with their children to contribute to such education, especially their children's teachers. The development of character is a process that requires the efforts of both the developing individual and the society and its schools. A society determined to enable its members to live well will treat character education as something to which every child has a right. Questions about the kinds of persons children will become, the contributions of good character to a flourishing life and how to balance various virtues and values in this process are therefore salient concerns for all schools. Interest is now being shown in character across a variety of UK schools. The aim of this Framework is to provide a *rationale* and a *practical outlet* for that interest.

No one doubts that belonging to a school community is a deeply formative experience that helps make students the kinds of persons they become. In a wide sense, character education permeates all subjects, wider school activities and general school ethos; it cultivates the virtues of character associated with common morality and develops students' understanding and embrace of what is excellent in diverse spheres of human endeavour. Schools do and should aid students in knowing the good, loving the good and doing the good. Schools should enable students to become good persons and citizens, able to lead good as well as 'successful' lives. Schooling is concerned centrally with the formation of character and benefits from an intentional and planned approach to character development.

Human flourishing is the widely accepted goal of life. To flourish is not only to be happy, but to fulfil one's potential. Flourishing is the aim of character education, which is critical to its achievement. *Human flourishing* requires *moral, intellectual* and *civic* virtues, *excellences* specific to diverse domains of practice or human endeavour, and generic virtues of *self-management* (known as *enabling* and *performance* virtues). All are necessary to achieve the highest potential in life.

Character education is about the acquisition and strengthening of virtues: the traits that sustain a well-rounded life and a thriving society. Schools should aim to develop confident and compassionate students who are effective contributors to society, successful learners and responsible citizens. Students also need to grow in their understanding of what is good or valuable, and their ability to protect and advance what is good. They need to develop a commitment to serving others, which is an essential manifestation of good character in action. Questions of character formation are inseparable from these educational goals and are fundamental to living well and living responsibly. Character development involves caring for and respecting others, as well as caring for and respecting oneself.

Character education is no novelty. If we look at the history of schooling from ancient to modern times, the cultivation of character was typically given pride of place, with the exception of a few decades towards the end of the twentieth century, when this aim disappeared from curricula, for a variety of reasons, in many Western democracies.

Contemporary character education is, however, better grounded academically than some of its predecessors, with firm support both from the currently dominant *virtue ethics* in moral philosophy and recent trends in social science, such as *positive psychology*, that have revived the concepts of character and virtue. Finally, a growing general public-policy consensus, across political parties and industry, suggests that the role of moral and civic character is pivotal in sustaining healthy economies and democracies.

What character education is

Character is a set of personal traits or dispositions that produce specific emotions, inform motivation and guide conduct. *Character education* is an umbrella term for all explicit and implicit educational activities that help young people develop positive personal strengths called *virtues*. Character education is more than just a subject; it has a place in the culture and functions of families, classrooms, schools and other institutions. Character education is about helping students grasp what is ethically important in situations and act for the right reasons, such that they become more autonomous and reflective. Students need to decide the kind of person they wish to become and to learn to choose between alternatives. In this process, the ultimate aim of character education is the development of *good sense* or practical wisdom: the capacity to choose intelligently between alternatives. This capacity involves knowing how to choose the right course of action in difficult situations, and it arises gradually out of the experience of making choices and growth of ethical insight.

What character education is not

Character education is *not* about moral indoctrination and mindless conditioning. The ultimate goal of all proper character education is to equip students with the intellectual tools to choose wisely of their own accord within the framework of a democratic society. Critical thinking is thus an ineluctable facet of a well-rounded character. Character and virtue are *not* essentially religious notions although they do clearly have a place in religious systems. Almost all current theories of virtue and character education happen to be couched in a post-religious language. Character and virtue are *not* paternalistic notions. If being 'paternalistic' means that character education goes against the wishes of students and their parents, empirical research shows the opposite. More generally speaking, the character of children cannot simply be put on hold at school until they reach the age where they have become wise enough to decide for themselves. Some form of character education will always take place in any school. The sensible question that can be asked about a school's character-education strategy is not, therefore, whether such education does occur, but whether it is intentional, planned, organised and reflective, or assumed, unconscious, reactive and random. The emphasis on character and virtue is *not* conservative or individualist – all about 'fixing the kids'. The ultimate aim of character education is not only to make individuals better persons but to create the social and institutional conditions within which all human beings can flourish. Character education is *not* about promoting the moral ideals of a particular moral system. Rather, it aims at the promotion of a core set of universally acknowledged (cosmopolitan) virtues and values.

Key principles

- Character is educable and its progress can be measured holistically, not only through self-reports but also more objective research methods.
- Character is important: it contributes to human and societal flourishing.
- Character is largely caught through role-modelling and emotional contagion: school culture and ethos are therefore essential.
- Character should also be taught: direct teaching of character provides the rationale, language and tools to use in developing character elsewhere in and out of school.
- Character is the foundation for improved attainment, better behaviour and increased employability.
- Character should be developed in partnership with parents, employers and other community organisations.
- Character results in academic gains for students, such as higher grades.
- Character education is about fairness and each child has a right to character development.
- Character empowers students and is liberating.
- Character demonstrates a readiness to learn from others.
- Character promotes democratic citizenship.

What virtues constitute good character?

Individuals can respond well or not to the challenges they face in everyday life, and the moral virtues are those character traits that enable human beings to respond appropriately to situations in any area of experience. These character traits enable people to live, cooperate and learn with others in a way that is peaceful, neighbourly and morally justifiable. Displaying moral and other virtues in admirable activity over the course of a life, and enjoying the inherent satisfaction that entails is what it means to live a flourishing life.

No definitive list of relevant areas of human experience and the respective virtues can be given, as the virtues will to a certain extent be relative to individual constitution, developmental stage and social circumstance. For example, temperance in eating will be different for an Olympic athlete and an office worker; what counts as virtuous behaviour for a teenager may not pass muster for a mature adult; and the virtues needed to survive in a war zone may not be the same as those in a peaceful rural community. There are also a great many virtues, each concerned with particular activities and potential spheres of human experience. It is, therefore, neither possible nor desirable to provide an exhaustive list of the moral virtues that should be promoted in all schools. Moreover, particular schools may decide to prioritise certain virtues over others in light of the school's history, ethos, location or specific student population. Nevertheless, a list of *prototypical* virtues – that will be recognised and embraced by representatives of all cultures and religions – can be suggested and drawn upon in character education. The list below contains examples of such virtues that have been foregrounded in some of the most influential philosophical and religious systems of morality – and that also resonate well with current efforts at character education in schools:

Virtue	Definition
Courage	Acting with bravery in fearful situations
Justice	Acting with fairness towards others by honouring rights and responsibilities
Honesty	Being truthful and sincere
Compassion	Exhibiting care and concern for others
Self-discipline	Acting well in the presence of tempting pleasures
Gratitude	Feeling and expressing thanks for benefits received
Humility/modesty	Estimating oneself within reasonable limits

Furthermore, every morally developing human being will need one extra virtue which the ancient Greeks called *phronesis*, which can also be called 'good sense' – the overall quality of knowing what to want and what not to want when the demands of two or more virtues collide, and to integrate such demands into an acceptable course of action. Living with good sense entails: considered deliberation, well founded judgement and the vigorous enactment of decisions. It reveals itself in foresight, in being clear sighted and far sighted about the ways in which actions will lead to desired goals. The ability to learn from experience (and make mistakes) is at the centre of it. To live with good sense is to be open-minded, to recognise the true variety of things and situations to be experienced. To live without 'good sense' is to live thoughtlessly and indecisively. 'Bad sense' shows itself in irresoluteness, or remissness in carrying out decisions and in negligence and blindness to our circumstances. To live without 'good sense' is to be narrow-minded and close-minded; it can reveal itself in an attitude of 'cocksure' – 'know-it-all' that resists reality. 'Good sense' cannot be confused with 'cunning'; 'cunning' reveals itself in non-moral straining for any self-chosen good. 'Good sense' forms part of all the other virtues; indeed, it constitutes the overarching *meta-virtue* necessary for good character. It requires a well-rounded assessment of situations, thinking through and looking ahead to potential actions and consequences.

Virtues are empowering and are the key to fulfilling an individual's potential. Because of the foundational role of the virtues in human flourishing, schools have a responsibility to cultivate the virtues, define and list those they want to prioritise and integrate them into all teaching and learning in and out of school. Students therefore need to learn their meanings and identify appropriate practices in which to apply them in their lives, *respecting themselves* (as persons of character) and rendering *service* to others.

In addition to the moral virtues, all human beings need personal traits that enable them to manage their lives effectively. These traits are sometimes called *performance virtues* and *enabling virtues*, to distinguish them from the specifically moral ones. In contemporary school-policy discourse, they are commonly referred to as 'soft skills'. One of the most significant of those is *resilience* or grit – the ability to bounce back from negative experiences. Others include determination, confidence, creativity and teamwork. All good programmes of character education will include the cultivation of performance virtues, but they will also explain to students that those virtues derive their ultimate value from serving morally acceptable ends, in particular from being enablers and vehicles of the moral virtues.

The goals of character education

It is common for a school to outline the goals of education in its mission statement, and a school that seeks to strengthen the character of its students should reaffirm its commitment to doing so in its mission statement.

Each school needs to describe the kinds of future citizens it wants to help develop and then outline the philosophy that underlies its approach. The philosophy and approach should involve clear ethical expectations of students and teachers and modelling by teachers to guide the building of individual virtues in students. Schools should provide opportunities for students to not just think and do, but also understand what it means to be and become a mature, reflective person. They should help prepare students for the tests of life, rather than simply a life of tests.

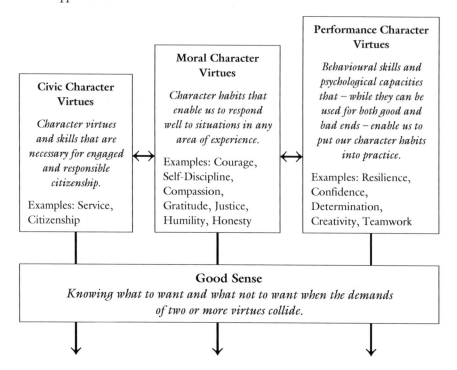

Civic Character Virtues

Character virtues and skills that are necessary for engaged and responsible citizenship.

Examples: Service, Citizenship

Moral Character Virtues

Character habits that enable us to respond well to situations in any area of experience.

Examples: Courage, Self-Discipline, Compassion, Gratitude, Justice, Humility, Honesty

Performance Character Virtues

Behavioural skills and psychological capacities that – while they can be used for both good and bad ends – enable us to put our character habits into practice.

Examples: Resilience, Confidence, Determination, Creativity, Teamwork

Good Sense
Knowing what to want and what not to want when the demands of two or more virtues collide.

Flourishing Individuals and Societies

School ethos based on character

The research evidence is clear: schools that are values-driven have high expectations and demonstrate academic success. They are committed and determined to develop the character of their students through the articulation, demonstration and commitment to core ethical virtues. Because the ethos of a school is the expression of the collective character of everyone, it is important for every member of a school community to have some basic understanding of what character is. Students and teachers therefore need to learn not only the names of character virtues, but display them in the school's thinking, attitudes and actions. Character virtues should be reinforced everywhere: on the playing fields, in classrooms, corridors, interactions between teachers and students, in assemblies, posters, head teacher messages and communications, staff training, and in relations with parents. They are critical in extra-curricular activities and should translate into positive feelings and behaviour. The process of being educated in virtue is not only one of acquiring ideas. It is about belonging and living within a community – for schools are, together with the family, one of the principal means by which students grow in virtue.

Teachers as character educators

Character education builds on what already happens in schools and most teachers see character cultivation as a core part of their role. Considerations of character, of the kind of person students hope to become, should be at the heart of teaching and education. The virtues acquired through experience by students are initially under the guidance of parents and teachers who serve as role models and moral exemplars.

In order to be a good teacher, one needs to be, or to become a certain *kind of person*: a person of good character who also exemplifies commitment to the value of what she teaches. The character and integrity of the teacher is more fundamental than personality or personal style in class, and it is no less important than mastery of subject content and techniques of instruction. Teaching a subject with integrity concerns more than helping students to acquire specific bits of knowledge and skills.

Good teaching is underpinned by an ethos and language that enables a public discussion of character within the school community so that good character permeates all subject teaching and learning. It also models commitment to the forms of excellence or goodness inherent in the subject matter: the qualities of craftsmanship, artistry, careful reasoning and investigations, beauty and power of language, and deep understanding made possible by the disciplines. Such commitment is important if students are to learn the value of what is taught and learn to do work that is good and personally meaningful.

Although a clear picture is emerging of the inescapability of character education, teachers often complain that they suffer from moral ambivalence and lack of self-confidence in their (inescapable) professional position as role models and character educators. Repeated empirical studies show that teachers find it difficult to address ethical issues in the classroom. Although many teachers possess a strong interest in moral issues, they are not always adequately trained to critically reflect upon and convey moral views to their students in a sophisticated way. Unfortunately, the recent surge in interest in character education has so far failed to make an impact on teacher education and training. Indeed, contemporary policy discourse, with its amoral, instrumentalist, competence-driven vocabulary, often seems to shy away from perspectives that embrace normative visions of persons in the context of their whole lives. The lack of teacher education programmes with a coherent approach to character education is most likely the result of more dominant principles of grade attainment and classroom management. This seems a lost opportunity, however, given the commonly expressed desire among trainee teachers to make a moral difference. It is fitting to end this Framework document with a call for increased attention to moral issues, in general, and character-educational issues, in particular, in teacher education and training.

Appendix B

Statement on teacher education and character education[1]

Parents entrust their children to schools, into the care of teachers, for the purposes of education. With young people spending a considerable proportion of their time in schools, it is important to consider the qualities possessed by teachers who have such a formative impact on their pupils. What makes a good teacher? What kind of person must he or she be? It is not only the content of what a teacher teaches directly, but what they model in practice, as ethical exemplars, which is important. As David Carr (2007) argues:

> It is often said that we remember teachers as much for the kinds of people they were than for anything they may have taught us, and some kinds of professional expertise may best be understood as qualities of character.

The role of the classroom teacher requires much public trust and a greater level of moral responsibility than many other professions. Good teachers are expected to challenge pupils' minds and shape their characters. As the Jubilee Centre (2015; Statement on Teacher Education) notes, 'the single most powerful tool you have to impact a student's character is your own character'. Good teaching should cultivate the virtues and promote good moral character. Teaching that is grounded primarily in subject knowledge and teaching expertise, skill or 'competence' does not capture the essential meaning of the occupation.

Schools ought to promote a positive moral climate that encourages teachers to exemplify the virtues that constitute such climates. The challenge facing teachers and teacher educators in this regard is whether to allow moral formation to occur unaided, letting pupils learn what they will, for good or bad, come what may; or whether to engage in intentional, transparent and deliberative approaches that attend seriously to the moral dimensions of teaching and schooling. In addition to setting examples to their pupils and peers, there are other reasons why good teachers should want their interactions with others to satisfy the requirements of morality: such reasons concern general moral aspirations towards others, professional aspirations and aspirations towards personal moral growth.

Virtues and teaching

Ethical development and character formation does not happen by chance. It should be embraced by a deliberate and planned pedagogy. As educators the language we use is a powerful tool developing character and helping pupils make progress in their moral development.

In 1995, the Universities Committee for the Education of Teachers (UCET) established a working party to formulate some ethical principles for teaching. The working party identified eleven principles fundamental to good or professionally acceptable teaching and they are worth summarising here (Tomlinson & Little, 2000: 152–154):

Teachers must have:

1 intellectual integrity;
2 vocational integrity;
3 moral courage;
4 altruism;
5 impartiality;
6 insight;
7 responsibility for their influence;
8 humility;
9 collegiality;
10 capacities for partnership; and
11 vigilance concerning professional responsibilities and aspirations.

This list identifies some of the key obligations of teachers, particularly their moral obligations, with a clear emphasis on courage, altruism, humility, and integrity.

No definitive list of relevant virtues can be given, but a list of prototypical virtues can be suggested and drawn upon for teacher education. The virtues may be categorised into four types, *moral, civic, performance* and *intellectual*. It is important for all four to work in collaboration for positive human flourishing. However, particular schools may choose to prioritise certain virtues (recognising a variety and diversity in educational practice) over others in light of a school's history, ethos, location or specific student population.

Teacher education should seek to prioritise the development of all four of the types of virtues.

These are:

Moral Virtues: Those virtues that enable us to respond well to situations in any area of experience. Examples of moral virtues include courage, self-discipline, compassion, gratitude, justice, humility and honesty.

Performance Virtues: Those virtues that can be used for both good and bad ends the qualities that enable us to manage our lives effectively. The virtue most commonly mentioned in this category is resilience – the ability to bounce back from negative experiences. Others include determination, confidence and teamwork.

The ultimate value of these virtues is being enablers and vehicles of the moral, civic and intellectual virtues.

Civic Virtues: Those virtues that are necessary for engaged and responsible citizenship and political literacy. They include service, citizenship and volunteering. Thus, part of good character involves the active display of civic virtues for the benefit of others and society more generally.

Intellectual Virtues: Those virtues that are necessary for right action and correct thinking. They are required for the pursuit of knowledge, truth and understanding.

It is important to single out what the Greeks called *phronesis*, but we can call 'good sense'. This is the overall quality of knowing what to want and what not to want when the demands of two or more virtues compete with one another and to integrate such demands into an acceptable course of action (see Cooke & Carr, 2014). Living with good sense entails considered deliberation, well founded judgement and the enactment of decisions. It is revealed in foresight, in being clear sighted and far sighted about the ways to achieve desired goals. The ability to learn from experience and mistakes is at the heart of 'good sense'. It is, therefore, an essential virtue for the education of teachers.

At the start of their careers, many teachers are motivated to choose their profession for its moral content (Sanger & Osguthorpe, 2011); further, research demonstrates that people enter the teaching profession from a desire to make a difference to children's lives and to develop good people (Arthur *et al.*, 2015). Sadly, however, this early moral aspiration is not adequately developed in teacher training and beyond. There is also a reported lack of moral *self-knowledge* among teachers. Indeed, Sockett & LePage (2002) found that a number of teachers at the beginning of a non-traditional graduate programme could not critically reflect on themselves as moral agents. An ideally good teacher is a certain sort of person, who exhibits pedagogical *phronesis* in their dealings with students. Such a view of teaching as a moral profession clearly calls for a richer account of the nature and requirements of teacher training, and even for the revival of the age-old idea of teaching as a moral vocation.

Teacher education and character education

Student teachers expect to engage with values and values-related issues during their formal education, and such engagement ought to influence their own values and attitudes. Personal and professional values often play a significant role in the selection process for entrance to teacher education and applicants ought to be encouraged to reflect on such values throughout teacher education courses and their lives as teachers. Recently, the APPG on Social Mobility and the Carter Review on Teacher Education have both called for character education to form part of teacher education. The official Teaching Standards for teacher education make clear that teachers must make the education of their pupils their first concern and that they are accountable for achieving the highest possible standards in their conduct. The expectations that underlie the judgement for the award of Qualified Teacher Status presuppose a high level of mutual respect between teacher, parent and pupil. The student teacher needs to achieve the required standards by demonstrating professional behaviour and showing respect for pupils, colleagues and parents, as well as for gaining the respect of others through their own actions and behaviours.

Good teacher education depends a great deal on the ethos of individual schools wherein trainees should learn how to become teachers with character. School culture is influenced by the wider educational culture and priorities of the era that are set out by the government and other authorities. The overwhelming, bureaucratic dynamic of some schools is likely to diminish moral judgement and decision making in favour of a network of tests and audits, engulfing students and teachers alike with an imperative to defer to authority for rewards and punishments. In other schools, however, teachers describe holistic school policies rooted in broad and encompassing philosophies. Attempts to improve the quality of teaching through standards, inspections, incentives, performance management, competency criteria, tests, indeed anything that is quantifiable and easily measured have too often resulted in quantification replacing wisdom. The worth of teaching, and teachers themselves, is largely seen in terms of the economic value of qualifications. Little attention is paid officially to purpose, to questions of meaning, and the ends to which a pupil's acquired knowledge, skills and understanding will be used. The teacher is portrayed as a technician charged with specific tasks which are measurable in outcome rather than on what the teacher is and can become. As Carr (2016) argues:

> A significant problem to which such work has responded has been recent official or centralist policy promotion of technicist models of professional practice that have sought to reduce teaching to the mastery of a repertoire of behaviourally conceived teaching skills or 'competences' for the purposes of teacher.

It is not possible to detail the full range of human abilities and qualities of a teacher within the concept of competence.

Debating whether or not teachers ought to engage in building the character of their students is a sign that we have asked the wrong question. The more important question is 'how do we prepare teachers to engage with the positive character formation of their pupils?'

Evidence

Parents are the primary educators of their children's character, but a poll conducted by Populus (2013a) shows that parents want all adults who have contact with their children to contribute to such education, especially teachers.

A 2015 Jubilee Centre study of 546 novice and experienced teachers and their educators found that ethics has always played a central role in good education and practice (Arthur *et al.*, 2015). The Jubilee Centre's work has sought to develop and advance previous research in the field. In 1993, Joseph and Efron's study examined 180 teachers' understandings of themselves as moral agents and discovered that teachers perceived their role not only as that of teaching subject matter, but also exhibiting and imparting moral values. Further studies have found that some teachers consider the moral dimensions of education to be even more important than academic success (Tuff, 2009). Across selected schools in Europe, Puurula & colleagues (2001) found that most teachers viewed affective education as part of their role. Although many teachers possess a strong interest in moral issues, they rarely consider themselves adequately trained to critically reflect upon these in any sophisticated way (Sockett & LePage, 2002). Indeed, experienced teachers typically have called for an increased focus on moral reflective practice in teacher training (Arthur *et al.*, 2015).

Recommendations for teacher education

The following recommendations seek to ensure that teacher education addresses the moral complexities of the teacher's role.

- encourage all new teachers to reflect on why they entered the profession: to define their sense of purpose. Teacher educators should stress the importance of the role in transforming both young people as well as their contribution to flourishing societies;
- increase the focus on the moral development of teachers in both initial teacher training and continued professional development;
- create space in courses for the critical, moral reflection on practice and how teachers might identify and/or address moral dilemmas;
- schools should recruit new teachers on their compatibility with a schools' mission and values based ethos; and
- ensure a greater recognition of the importance of mentoring in the education of teachers. This would include giving proper time, space, recognition and reward to those who carry out this extremely important role.

Conclusion

The conception of teaching as a moral profession is not a recent one. It is however one that has lost ground to other competing agendas in recent years. The emphasis on the character and conduct of teachers themselves requires an appropriate moral focus in the education of teachers. The character and integrity of the teacher is fundamental and it is no less important than mastery of subject content and teaching techniques. This is why teachers should not only exemplify positive character traits to their pupils, but also help the pupils to reflect on their own character strengths and weaknesses.

Knowledge of the virtues will not necessarily change behaviour. A pupil can understand, through teaching, what the most desirable virtue to display in certain circumstances may be, but be unable to translate this knowledge into positive action. This is why the gap between understanding virtues, on the one hand, and virtues in action, on the other, requires modelling by teachers and parents. In this sense, teacher education should be understood as a process of formation of the person as a teacher. Proposals to promote and encourage character building, indeed the flourishing of the next generation, ought to be welcomed by all.

> For centuries, the concept of the teacher as a moral educator of the new generation has endured as both a stated objective of the professional role and an implicit inevitability of its moral agency...Moral education, as it is broadly conceived, includes both what teachers as ethical exemplars model in the course of their daily practice and what moral lessons they teach directly either through the formal curriculum or the informal dynamics of classroom and school life.
>
> (Campbell, 2003: 47).

Note

1 This statement was developed through a consultation at St. George's House, Windsor, on 9 and 10 September 2015. It recaps much of the content of Chapter 1 while adding specific recommendations. The consultation was initiated by the Jubilee Centre for Character and Virtues and attended by teacher educators, teachers and other representatives from the following organisations:

University of Birmingham
Queen Elizabeth's Grammar School, Ashbourne
Oxford Brookes University
The University of Birmingham School
Holy Cross Catholic Primary School
Museum of World Religions
Ark Boulton Academy, Birmingham
Redhill School, Stourbridge
Wellington College
University of York
University of Edinburgh
Teach First
DEMOS
University of Sussex
The Church of England Office
SSAT
Arnett Hills JM Primary School
Wigmore High School
Kings Langley School, Herts
Kelhelland School, Cornwall
Floreat Brentford and Wandsworth
Kings Leadership School

The Laurels School
ACE

For more information about the statement please contact
The Jubilee Centre for Character and Virtues
w: www.jubileecentre.ac.uk
e: jubileecentre@contacts.bham.ac.uk
t: 0121 414 3602

References

Adams, R. M. (2006) *A Theory of Virtue: Excellence in being for the good*. Oxford: Oxford University Press.

Allport, G. W. (1937) *Personality: A psychological interpretation*. New York: Holt.

Annas, J. (1993) *The Morality of Happiness*. Oxford: Oxford University Press.

Annas, J. (2011) *Intelligent Virtue*. Oxford: Oxford University Press.

Aristotle (1975) *The Nicomachean Ethics*, trans. H. Rackham. Cambridge, MA: Harvard University Press.

Aristotle (1985) *Nicomachean Ethics*, trans. T. Irwin. Indianapolis: Hackett Publishing.

Arthur, J. (2001) *Schools and Community*. London: Routledge.

Arthur, J. (2003) *Education with Character: The moral economy of schooling*. London: RoutledgeFalmer.

Arthur, J. (2005) The Re-Emergence of Character Education in British Education Policy. *British Journal of Educational Studies*, 53(3), pp. 239–254.

Arthur, J. (2010a) *Of Good Character: Exploration of virtues and values in 3–25 year olds*. Exeter: Imprint Academic.

Arthur, J. (2010b) *Citizens of Character: New directions in character and values education*. Exeter: Imprint Academic.

Arthur, J. (2011) Personal Character and Tomorrow's Citizens: Student expectations of their teachers. *International Journal of Educational Research*, 50(3), pp. 184–189.

Arthur, J. and Carr, D. (2013) Character in Learning for Life: A virtue-ethical rationale for recent research on moral and values education. *Journal of Beliefs & Values*, 34(1), pp. 26–35.

Arthur, J., Harrison, T., Carr, D., Kristjánsson, K. and Davison, I. (2014) *The Knightly Virtues: Enhancing Virtue Literacy through Stories*. Research report. Birmingham: University of Birmingham, Jubilee Centre for Character and Virtues. Retrieved 15 October, 2014, from http://www.jubileecentre.ac.uk/userfiles/jubileecentre/pdf/KV%20New%20PDF/KnightlyVirtuesReport.pdf.

Arthur, J., Kristjánsson, K., Cooke, S., Brown, E. and Carr, D. (2015a) *The Good Teacher: Understanding virtues in practice*. Research report. Birmingham: University of Birmingham, Jubilee Centre for Character and Virtues. Retrieved 20 July, 2015, from www.jubileecentre.ac.uk/userfiles/jubileecentre/pdf/Research%20Reports/The_Good_Teacher_Understanding_Virtues_in_Practice.pdf.

Arthur, J., Kristjánsson, K., Walker, D., Sanderse, W., Jones, C., Thoma, S., Curren, R. and Roberts, M. (2015b) *Character Education in UK Schools*. Research report. Birmingham: Jubilee Centre for Character and Virtues. Retrieved 9 April, 2015, from http://www.jubileecentre.ac.uk/userfiles/jubileecentre/pdf/Research%20 Reports/Character_Education_in_UK_Schools.pdf.

Arthur, J., Harrison, T. and Taylor, E. (2015c) *Building Character through Youth Social Action*. Research report. Birmingham: University of Birmingham, Jubilee Centre for Character and Virtues. Retrieved 1 October 15, 2015, from http://www.jubileecentre.ac.uk/userfiles/jubileecentre/pdf/Research%20Reports/Building_Character_Through_Youth_Social_Action.pdf.

Arthur, J., Harrison, T. and Davison, I. (2015d) *Levels of Virtue Literacy in Catholic, Church of England and Non-Faith Schools in England: A research report*, International Studies in Catholic Education. Retrieved 30 October, 2015, from http://www.tandfonline.com/doi/abs/10.1080/19422539.2015.1072957.

Arweck, E., Nesbitt, E. and Jackson, R. (2005) Common Values for the Common School? Using two values education programmes to promote 'spiritual and moral development'. *Journal of Moral Education, 34*(3), pp. 325–342.

Badwar, N. K. (2014) *Well-Being. Happiness in a worthwhile life*. Oxford: Oxford University Press.

Baumeister, R. F. and Exline, J. J. (1999) Virtue, Personality, and Social Relations: Self-control as the moral muscle. *Journal of Personality, 67*(6), pp. 1165–1194.

Baumeister, R. F. and Thierney, J. (2011) *Willpower: Rediscovering the greatest human strength*. New York: Penguin.

Benninga, J. S., Berkowitz, M. W., Kuehn, P. and Smith, K. (2003) The Relationship of Character Education Implementation and Academic Achievement in Elementary Schools. *Journal of Research in Character Education, 1*(1), pp. 19–32.

Berkowitz, M. W. (2012) Navigating the Semantic Minefield of Promoting Moral Development. Retrieved 13 April, 2012, from http://amenetwork.org/oped/?p=40#more-40.

Berkowitz, M. W. and Bier, M. C. (2006) What Works in Character Education: A research-driven guide for educators. Washington, D.C., Character Education Partnership. Retrieved 13 April, 2013, from http://characterandcitizenship.org/images/files/wwcepractitioners.pdf .

Biesta, G. J. (2014) How does a competent teacher become a good teacher? On judgement, wisdom, and virtuosity in teaching and teacher education. In R. Hollbronn and L. Foreman-Peck (eds), *Philosophical Perspectives on Teacher Education*. Oxford: Wiley-Blackwell.

Blasi, A. (1980) Bridging Moral Cognition and Moral Action: A critical review of the literature. *Psychological Bulletin, 88*(1), pp. 1–45.

Brooks, D. (2015) *The Road to Character*. New York: Allen Lane.

Bruner, J. (1960) *The Process of Education*. Cambridge MA: Harvard University Press.

Campbell, E. (2003) *The Ethical Teacher*. Maidenhead: Open University Press.

Campbell, E. (2008) Teaching Ethically as a Moral Condition of Professionalism. In L. Nucci, D. Narváez, and T. Krettenauer (eds), *The International Handbook of Moral and Character Education*, New York: Routledge. Pp. 101–118.

Campbell, V. and Bond, R. (1982) Evaluation of a Character Education Curriculum. In D. McClelland (ed.), *Education for Values*. New York: Irvington Publishers.

Carr, D. (1991) *Educating the Virtues. An essay on the philosophical psychology of moral development and education*. London, New York: Routledge.

Carr, D. (1993) Moral Values and the Teacher: Beyond the paternal and the permissive. *Journal of Philosophy of Education, 27*(2), pp. 193–207.

Carr, D. (1996) After Kohlberg: Some implications of an ethics of virtue for the theory of moral education and development. *Studies in Philosophy and Education*, 15(4), pp. 353–370.

Carr, D. (2007) Character in Teaching. *British Journal of Educational Studies*, 55(4), pp. 369–389.

Carr, D. (2012) *Educating the Virtues: Essay on the philosophical psychology of moral development and education*. London: Routledge.

Carr, D. (2017) Virtue Ethics and Education. In N. Snow (ed.), *Oxford Handbook of Virtue*. Oxford: Oxford University Press.

Carr, D. and Harrison, T. (2015) *Educating Character through Stories*. Exeter: Imprint Academic.

Chen, Y. L. (2013) A Missing Piece of the Contemporary Character Education Puzzle: The individualisation of moral character. *Studies in Philosophy and Education*, 32(4), pp. 345–360.

Clarendon Commission (1864) *On the Principal Public Schools*. London: HMSO.

Colby, A., and Damon, W. (1992) *Some Do Care: Contemporary lives of moral commitment*. New York: Free Press.

Comenius, J. A. (1907) *The Great Didactic*, trans. M. W. Keatinge. London: Adam and Charles Black.

Cooke, S. and Carr, D. (2014) Virtue, Practical Wisdom and Character in Teaching. *British Journal of Educational Studies*, 62(2), pp. 91–110.

Curren, R. (2010) Aristotle's Educational Politics and the Aristotelian Renaissance in Philosophy of Education. *Oxford Review of Education*, 36(5), pp. 543–559.

Curren, R. (2014) Measures of Goodness. Keynote speech presented at the Jubilee Centre Conference *Can Virtue be Measured?* 11 January, Oriel College, Oxford. Retrieved 12 January, 2014, from http://www.jubileecentre.ac.uk/userfiles/jubileecentre/pdf/conference-papers/can-virtue-be-measured/curren-randall.pdf.

Curzer, H. (2002) Aristotle's Painful Path to Virtue. *Journal of History of Philosophy*, 40(1), pp. 141–162.

Curzer, H. (2005) How Good People do Bad Things. Aristotle on the misdeeds of the virtuous. *Oxford Studies in Ancient Philosophy*, 28, pp. 233–256.

Curzer, H. (2012) *Aristotle and the Virtues*. Oxford: Oxford University Press.

Curzer, H. (2014) Tweaking the Four-Component Model. *Journal of Moral Education*, 43(1), pp. 104–123.

Damon, W. (1988) *The Moral Child: Nurturing children's natural moral growth*. New York: Free Press.

Damon, W. (2008) *Moral Child: Nurturing children's natural moral growth*. New York: Simon and Schuster.

De Raad, B. and Van Oudenhoven, J. P. (2011) A Psycholexical Study of Virtues in the Dutch Language, and Relations between Virtues and Personality. *European Journal of Personality*, 25(1), pp. 43–52.

Department for Education and Employment (1997) *Excellence in Schools*. London: The Stationery Office.

Department for Education and Employment (1999) *National Curriculum for England*. London: The Stationery Office.

Department for Education and Skills (2001) *Schools: Achieving success*. London: The Stationery Office.

Doris, J. (2002) *Lack of Character: Personality and moral behavior*. Cambridge: Cambridge University Press.

Durlak, J. A., Weissberg, R. P., Dymnicki, A. B., Taylor, R. D. and Schellinger, K. B. (2011) The Impact of Enhancing Students' Social and Emotional Learning: A meta-analysis of school-based universal interventions. *Child Development*, *82*(1): 405–432.

Evans, J. (2011) Our Leaders are all Aristotelians now. *Public Policy Research*, *17*(4), pp. 214–221.

Fallona, C. (2000) Manner in Teaching: A study in observing and interpreting teachers' moral virtues. *Teaching and Teacher Education*, *16*, pp. 681–695.

Fiedler, S., Glöckner, A., Nicklisch, A. and Dickert, S. (2013) Social Value Orientation and Information Search in Social Dilemmas: An eye-tracking analysis. *Organizational Behavior and Human Decision Processes*, *120*(2), pp. 272–284.

Fowers, B. (2005) *Virtue and Psychology: Pursuing excellence in ordinary practices.* Washington, D.C.: American Psychological Association.

Fowers, B. J. (2014) Assessing Virtue: Lessons from the subfields of psychology. Paper delivered at the Jubilee Centre Conference *Can Virtue Be Measured?* 10 January, Oriel College, Oxford. Retrieved 12 January, 2014, from http://www.jubilee-centre.ac.uk/userfiles/jubileecentre/pdf/conference-papers/can-virtue-be-measured/fowers-blaine.pdf.

Frimer, J. A., Walker, L. J., Lee, B. H., Riches, A. and Dunlop, W. L. (2012) Hierarchical Integration of Agency and Communion: A study of influential moral figures. *Journal of Personality*, *80*(4), pp. 1117–1145.

Fullinwider, R. K. (1989) Moral Conventions and Moral Lessons. *Social Theory and Practice*, *15*(3), pp. 321–338.

Garrett, J.E. (1993) The Moral Status of 'the Many' in Aristotle. *Journal of the History of Philosophy*, *31*(2), pp. 171–189.

Gilligan, C. (1982) *In a Different Voice. Psychological theory and women's development.* Cambridge, MA: Harvard University Press.

Glasser, W. (1969) *Schools without Failure.* New York: Harper and Row, p. 186.

Goodwin, G. P., Piazza, J. and Rozin, P. (2014) Moral Character Predominates in Person Perception and Evaluation. *Journal of Personality and Social Psychology*, *106*(1), pp. 148–168.

Greene J., Sommerville R. B., Nystrom L. E., Darley J. M. and Cohen J. D. (2001) An fMRI Investigation of Emotional Engagement in Moral Judgment. *Science*, *293*(14 September), pp. 2105–2108.

Guitton, J. (1964) *A Student's Guide to Intellectual Work.* University of Notre Dame Press.

Halstead, M. and Taylor, M. (2000a) *The Development of Values, Attitudes and Personal Qualities: A review of recent research.* Slough: NFER.

Halstead, M. and Taylor, M. (2000b) Learning and Teaching about Values: A review of recent research. *Cambridge Journal of Education*, *30*(2).

Harrison, T. (2014) Does the Internet Influence the Character Virtues of 11–14 Year Olds in England. PhD Thesis. Birmingham: University of Birmingham.

Hofstee, W. K. B. (1990) The Use of Everyday Personality Language for Scientific Purposes. *European Journal of Personality*, *4*(1), pp. 77–88.

Huitt, W. (2004) Moral and Character Development. *Educational Psychology Interactive.* Valdosta, GA: Valdosta State University. Retrieved 18 January, 2010, from http://www.edpsycinteractive.org/morchr/morchr.html.

Hursthouse, R. (2007) Environmental Virtue Ethics. In R. L. Walker and P. J. Ivanhoe (eds), *Working Virtue: Virtue ethics and contemporary moral problems* (pp. 155–171). Oxford: Clarendon Press.

Hursthouse, R. (2012) Virtue Ethics. In E. N. Zalta (ed.), *Stanford Encyclopaedia of Philosophy* (Fall 2013 edition). Retrieved 30 October, 2015, from http://plato.stanford.edu/archives/fall2013/entries/ethics-virtue/.

Jayawickreme, E., Meindl, P., Helzer, E. G., Furr, R. M. and Fleeson, W. (2014) Virtuous States and Virtuous Traits: How the empirical evidence regarding the existence of broad traits saves virtue ethics from the situationist challenge. *Theory and Research in Education, 12*(3), pp. 283–308.

Joseph, P. B. and Efron, S. (1993) Moral Choices/Moral Conflicts: Teachers' self-perceptions, *Journal of Moral Education, 22*(3), pp. 201–221.

Jubilee Centre for Character and Virtues (2013a) *Populus Survey.* Retrieved 13 July, 2014, from http://www.jubileecentre.ac.uk/471/character-education/populus-survey.

Jubilee Centre for Character and Virtues (2013b) *A Framework for Character Education in Schools.* Retrieved 12 January, 2014, from http://jubileecentre.ac.uk/userfiles/jubileecentre/pdf/other-centre-papers/Framework.pdf.

Jubilee Centre for Character and Virtues (2014a) *Secondary Programme of Study: A taught course for 11–16 year olds.* Birmingham: University of Birmingham. Retrieved 30 October, 2015, from http://jubileecentre.ac.uk/1636/character-education.

Jubilee Centre for Character and Virtues (2014b) *Teaching Character Through the Curriculum.* Birmingham: University of Birmingham. Retrieved 30 October, 2015, from http://www.jubileecentre.ac.uk/userfiles/jubileecentre/pdf/Teaching_Character_Through_The_Curriculum1.pdf.

Jubilee Centre for Character and Virtues (2015a) *Primary Programme of Study: A taught course for 4–11 year olds.* Birmingham: University of Birmingham. Retrieved 30 October, 2015, from http://jubileecentre.ac.uk/1635/character-education.

Jubilee Centre for Character and Virtues (2015b) Statement on Teacher Education and Character Education. Birmingham: University of Birmingham. Retrieved from http://www.jubileecentre.ac.uk/userfiles/jubileecentre/pdf/character-education/Statement_on_Teacher_Education_and_Character_Education.pdf.

Kawakami, K., Dunn, E., Karmali, F. and Dovidio, J. F. (2009) Mispredicting Affective and Behavioral Responses to Racism. *Science Magazine, 323*(5911), pp. 276–278.

Kern, M. L., Eichstaedt, J. C., Schwartz, H.A., Dziurzynski, L., Ungar, L. H., Stillwell, D. J., Kosinski, M., Ramones, S. M. and Seligman, M. E. P. (2014) What's It Like to Be 'Neurotic'? An open vocabulary approach to personality (submitted paper).

Kesebir, P. and Kesebir, S. (2012) The Cultural Salience of Moral Character and Virtue declined in Twentieth Century America. *Journal of Positive Psychology, 7*(6), pp. 471–480.

Kohlberg, L. (1958) *The Development of Modes of Moral Thinking and Choice in the Years 10–16.* Chicago, Ill: Department of photo duplication, University of Chicago Library.

Kohlberg, L. (1981) *The Philosophy of Moral Development: Moral stages and the idea of justice.* San Francisco, CA: Harper & Row.

Kristjánsson, K. (2006a) Emulation and the Use of Role Models in Moral Education. *Journal of Moral Education, 35*(1), pp. 37–49.

Kristjánsson, K. (2006b) *Justice and Desert-Based Emotions.* Aldershot: Ashgate.

Kristjánsson, K. (2007) *Aristotle, Emotions and Education.* Aldershot: Ashgate.

Kristjánsson, K. (2010) *The Self and Its Emotions.* Cambridge: Cambridge University Press.

Kristjánsson, K. (2013a) *Virtues and Vices in Positive Psychology: A philosophical critique*. Cambridge: Cambridge University Press.

Kristjánsson, K. (2013b) Ten Myths about Character, Virtue and Virtue Education – And three well-founded misgivings. *British Journal of Educational Studies, 61*(3).

Kristjánsson, K. (2014a) Phronesis and Moral Education. Trading beyond the truisms. *Theory and Research in Education, 12*(2), pp. 151–171.

Kristjánsson, K. (2014b) There is Something about Aristotle: The pros and cons of Aristotelianism in contemporary moral education. *Journal of Philosophy of Education, 48*(1).

Kristjánsson, K. (2014c) On the Old Saw that Dialogue is a Socratic but not an Aristotelian Method of Moral Education. *Educational Theory, 64*(4), 333–348.

Kristjánsson, K. (2015) *Aristotelian Character Education*. London: Routledge.

Lapsley, D. K. and Narvaez, D. (2006) Character Education. In W. Damon and R. M. Lerner (eds), *Handbook of Child Psychology, Vol. 4: Child psychology in practice*, New York: Wiley. Pp. 248–296.

Lauwerys, J. A. and Hans, N. (eds) (1951) *The Yearbook of Education*. London: University of London Institute of Education and Evans Publishing.

Lickona, T. (1991) *Educating for Character: How our schools can teach respect and responsibility*. New York: Bantam USA.

Lickona, T. (1996) Eleven Principles of Effective Character Education. *Journal of Moral Education, 25*(1), pp. 93–100.

Lyseight-Jones, P. (1998) 'It is Not a Good Time for Children': Assessment issues within personal and social development. In S. Inman, M. Buck and H. Burke (eds), *Assessing Personal and Social Development: Measuring the unmeasurable?*, London: Falmer Press. Pp. 33–48.

MacIntyre, A. (1981) *After Virtue*. London: Duckworth.

MacIntyre, A. (1999) *Dependent Rational Animals: Why human beings need the virtues*. Chicago, Ill.: Open Court.

MacIntyre, A. (2007, 3rd ed.) *After Virtue: A study in moral theory*. Notre Dame, Ind.: University of Notre Dame Press.

Marenbon, J. (1996) *A Moral Maze: Government values in education*. London: Politeia.

McCall, C. (2009) *Transforming Thinking: Philosophical inquiry in the primary and secondary classroom*. Abingdon: Routledge.

McClellan, B. E. (1992) *Schools and the Shaping of Character: Moral education in America. 1607–present*. Clearing House for Social Studies: Indiana University.

McCrae, R. R. (2009) The Five-Factor Model of Personality Traits: Consensus and controversy. In P. J. Corr and G. Matthews (eds), *The Cambridge Handbook of Personality Psychology*, Cambridge: Cambridge University Press. Pp. 148–161.

McGrath, R. E. (2014) Bridging the Gap between Psychological and Cultural Perspectives on Virtue and Strength. Paper delivered at the Jubilee Centre Conference *Can Virtue be Measured?* 10 January, 2014, Oriel College, Oxford. Retrieved 12 January, 2014, from http://www.jubileecentre.ac.uk/userfiles/jubileecentre/pdf/conference-papers/can-virtue-be-measured/mcgrath-robert.pdf.

McGrath, R. E. (2015) Character Strengths in 75 Nations: An update. *Journal of Positive Psychology, 10*(1), pp. 41–52.

Miller, C. (2013) *Moral Character: An empirical theory*. Oxford: Oxford University Press.

Miller, C. B. (2014) *Character and Moral Psychology*. Oxford: Oxford University Press.

Mill, J. S. (1989) *On Liberty and Other Writing*. Cambridge: Cambridge University Press.

Ministry of Education (1949) *Citizens Growing Up: At home, in school and after*. London: HM Stationery Office.

Morris, I. (2015) *Learning to Ride Elephants: Teaching happiness and wellbeing in schools*. London: Continuum International Publishing.

Murphy, J. B. (2015) Does Habit Interference Explain Moral Failure? *Review of Philosophy and Psychology*, 6(2): 255–273. Retrieved 11 November, 2015, from http://link.springer.com/article/10.1007%2Fs13164-014-0220-5.

Narvaez, D. (2005) The Neo-Kohlbergian Tradition and Beyond: Schemas, expertise and character. In G. Carlo and C. Pope-Edwards (eds), Nebraska Symposium on Motivation, vol. 51: Moral motivation through the lifespan, Lincoln, NE: University of Nebraska Press. Pp. 119–163.

Narvaez, D. and Rest, J. (1995) The Four Components of Acting Morally. In W. Kurtines and J. Gewirtz (eds), *Moral Behaviour and Moral Development: An introduction*, New York: McGraw Hill. Pp. 385–400.

Nash, R. J. (1997) *Answering the 'Virtuecrats': A Moral conversation on character education*. New York: Teachers College Press.

Newsome, D. (1961) *Godliness and Good Learning*. London: John Murray.

Noftle, E. E., Schnitker, S. A. and Robins, R. W. (2011) Character and Personality: Connections between positive psychology and personality psychology. In K. M. Sheldon, T. B. Kashdan and M. F. Steger (eds), *Designing Positive Psychology: Taking stock and moving forward*, Oxford: Oxford University Press. Pp. 207–227.

Nucci, L. P., Krettenauer, T. and Narváez, D. (eds) (2008) *Handbook of Moral and Character Education*. London: Routledge.

Nussbaum, M. C. (1990) Aristotelian Social Democracy. In R. B. Douglass, G. Mara and H. Richardson (eds), *Liberalism and the Good*, London: Routledge, pp. 203–252.

Nussbaum, M. C. (1993) Non-Relative Virtues: An Aristotelian approach. In M. Nussbaum and A. Sen (eds), *The Quality of Life*, New York: Oxford Clarendon Press. Pp. 242–269.

Oancea, A. and Pring, R. (2008) The Importance of Being Thorough: On systematic accumulations of 'what works' in education research. *Journal of Philosophy of Education*, 42(S1), pp. 15–39.

Owen, R. D. (1824) *An Outline of the Education System at New Lanark*. Glasgow: New Harmony Gazette.

Park, N. and Peterson, C. (2006) Moral Competence and Character Strengths among Adolescents: The development and validation of the values in action inventory of strengths for youth. *Journal of Adolescence*, 29(6), pp. 891–909.

Park, N. and Peterson, C. (2009) Strengths of Character in Schools. In R. Gilman, E. S. Huebner and M. J. Furlong (eds), *Handbook of Positive Psychology in Schools*, New York: Routledge. Pp. 65–76.

Payne, B. K. and Gawronski, B. (2010) A History of Implicit Social Cognition: Where is it coming from? Where is it now? Where is it going? In B. Gawronski, and B. K. Payne (eds), *Handbook of Implicit Social Cognition: Measurement, theory, and applications*, New York: Guilford Press. Pp. 1–15.

Pear, T. H. (1951) The Training of Character in Some English Schools. In J. A. Lawerys and N. Harris (eds), *The Yearbook of Education*, London: University of London Institute of Education and Evans Publishing.

Perugini, M. and Leone, L. (2009) Implicit Self-Concept and Moral Action. *Journal of Research in Personality*, 43(5), pp. 747–754.

Peterson, C. and Seligman, M. E. P. (2004) *Character Strengths and Virtues: A handbook and classification*. Oxford: Oxford University Press.

Power, C. (1998) The Just Community Approach to Moral Education. *Journal of Moral Education, 17*(3), pp. 195–208.

Pring, R. A. (1992) Academic Responsibility and the Professional Relevance. Inaugural lecture delivered before the University of Oxford on 8 May 1991. Oxford: Clarendon Press.

Rest, J. (1986) *Moral Development: Advances in research and theory*. New York: Prager.

Rest, J., Narvaez, D., Bebeau, M. and Thoma, S. (1999) A Neo-Kohlbergian Approach: The DIT and schema theory. *Educational Psychology Review, 11*(4), pp. 291–324.

Revell, L. and Arthur, J. (2007) Character Education in Schools and the Education of Teachers. *Journal of Moral Education, 36*(1), pp. 79–92.

Rose, D. (2004) The Potential of Role Model Education. In K. Kristjánsson (2006) Emulation and the Use of Role Models in Moral Education. *Journal of Moral Education, 35*(2), pp. 37–49. Retrieved 30 October, 2015, from http://www.infed.org/biblio/role_model_education.htm.

Rothblatt, S. (1976) *Tradition and Change in English Liberal Education*. London: Faber and Faber.

Russell, D. C. (2012) *Practical Intelligence and the Virtues*. Oxford University Press.

Russell, D. C. (2014a) Aristotelian Virtue Theory: After the person–situation debate. *Revue Internationale de Philosophie, 68*(267), pp. 37–63.

Russell, D. C. (2014b) What Virtue Ethics Can Learn from Utilitarianism. In B. Eggleston and D. Miller (eds), *The Cambridge Companion to Utilitarianism*, Cambridge: Cambridge University Press. Pp. 258–279.

Ryan, K. (1993) Mining the Values in the Curriculum. *Educational Leadership, 51*(3), pp. 16–18.

Ryan, K. and Bohlin, K. (1999) *Building Character in Schools*. San Francisco: Jossey-Bass.

Ryle, G. (1975) Can Virtue Be Taught? In R. F. Dearden, P. H. Hirst and R. S. Peters (eds), (2012) *Education and the Development of Reason*. London: Routledge and Kegan Paul.

Sanderse, W. (2012) *Character Education: A neo-Aristotelian approach to the philosophy, psychology and education of virtue*. Delft: Eburon.

Sanderse, W. (2013) The Meaning of Role Modelling in Moral and Character Education. *Journal of Moral Education, 42*(1), 28–42.

Sanderse, W. (2015) An Aristotelian Model of Moral Development. *Journal of the Philosophy of Education, 49*(3), pp. 382–398.

Sanderse, W. (2016) Aristotelian Action Research: Its Value for Studying Character Education in Schools. *Educational Action Research*. In press. DOI: 10.1080/09650792.2015.1067161.

Sandler, R. (2007) *Character and Environment: A virtue-oriented approach to environmental ethics*. New York: Columbia University Press.

Sanger, M. N. and Osguthorpe, R. D. (2011) Teacher Education, Pre-Service Teacher Beliefs, and the Moral Work of Teaching. *Teaching and Teacher Education, 27*(3), pp. 569–578.

Sanger, M. N. and Osguthrorpe, R. O. (2013) *The Moral Work of Teaching and Teacher Education*. New York: Teachers Press.

Schueller, S. M. (2014) Virtue in Real Life: Using smartphones to coordinate self, observer, and behavioral data of virtue. Paper delivered at the Jubilee Centre

Conference *Can Virtue Be Measured?* Oriel College, Oxford. Retrieved 12 January, 2014, from http://www.jubileecentre.ac.uk/userfiles/jubileecentre/pdf/conference-papers/can-virtue-be-measured/schueller-stephen.pdf.

Schwartz, B. and Sharpe, K. E. (2010) *Practical Wisdom: The right way to do the right thing.* New York: Riverhead Books.

Seider, S. (2012) *Character Compass: How powerful school culture can point students toward success.* Cambridge: Harvard Education Press.

Sherman, N. (1989) *The Fabric of Character: Aristotle's theory of virtue.* Oxford: Clarendon Press.

Smith, T.W. (2001) *Revaluing Ethics. Aristotle's dialectical pedagogy.* New York: State University of New York Press.

Snow, N. (2014) Virtue Intelligence. Keynote speech presented at the Jubilee Centre Conference *Can Virtue Be Measured?* Oriel College, Oxford. Retrieved 12 January, 2014, from http://www.jubileecentre.ac.uk/userfiles/jubileecentre/pdf/conference-papers/can-virtue-be-measured/snow-nancy.pdf.

Snyder, F. J., Vuchinich, S., Acock, A., Washburn, I. J. and Flay, R. (2012) Improving Elementary School Quality through the Use of a Social-Emotional and Character Development Program: A matched-pair, cluster-randomized, controlled trial in Hawai'i. *Journal of School Health, 82*(1), pp. 11–20.

Sockett, H. (1993) *The Moral Base for Teacher Professionalism.* New York: Teachers College Press.

Sockett, H. and LePage, P. (2002) The Missing Language of the Classroom. *Teaching and Teacher Education, 18*(2), pp. 159–171.

Stohr, K. (2002) Moral Cacophony: When continence is a virtue. *Journal of Ethics, 7*(4), pp. 339–363.

Steutel, J. and Spiecker, B. (2004) Cultivating Sentimental Dispositions through Aristotelian Habituation. *Journal of Philosophy of Education, 38*(4), 531–549.

Stoll, S. K. and Beller, J. M. (1998) Can Character be Measured? *Journal of Physical Education, Recreation and Dance, 69*(1), pp. 19–24.

Swann, W. B., Jr. (1996) *Self-Traps: The elusive quest for higher self-esteem.* New York: W. H. Freeman and Co.

Taunton Commission (1868) *Schools Enquiry Commission.* London: HMSO.

Thoma, S. (2006) Research on the Defining Issues Test. In M. Killen and J. G. Smetana (eds), *Handbook of Moral Development*, Mahwah, NJ: Erlbaum, pp. 67–92.

Thoma, S. (2014) Measuring Moral Judgements from a Neo-Kohlbergian Perspective. Keynote speech presented at the Jubilee Centre Conference Can Virtue be Measured? Oriel College, Oxford. Retrieved 12 January, 2014, from http://www.jubileecentre.ac.uk/userfiles/jubileecentre/pdf/conference-papers/can-virtue-be-measured/thoma-steve.pdf

Thoma, S., Derryberry, P. and Crowson, H. M. (2013) Describing and Testing an Intermediate Concept Measure of Adolescent Moral Thinking. *Journal of Educational and Developmental Psychology, 10*(2), pp. 239–252.

Tomlinson, J. and Little, V. (2000) A Code of the Ethical Principles Underlying Teaching as a Professional Activity. In R. Gardner, R. Cairns and D. Lawton (2000) *Education for Values: Morals, Ethics, and Citizenship in Contemporary Teaching.* London: Kogan Page Ltd.

Tough, P. (2013) *How Children Succeed: Grit, curiosity and the hidden power of character.* London: Random House.

Tuff, L. (2009) *Teacher Perception and Character Education.* Unpublished thesis: University of Lethbridge.

Vasalou, S. (2012) Educating Virtue as a Mastery of Language. *Journal of Ethics*, *16*(1), pp. 67–87.

Walker, D. I., Roberts, M. P. and Kristjánsson, K. (2015) Towards a New Era of Character Education in Theory and in Practice. *Educational Review*, *67*(1), pp. 79–96.

Warnick, B. (2009) *Imitation and Education. A philosophical enquiry into learning by example*. New York: State University of New York Press.

White, J. (1990) *Education and the Good Life: Beyond the national curriculum*. London: Kogan Page.

Wiley, L. S. (1998) *Comprehensive Character-building Classrooms: A handbook for teachers*. Manchester, NH: Character Development Foundation.

Wilson, J. (1993) *Reflections and Practice: Teacher Education and the Teacher Profession*. University of Western Ontario: Althouse Press.

Wynne, E. (1991) Character and Academics in the Elementary School. In J. Benninga (ed.), Moral Character and Civic Education in the Elementary School. New York: Teachers College Press.

Wynne, E. and Walberg, H. (1985) The Complementary Goals of Character Development and Academic Excellence. *Educational Leadership*, *43*(4), pp. 15–18.

Yu, J. (2007) *The Ethics of Confucius and Aristotle: Mirrors of virtue*. London: Routledge.

Index

204   *Index*

Made in the USA
Columbia, SC
09 January 2021